Show Me Microsoft® Office FrontPage 2003

Steve Johnson

Perspection, Inc.

Que Publishing
800 East 96th Street
Indianapolis, IN 46240 USA

Show Me Microsoft® Office FrontPage 2003

International Standard Book Number: 0-7897-3006-5

Library of Congress Catalog Card Number: 2003108707

Printed in the United States of America

First Printing: September 2003

06 05 04 03   4 3 2 1

Que Publishing offers excellent discounts on this book when ordered in quantity for bulk purchases or special sales. For information, please contact:

> U.S. Corporate and Government Sales
>
> 1-800-382-3419
>
> corpsales@pearsontechgroup.com

For sales outside the U.S., please contact:

> International Sales
>
> 1-317-428-3341
>
> International@pearsontechgroup.com

Trademarks

Warning and Disclaimer

Publisher
Paul Boger

Associate Publisher
Greg Wiegand

Managing Editor
Steve Johnson

Author
Steve Johnson

Project Editor
Holly Johnson

Technical Editor
Matt West

Production Editor
Beth Teyler

Page Layout
Kate Lyerla
Joe Kalsbeek
Ryan Suzuki
Matt West

Interior Designers
Steve Johnson
Marian Hartsough

Indexer
Katherine Stimson

Proofreader
Beth Teyler

Team Coordinator
Sharry Lee Gregory

Acknowledgements

a

Perspection, Inc.

Show Me Microsoft Office FrontPage 2003 has been created by the professional trainers and writers at Perspection, Inc. to the standards you've come to expect from Que publishing. Together, we are pleased to present this training book.

Perspection, Inc. is a software training company committed to providing information and training to help people use software more effectively in order to communicate, make decisions, and solve problems. Perspection writes and produces software training books, and develops multimedia and Web-based training. Since 1991, we have written more than 60 computer books, with several bestsellers to our credit, and sold over 4.5 million books.

This book incorporates Perspection's training expertise to ensure that you'll receive the maximum return on your time. You'll focus on the tasks and skills that increase productivity while working at your own pace and convenience.

We invite you to visit the Perspection Web site at:

www.perspection.com

Acknowledgements

The task of creating any book requires the talents of many hard-working people pulling together to meet impossible deadlines and untold stresses. We'd like to thank the outstanding team responsible for making this book possible: the writer, Steve Johnson; the project editor, Holly Johnson; the technical editor, Matt West; the production team, Kate Lyerla, Joe Kalsbeek, Ryan Suzuki, and Matt West; the proofreader, Beth Teyler; and the indexer, Katherine Stimson.

At Que publishing, we'd like to thank Greg Wiegand for the opportunity to undertake this project, Sharry Gregory for administrative support, and Sandra Schroeder for your production expertise and support.

Perspection

Dedication

Most importantly, I would like to thank my wife Holly, and my three children, JP, Brett, and Hannah, for their support and encouragement during the project. I would also like to thank Sarah Bartholomaei for her tender loving care and dedication towards our children during the deadline times.

About The Author

Steve Johnson has written more than twenty books on a variety of computer software, including Microsoft Office XP, Microsoft Windows XP, Macromedia Director MX and Macromedia Fireworks, and Web publishing. In 1991, after working for Apple Computer and Microsoft, Steve founded Perspection, Inc., which writes and produces software training. When he is not staying up late writing, he enjoys playing golf, gardening, and spending time with his wife, Holly, and three children, JP, Brett, and Hannah. When time permits, he likes to travel to such places as New Hampshire in October, and Hawaii. Steve and his family live in Pleasanton, California, but can also be found visiting family all over the western United States.

We Want To Hear From You!

As the reader of this book, *you* are our most important critic and commentator. We value your opinion and want to know what we're doing right, what we could do better, what areas you'd like to see us publish in, and any other words of wisdom you're willing to pass our way.

As an associate publisher for Que, I welcome your comments. You can email or write me directly to let me know what you did or didn't like about this book—as well as what we can do to make our books better.

Please note that I cannot help you with technical problems related to the topic of this book. We do have a User Services group, however, where I will forward specific technical questions related to the book.

When you write, please be sure to include this book's title and author as well as your name, email address, and phone number. I will carefully review your comments and share them with the author and editors who worked on the book.

Email: feedback@quepublishing.com

Mail: Greg Wiegand
         Que Publishing
         800 East 96th Street
         Indianapolis, IN 46240 USA

For more information about this book or another Que title, visit our Web site at *www.quepublishing.com*. Type the ISBN (excluding hyphens) or the title of a book in the Search field to find the page you're looking for.

Contents

C

HOMESENSE

Introduction

Welcome to *Show Me Microsoft Office FrontPage 2003*, a visual quick reference book that shows you how to work efficiently with Microsoft Office FrontPage 2003. This book provides complete coverage of basic and intermediate FrontPage 2003 skills.

Find the Best Place to Start

You don't have to read this book in any particular order. We've designed the book so that you can jump in, get the information you need, and jump out. However, the book does follow a logical progression from simple tasks to more complex ones. Each task is no more than two pages long. To find the information that you need, just look up the task in the table of contents, index, or troubleshooting guide, and turn to the page listed. Read the task introduction, follow the step-by-step instructions along with the illustration, and you're done.

What's New

If you're searching for what's new in FrontPage 2003, just look for the icon: New!. The new icon appears in the table of contents so you can quickly and easily identify a new or improved feature in FrontPage 2003. A complete description of each new feature appears in the New Features guide in the back of this book.

How This Book Works

Each task is presented on no more than two facing pages, with step-by-step instructions in the left column and screen illustrations in the right column. This arrangement lets you focus on a single task without having to turn the page.

Step-by-Step Instructions

This book provides concise step-by-step instructions that show you "how" to accomplish a task. Each set of instructions include illustrations that directly correspond to the easy-to-read steps. Also included in the text are timesavers, tables, and sidebars to help you work more efficiently or to teach you more in-depth information. A "Did You Know?" provides tips and techniques to help you work smarter, while a "See Also" leads you to other parts of the book containing related information about the task.

Real World Examples

This book uses real world examples to help convey "why" you would want to perform a task. The examples give you a context in which to use the task. You'll observe how *Home Sense, Inc.,* a fictional home improvement business, uses FrontPage 2003 to get the job done.

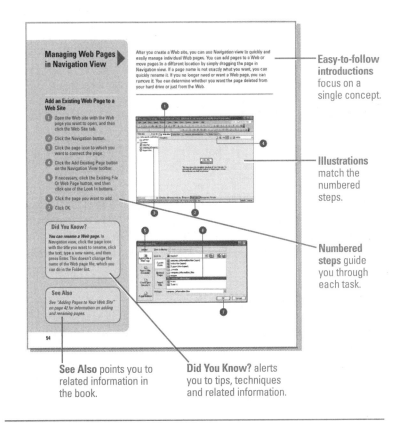

Easy-to-follow introductions focus on a single concept.

Illustrations match the numbered steps.

Numbered steps guide you through each task.

See Also points you to related information in the book.

Did You Know? alerts you to tips, techniques and related information.

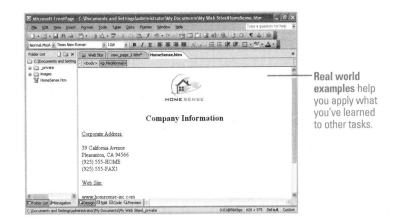

Real world examples help you apply what you've learned to other tasks.

Troubleshooting Guide

This book offers quick and easy ways to diagnose and solve common FrontPage 2003 problems that you might encounter. The troubleshooting guide helps you determine and fix a problem using the task information you find. The problems are posed in question form and are grouped into categories that are presented alphabetically.

Troubleshooting points you to information in the book to help you fix your problems.

Show Me Live Software

In addition, this book offers companion software that shows you how to perform most tasks using the live program. The easy-to-use VCR-type controls allow you to start, pause, and stop the action. As you observe how to accomplish each task, Show Me Live highlights each step and talks you through the process. The Show Me Live software is available free at *www.perspection.com* or *www.quepublishing.com/showme*.

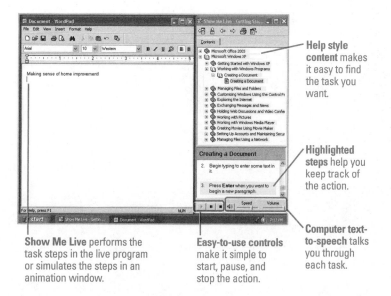

Help style content makes it easy to find the task you want.

Highlighted steps help you keep track of the action.

Computer text-to-speech talks you through each task.

Show Me Live performs the task steps in the live program or simulates the steps in an animation window.

Easy-to-use controls make it simple to start, pause, and stop the action.

Getting Started with FrontPage

Introduction

Microsoft Office FrontPage 2003 is a program that empowers even the most inexperienced computer user with the tools to create and launch a **Web site** or **Web page**. From the planning stages through the development process, this chapter is designed to familiarize you with the terminology and overall operation of FrontPage.

If you're upgrading to FrontPage 2003 from a previous version, this chapter describes how to prepare and install FrontPage 2003. The temptation is to insert the FrontPage 2003 CD and start the installation, but you can avoid problems by making sure your computer is ready for FrontPage 2003. Before you install FrontPage 2003, you need to check your computer hardware and software and make several setup decisions that relate to your computer. The Office Setup Wizard walks you through the installation process.

After installing FrontPage, you will find many of the same elements that you've come to know from other Microsoft Office 2003 programs. The components of the overall window contain the menu bar, title bar, toolbars and task panes that make using FrontPage an easy transition. You'll notice that many of the same functions on the menus and toolbars are the same as Word, Excel, or other Office applications, but do include many additions specific to FrontPage. Searching, using the dialog boxes and help features, along with getting updates from the Web and detecting and repairing problems, all work the same way as they do in Office 2003 programs.

Once you've familiarized yourself with the look and feel of FrontPage, you can begin using it by creating a simple Web page. You can insert, copy and paste text and get it ready to add more specific elements as your skills progress. After creating your page, you can save it to work on later.

What You'll Do

Prepare for FrontPage 2003

Support FrontPage on Your Web Server

Install FrontPage 2003

Start FrontPage

View the FrontPage Window

Work with Menus and Toolbars

Work with Dialog Boxes

Use Task Panes

Create a Simple Web Page

Save a Web Page

Open an Existing Web Page

Find a File or Text in a File

Get Help While You Work

Get Help from the Office Assistant

Get FrontPage Updates on the Web

Detect and Repair Problems

Close a Web Page and Exit FrontPage

Preparing to Install FrontPage 2003

System Requirements

Before you can install FrontPage, you need to make sure your computer meets the minimum system requirements. You need to have a computer with the following minimum configuration:

- An Intel Pentium 233-megahertz (MH) processor, Pentium III recommended.

- 128 megabytes (MB) of RAM or above recommended.

- 180 MB of available hard disk space.

- Microsoft Windows 2000 with Service Pack 3 (SP3) or later; Windows XP or later.

Microsoft Office FrontPage 2003 has multiple server-related features that work with specific environments. Server configurations and options are available for:

- FrontPage version 2002 without FrontPage Server Extensions

- FrontPage 2002 with Server Extensions for FrontPage 2002

- Microsoft SharePoint Team Services from Microsoft

- Microsoft Windows SharePoint Services

If you are not sure that your computer meets the minimum requirements, you can check your computer for the information. In Microsoft Windows XP, you can check system information on your computer using the System Information accessory. Click the Start button on the taskbar, point to All Programs, point to System Tools, and then click System Information. You can also access the System Information accessory from within FrontPage. Click the Help menu, click About Microsoft Office FrontPage, and then click System Info. In the System Information window, click System Summary to find out the information you need about your computer.

Computer system information

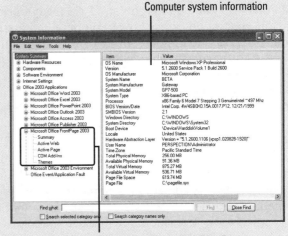

Select an option to view FrontPage system related information

Supporting FrontPage on Your Web Server

A Web site resides on a Web server, a computer dedicated to making Web pages available to people who want to visit the site. FrontPage supports three different types of Web servers: non-extended, extended, and Windows SharePoint Services.

A **non-extended** Web server is a generic Web server that uses Internet File Transfer Protocol (FTP), Distributed Authoring and Versioning (WebDAV), or Windows file system to transfer FrontPage files for delivery over the Web. A non-extended Web server doesn't use FrontPage server software (FrontPage Server Extensions), which prevents you from using extended functionality in FrontPage to use hit counters, e-mail Web results, and collect information from a database.

An **extended** Web server is a generic Web server that uses FrontPage Server Extensions. The server extensions allow you to add hit counters, e-mail Web results, and collect information from a database using Active Server Pages (ASP) or Microsoft ASP.NET. FrontPage 2003 doesn't comes with a new version of FrontPage Server Extensions. Instead, you can use FrontPage 2002 Server Extensions, which are compatible and available from Microsoft's MSDN Web site, or Windows SharePoint Services.

Windows SharePoint Services is an engine that enables you to create Web sites to share information. SharePoint sites provide communities for team collaboration, enabling users to work together on documents, tasks, and projects. Windows SharePoint Services is part of Windows .NET Server 2003. To install Windows SharePoint Services, you need to install Windows .NET Server 2003 first; see Chapter 13, "Working Together on a SharePoint Team Site," for more details.

When you install FrontPage, you don't need to know what type of Web server you'll use to deliver your Web site, but you'll need to know it when you start creating Web pages, so you can take advantage of the FrontPage features provided by the Web server and avoid the ones it doesn't support.

You can customize FrontPage to enable the features you want and disable the ones you don't by using the Page Option dialog box. To enable FrontPage Server Extensions or SharePoint Services, simply click the Tools menu, click Page Options, click the Authoring tab, click the FrontPage And SharePoint Technologies list arrow, select the option you want to use, select the Browse-time Web Components check box or select the SharePoint Services check, and then click OK.

Select a technology option

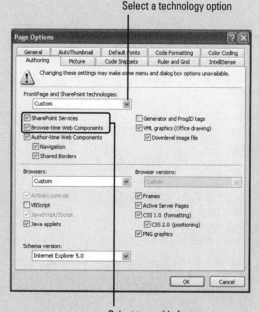

Select to enable features

Installing FrontPage 2003

The Microsoft Office FrontPage Setup Wizard guides you step-by-step through the process of installing FrontPage 2003. When you install FrontPage, you have several options: upgrade (from a previous version), complete, minimal, typical, and custom. The Upgrade option keeps your current FrontPage settings and installs the new version. The Complete option installs the entire FrontPage software package, which takes up the most storage on your hard drive. The Minimal option installs only the required files, which takes up the least amount of hard drive space. The Typical option installs the common FrontPage components. If you want to install specific components, such as .NET Programmability Support or Office shared features and tools, you can select the Custom option, which requires you to select additional options as you step through the FrontPage Setup Wizard.

Install FrontPage

① Insert the Microsoft Office FrontPage 2003 CD into your CD-ROM drive.

The Microsoft Office FrontPage Setup Wizard appears.

② Type the 25-character product key, and then click Next.

③ Type the user information requested, and then click Next.

④ Select the I Accept This Agreement check box, and then click Next.

⑤ Click the option for the type of installation you want, and then click Next.

⑥ Click Install.

⑦ To check for updates on the Web, select the Check The Web For Updates And Additional Downloads check box.

⑧ When you're done, click Finish.

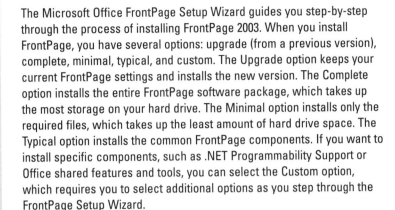

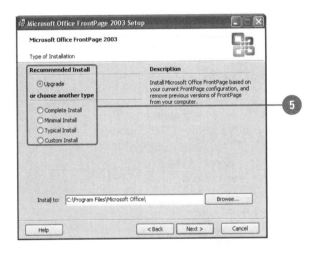

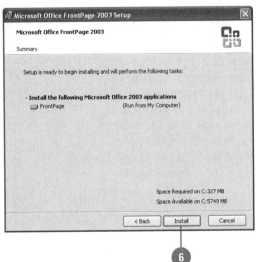

Install FrontPage Using Custom Options

1. Insert the FrontPage CD into your CD-ROM drive.

   The Microsoft Office FrontPage Setup Wizard appears.

2. Type the 25-character product key, and then click Next.

3. Type the user information requested, and then click Next.

4. Select the I Accept This Agreement check box, and then click Next.

5. Click the Custom option, and then click Next.

6. Click the plus sign (+) to expand custom options.

7. Click the icon next to the option you want to change, and then click the option you want.

   ◆ **Run From.** Installs the feature to run from your hard disk, network, or CD.

   ◆ **Run All From.** Installs all components to run from your hard disk, network, or CD.

   ◆ **Installed On First Use.** Setup doesn't install the feature, but installs it the first time you try to use it.

   ◆ **Not Available.** Setup doesn't install the feature.

8. Click Next to continue.

9. Click Install.

10. When you're done, click Finish.

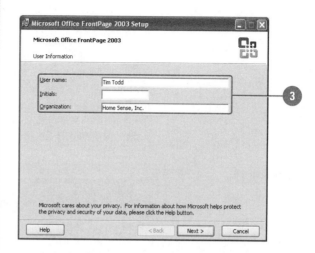

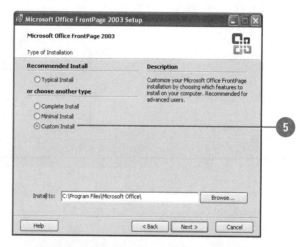

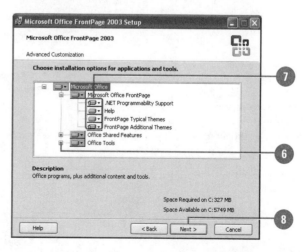

Starting FrontPage

When you first open FrontPage, the program window opens, displaying a blank new page, menus, toolbars, and a taskbar. The Title bar across the top of the screen contains the program and Web site name, with the Menu bar directly below it, and the Standard and Formatting toolbars below the Menu bar. The task pane provides options that relate to the current task. The View tabs—which offer access to Design, Split, Code, and Preview modes—occupy a small area at the bottom of the screen. These tabs allow you to view pages from different perspectives; the program's default is Design view.

Start FrontPage Using the Start Menu

1. Click the Start button on the taskbar.

2. Point to All Programs.

3. Click Microsoft Office.

4. Click Microsoft Office FrontPage 2003.

5. If a message alert appears, asking you to make FrontPage your default editor, clear the Always Perform This Check When Starting FrontPage check box, and then click Yes or No.

   The first time you start an Office program, an Activation Wizard opens; follow the instructions to activate the product.

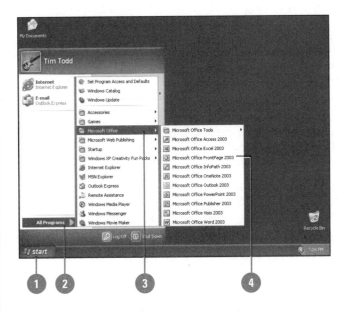

Did You Know?

You should close the blank page before creating a new site. Before you begin working on a new site, close the blank page that opens when you start FrontPage 2003. If you don't, it will be added automatically as the first page of your Web site.

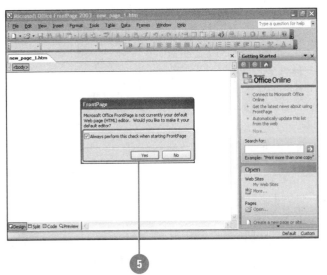

Viewing the FrontPage Window

Web Site and Document tabs
The tabs provide easy access to the Web site and Web pages.

Menu bar
The eleven menus provide access to all FrontPage options.

Title bar
The document name and Microsoft FrontPage appear in the title bar. *new_page_1.htm* is a temporary name FrontPage uses until you assign a new one.

Insertion point
The blinking insertion point (also called a cursor) shows you where the next character will appear.

Close button

Standard and Formatting toolbars
These and other toolbars contain buttons that provide quick access to a variety of commands and features.

Task pane
The task pane provides options related to the current task.

View buttons
Click to see your Web content in different ways.

Web Page
You enter text and graphics here.

Status bar
The status bar provides information about current settings and commands.

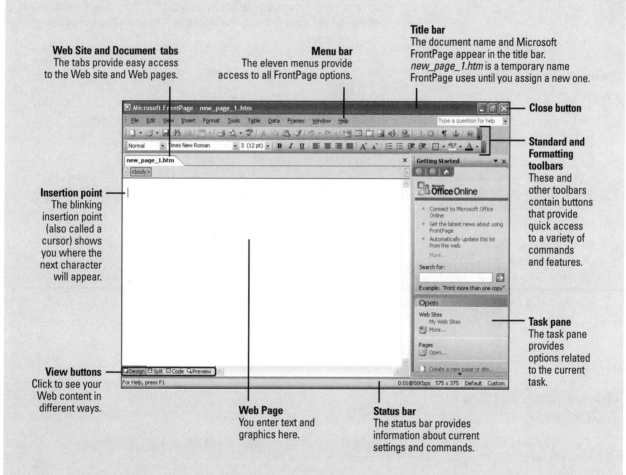

1

Working with Menus and Toolbars

All FrontPage commands are organized on menus on the menu bar, and each menu contains a list of related commands. A **short menu** displays often used commands, and an **expanded menu** displays all commands available on that menu. A menu command followed by an ellipsis (...) indicates that a **dialog box** opens, so you can provide additional information. An arrow to the right of a command indicates that a submenu opens, displaying related commands. An icon to the left means a toolbar button is available for that command. Toolbars contain buttons you can click to carry out commands you use frequently. A keyboard combination to the right of a menu command indicates a **shortcut key** is available for the command.

Choose a Command Using a Menu

1. Click a menu name on the menu bar to display a list of commands.

2. If necessary, click the expand arrow to expand the menu and display more commands, or wait until the expanded list of commands appears.

3. Click the command you want, or point to the arrow to the right of the menu command to display a submenu of related commands, and then click the command.

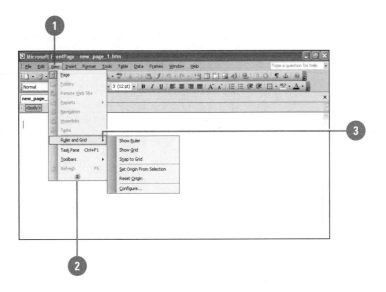

Choose a Command Using a Toolbar Button

1. If you're not sure what a toolbar button does, point to it to display a ScreenTip.

2. To choose a command, click the Toolbar button or click the Toolbar Options list arrow.

   When you select a button from the list arrow, the button appears on the toolbar, showing only the buttons you use most often.

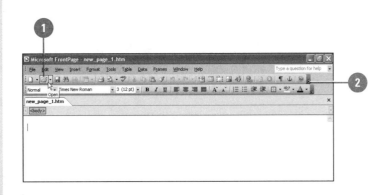

Choose a Command Using a Shortcut Key

◆ To choose a command using a shortcut key, press and hold the first key, and then press the other key. For example, press and hold Ctrl, and then press O to perform the Open command.

Shortcut key

Display or Hide a Toolbar

1 Click the View menu, and then point to Toolbars.

2 Click the unchecked toolbar you want to display or the checked toolbar you want to hide.

Did You Know?

You can move and reshape a toolbar. To move a toolbar to another location, click a blank area of the toolbar (not a button), and then drag the toolbar to a new location. To change the shape of a floating toolbar, position the mouse pointer over the edge of the toolbar, and then drag to reshape it.

The commands and buttons on menus and toolbars respond to your work habits. As you select menu commands or toolbar buttons, those commands and toolbar buttons are promoted to the short menu and shared toolbar if they were not already there.

Working with Dialog Boxes

A **dialog box** is a special window that opens when FrontPage needs additional information from you in order to complete a task. You can indicate your choices by selecting a variety of option buttons and check boxes; in some cases, you type the necessary information in the boxes provided. Some dialog boxes consist of a single window, while others contain **tabs** that you click to display additional sets of options.

Choose Dialog Box Options

All FrontPage dialog boxes contain the same types of options, including:

◆ **Tabs.** Click a tab to display its options. Each tab groups a related set of options.

◆ **Option buttons.** Click an option button to select it. You can usually select only one.

◆ **Spin box.** Click the up or down arrow to increase or decrease the number, or type a number in the box.

◆ **Check box.** Click the box to turn on or off the option. A checked box means the option is selected; a cleared box means it's not.

◆ **List box.** Click the list arrow to display a list of options, and then click the option you want.

◆ **Text box.** Click in the box, and then type the requested information.

◆ **Button.** Click a button to perform a specific action or command. A button name followed by an ellipsis (...) opens another dialog box.

◆ **Preview box.** Many dialog boxes show an image that reflects the options you select.

Tabs

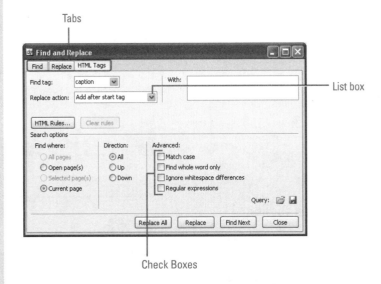

List box

Check Boxes

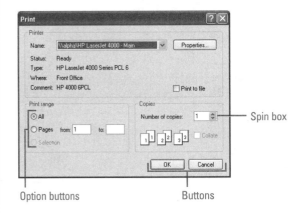

Option buttons

Spin box

Buttons

Using Task Panes

When you start FrontPage, a task pane appears by default on the right side of the program window. The task pane displays various options that relate to the current task. There are several types of options available on the task pane. You can search for information, select options, and click links, like the ones on a Web page, to perform commands. You can also display different task panes, move back and forth between task panes, and close a task pane to provide a larger work area.

Use the Task Pane

1. When you start FrontPage, the task pane appears on the right side of your screen.

2. Click an option on the task pane.

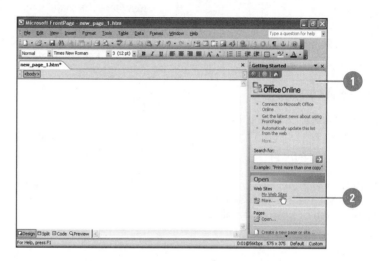

Open and Close Task Panes

1. Click the View menu, and then click Task Pane.

2. To open another task pane, click the list arrow on the task pane title bar, and then click the task pane you want.

3. To switch between task panes, click the Back and Forward task pane buttons.

4. Click the Close button on the task pane.

Creating a Simple Web Page

When you start FrontPage, a blank new page appears, ready for you to enter text. By default, this page is titled new_page_1.htm. You can create new Web pages and sites in several ways: using the New command on the File menu, the Create New Normal Page button on the Standard toolbar, and by the New task pane. FrontPage numbers new pages consecutively. The insertion point (blinking cursor bar) appears in the page where text will appear when you type. As you type, text moves, or **wraps**, to a new line when the previous one is full. You can move the insertion point anywhere within the page so that you can insert new text and **edit** (or insert, revise, or delete) existing text. You can copy or move items (including blocks of text) from one place to another within a Web page, or from other programs.

Create a Web Page

1. Click the File menu, and then click New.

2. Click Blank Page.

3. Begin typing, and then press Enter when you want to begin a new paragraph or insert a blank line.

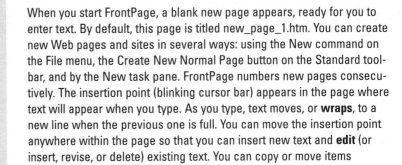

Edit Text in a Web Page

1. Click where you want to insert text, or select the text you want to edit.

2. Make the change you want:

   ◆ Type to insert new text.

   ◆ Press Enter to begin a new paragraph or insert a blank line.

   ◆ Press Backspace or Delete to erase text to the left or right of the insertion point.

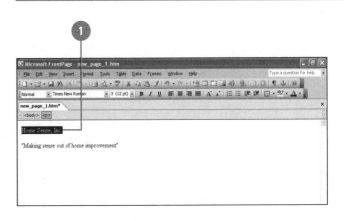

Copy and Paste Text in a Web Page

① In the Web page you are copying from, select the item you want to copy.

② Click the Copy button on the Standard toolbar.

TIMESAVER *To copy a selected item, press Ctrl+C.*

③ Click the location where you want to insert the item to position the insertion point.

④ Click the Paste button on the Standard toolbar.

TIMESAVER *To paste an item, press Ctrl+V.*

⑤ Click the Paste Options button, and then click an option to customize the way the text appears.

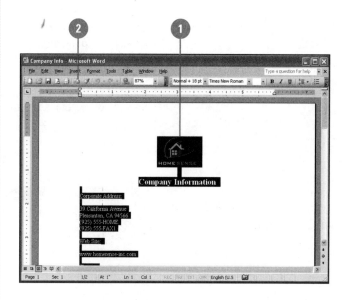

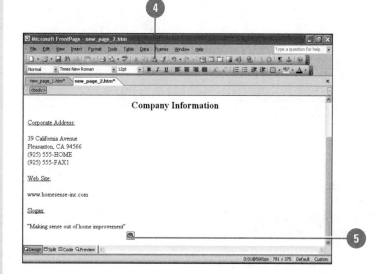

Saving a Web Page

Saving your files frequently ensures that you don't lose work during an unexpected power loss. The first time you save a Web page, specify a file name and folder in the Save As dialog box. The next time you save using the Save button on the Standard toolbar or Save command on the File menu, FrontPage saves the file with the same name in the same folder. If you want to change a file's name or location, you can use the Save As dialog box again to create a copy of the original file.

Save a Web Page

1. Click the File menu, and then click Save As.

2. Click an icon on the Places bar to open a frequently used folder.

3. If necessary, click the Save In list arrow, and then click the drive where you want to save the page.

4. Double-click the folder in which you want to save the page.

5. Type a name for the page, or use the suggested name.

6. Click Save.

7. If the Embedded Files dialog box appears, click OK to save the files.

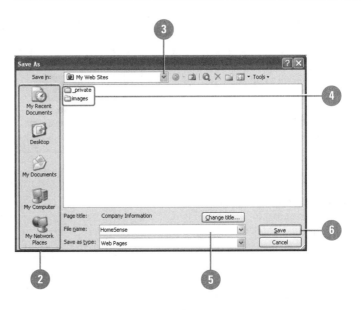

Did You Know?

You can delete or rename a file in a dialog box. In the Open or Save As dialog box, click the file, click the Tools list arrow, and then click Delete or Rename.

You can move or copy a file quickly in a dialog box. In the Open or Save As dialog box, right-click the file you want to move or copy, click Cut or Copy, open the folder where you want to paste the file, right-click a blank area, and then click Paste.

Saved file in Design view

Saved file in Folder list

Save a Web Page in a New Folder

1. Click the File menu, and then click Save As.

2. Locate and select the drive and folder where you want to create the new folder.

3. Click the Create New Folder button.

4. Type the new folder name, and then click OK.

5. Type a name for the file, or use the suggested one.

6. Click Save.

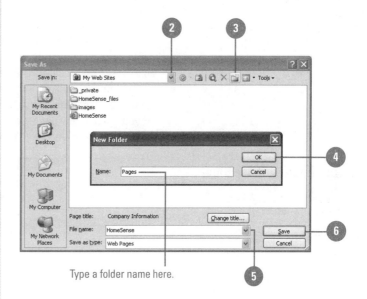

Type a folder name here.

Did You Know?

You don't need to worry about file name extensions. When you name a file, you do not have to type the file name extension. FrontPage adds the correct file name extension to the name you give your file. However, if you clear the Hide Extensions For Known File Types check box on the View tab in the Folders Options dialog box (in My Documents, click the Tools menu, and then click Folder Options), you need to include the extension in the file name.

Opening an Existing Web Page

Opening a Web page is a simple procedure and can be accomplished using the Open button list arrow on the Standard toolbar. You can open a Web page from your local hard drive, a network drive, or a Web server using an Uniform Resource Locator (URL). If you can't recall a file's name or location, use the Search feature in the Open dialog box to locate the file, based on the information (or **criteria**) you can recall, such as its creation date, content, author, size, and so forth. By default, FrontPage opens the last Web site you worked on every time you open the program. If you open a new page while another site is still open, the new page opens in a new FrontPage window.

Open a Web Page in Page View

1. Click the View menu, and then click Page.

2. Click the Open button list arrow on the Standard toolbar, and then click Open.

3. Click an icon on the Places bar to open a frequently used folder.

4. If necessary, click the Look In list arrow, and then select the folder location of the Web page you want to open.

5. Select the page you want to open from the page list in the working folder, or type the URL of the page you want.

6. If you can't find the file, you can use the Search command on the Tools menu.

7. Click Open.

Did You Know?

You can open a recently opened Web page. If you've recently accessed a Web page, you can use the File menu to quickly open it again. Click the File menu, click Recent Files, and then click the file you want.

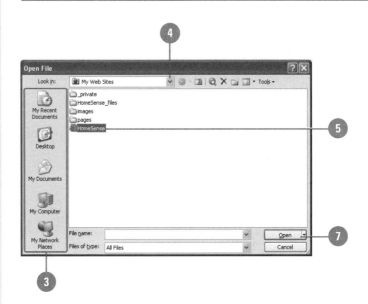

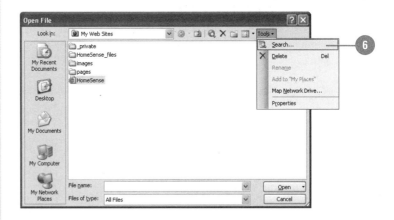

Finding a File or Text in a File

The search feature available in the Open dialog box is also available using the Search task pane. You can use the Search task pane to find a file's name or location as well as search for specific text in a Web page. This becomes handy when you recall the content of a page, but not the name. When you perform a search, try to use specific or unique words to achieve the best results.

Find a File or Text in a File

1. Click the File menu, and then click File Search.

2. Type the name of the file you are looking for, or any distinctive words or phrases in the Web page.

3. Click the Search In list arrow, and then select or clear the check boxes to indicate where you want the program to search.

   Click the plus sign (+) to expand a list.

4. Click the Results Should Be list arrow, and then select or clear the check boxes to indicate the type of files you want to find.

5. Click Go.

6. To revise the find, click Modify.

7. When the search results appear, point to a file, click the list arrow, and then click the command you want.

8. When you're done, click the Close button on the task pane.

Did You Know?

You can use wildcards to search for file names. When you recall only part of the file name you want to open, type a question mark (?) for any one unknown character or an asterisk (*) for two or more unknown characters.

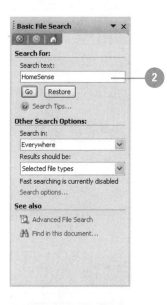

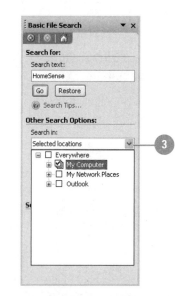

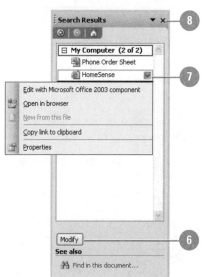

Getting Help While You Work

At some time, everyone has a question or two about the program they are using. The Office Online Help system provides the answers you need. You can search an extensive catalog of Help topics using a table of contents to locate specific information, or you can get context sensitive help in a dialog box. You can also ask your question in the Type A Question For Help box located on the right side of the menu bar. When you use any of these help options, a list of possible answers is shown to you in the Search Results task pane, with the most likely answer to your question at the top of the list.

Get Help Without the Office Assistant

1 Click the Help button on the Standard toolbar.

TIMESAVER *Press F1 to quickly open Help.*

2 Locate the Help topic you want.

◆ Type one or more keywords in the Search For box, and then click the Start Searching button.

◆ Click Table Of Contents, and then click a topic.

The topic you want appears in the right pane.

3 Read the topic, and then click any hyperlinks to get information on related topics or definitions.

4 When you're done, click the Close button.

5 Click the Close button on the task pane.

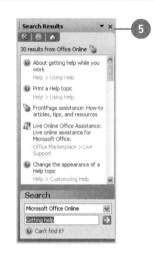

Get Help While You Work

1. Click the Type A Question For Help box.

2. Type your question, and then press Enter.

3. Click the topic that you want to read about.

4. When you're done, click the Close button.

5. Click the Close button on the task pane.

Get Help in a Dialog Box

1. Display the dialog box in which you want to get help.

2. Click the Help button.

3. Click the item in the dialog box in which you want information.

   A ScreenTip displays information about the dialog box item.

4. Click a blank area to remove the ScreenTip.

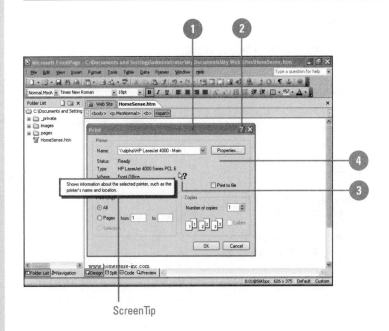

ScreenTip

Getting Help from the Office Assistant

Often the easiest way to learn how to accomplish a task is to ask someone who knows. Now, with Office, that knowledgeable friend is always available in the form of the Office Assistant. The **Office Assistant** is an animated Help feature that you can use to access information that is directly related to the task you need help with. Using everyday language, just tell the Office Assistant what you want to do and it walks you through the process step by step. You can turn this feature on and off whenever you need to. If the personality of the default Office Assistant—Clippit—doesn't appeal to you, choose from a variety of other Office Assistants.

Ask the Office Assistant for Help

1. Click the Help menu, and then click Show Office Assistant.

2. If necessary, click the Office Assistant to display the help balloon.

3. Type your question about a task you want help with.

4. Click Search.

5. Click the topic you want help with, and then read the information.

6. After you're done, click the Close button.

7. To refine the search, click the Search list arrow, select a search area, and then click the Start Searching button.

8. When you're done, click the Close button on the task pane.

9. Click the Help menu, and then click Hide The Office Assistant.

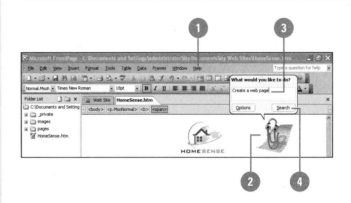

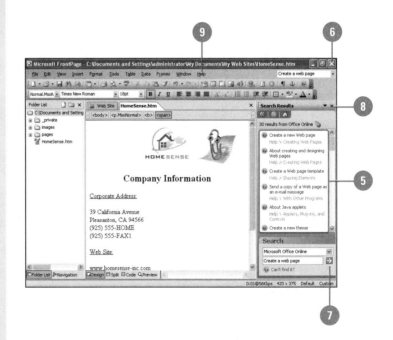

Hide the Office Assistant

1. Right-click the Office Assistant.

2. Click Hide.

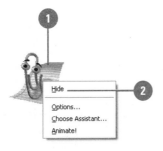

Turn Off the Office Assistant

1. Right-click the Office Assistant, and then click Options, or click the Options button in the Assistant window.

2. Click the Options tab.

3. Clear the Use The Office Assistant check box.

4. Click OK.

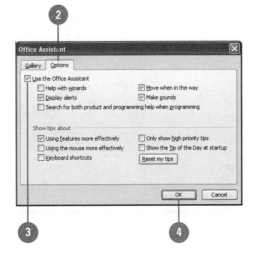

Did You Know?

You can change the Assistant character. Right-click the Assistant, and then click Choose Assistant. Click the Next and Back buttons to view the available Assistants, and then click OK. You might be asked to insert the original installation CD.

Getting FrontPage Updates on the Web

FrontPage offers a quick and easy way to get updates of any new software downloads that improve the stability and security of the program. From the Help menu, simply select the Check For Updates command to connect to the Microsoft Office Online Web site, where you can have your computer scanned for necessary updates, and then choose which Office updates you want to download and install. You can use Microsoft Office Online Web site to check out other options that are available. Using the Office Online links on the FrontPage Help task pane, you can check out FrontPage-related news, obtain the most up-to-date help from Microsoft, and locate training and assistance with any aspect of FrontPage.

Get FrontPage Updates on the Web

1. Click the Help menu, and then click Check For Updates.

   The Microsoft Office Online Web site opens, displaying the Downloads page.

2. Click Check For Updates to find out if you need FrontPage updates, and then choose the updates you want to download and install.

3. When you're done, click the Close button.

Get the Latest Information on FrontPage

1. Click the Help button on the toolbar.

2. Click one of the Office Online links for information on a FrontPage feature.

    ◆ Click Assistance to go to the Assistance Home Web page for information on ways to maximize the features you want to use in FrontPage for greater efficiency.

    ◆ Click Training to go to the Training Home Web page to learn how to use the tools in FrontPage more effectively.

    ◆ Click Communities to go the Microsoft Office Newsgroup Web page to communicate with other FrontPage users.

    ◆ Click Downloads to go the Downloads Home Web page and get the very latest information on FrontPage.

3. When you're done, click the Close button to go back to FrontPage.

4. Click the Close button on the task pane.

Detecting and Repairing Problems

To help you keep FrontPage running at its best, Office comes with its own diagnostic and repair tools. If you find that FrontPage is not behaving as you think it should, its core files might have been damaged or inadvertently deleted. Running the Detect and Repair tool restores FrontPage's default settings and finds and fixes problems that might diminish the performance of FrontPage. Before you begin the Detect and Repair procedure, make sure you close all programs that are running. If the Detect and Repair procedure doesn't fix the problem you are encountering, try reinstalling FrontPage. The FrontPage 2003 setup programs can help you reinstall or repair the program. It can also add or remove program features, or uninstall it. If an Office program gets stuck exiting or stops responding during an operation, you can use the Microsoft Office Application Recovery program to exit the program, send an error report to Microsoft, and try to recover your unsaved work.

Detect and Repair Problems

1. Click the Help menu, and then click Detect And Repair.

2. To save your shortcuts, select the Restore My Shortcuts While Repairing check box.

3. To save the settings you have specified for your FrontPage features, clear the Discard My Customized Settings And Restore Default Settings check box.

4. Click Start to begin the process.

5. If necessary, insert the Microsoft Office FrontPage 2003 CD.

6. Click OK when the procedure is complete.

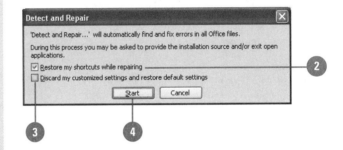

Did You Know?

You can run Detect and Repair from the setup program. In the Control Panel (Classic view), double-click Add Or Remove Programs, click Microsoft Office FrontPage 2003, click Change, click the Reinstall Or Repair option, click Next, click Repair Errors In My FrontPage Installation, and then click Install.

Recover an Office Program

1. Click the Start button on the taskbar, point to All Programs, and then point to Microsoft Office.

2. Point to Microsoft Office Tools, and then click Microsoft Office Application Recovery.

3. Click the Office program you want to recover.

4. Click Restart Application or End Application.

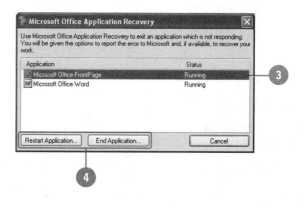

Perform Maintenance on Office Programs

1. In Windows Explorer, double-click the Setup icon on the Office CD.

2. Click one of the following maintenance buttons:

   ◆ **Add Or Remove Features.** To determine which, and when, features are installed or removed

   ◆ **Reinstall Or Repair.** To repair or reinstall Office

   ◆ **Uninstall.** To uninstall Office

3. Click Next, and then follow the wizard instructions to complete the maintenance.

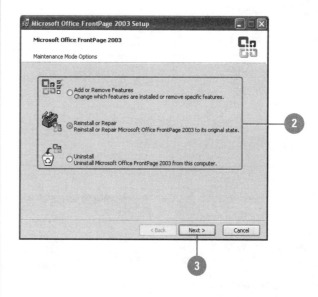

Closing a Web Page and Exiting FrontPage

After you finish working on a Web, you can close it and open another one, or close it and quit FrontPage. Closing a Web makes more computer memory available for other processes. Closing a Web is different from quitting FrontPage: after you close a Web, FrontPage is still running. When you're finished using FrontPage, you can quit the program.

Close a Web Page or Site

1. Click the File menu, and then click Close or Close Site.

   TIMESAVER *Click the Window menu, and then click Close All Pages to close all open Web pages.*

2. Click Yes to save any Web changes; click No to close the Web without saving any changes; or click Cancel to return to the Web without closing it.

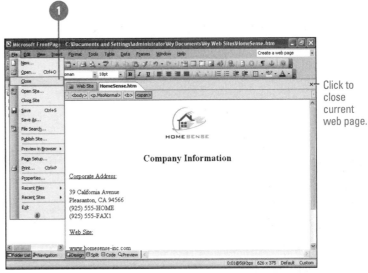

Click to close current web page.

Exit FrontPage

1. Click the File menu, and then click Exit, or click the Close button on the FrontPage program window title bar.

2. Click Yes to save any Web changes, or click No to ignore any changes.

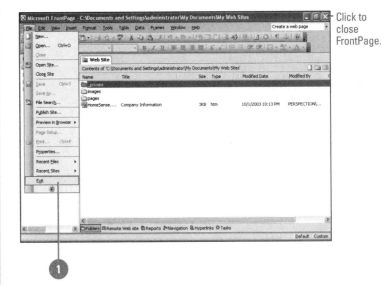

Click to close FrontPage.

Creating a Web Site

Introduction

Before jumping in and letting your creative energy take over, it's wise to plan out what you want your Web site to accomplish. Taking the time now to plan your overall ideas and getting them down on paper will save you hours of work later on. Maybe you want to create a business site that will have a corporate style to it. Perhaps you're a hobbyist who wants to display your favorite collection. Either way, having an image and content to match your product, will take some planning and research.

Microsoft Office FrontPage 2003 helps you create a Web site in two general ways—by a template or a wizard. A **template** opens a Web site with predefined headings, links, and place-holder text that specifies what information you should enter. A **wizard** walks you through the steps to create a finished document (or page) tailored to your preferences. There are six different views in FrontPage that help you work more efficiently. Some of the views include the Folders view, which displays all files and folders currently under construction. Another, the Navigation view, shows the structure of the pages in the form of a flowchart.

As far as content, FrontPage makes it easy to import a file, folder or an entire Web site. There is a wizard, called the Import Web Site Wizard, that can step you through the process. If you find that you need to insert a page or two into your site, you can do it through a blank page, or even using a template to add a page or two. Once you start gathering all this data for your site, it might be helpful to apply a theme, or an overall style. There are pre-defined themes available, or you can take one, and customize it to your preferences. With all the work that you are doing on your site, remembering to save it often is crucial to your project. When using a wizard, FrontPage automatically names your pages, or you can rename them to something more meaningful to you.

Planning a Web Site

Before you begin developing your Web site in FrontPage, there are several issues to consider and a few decisions to make. First, of course, is the question of what type of **Web page** or **Web site** you want to build. What is the focus of your design? Are you looking to create a personal page or site? Maybe you want to create a business site. Perhaps you're a hobbyist, anxious to display your extensive knowledge and imagery on your favorite subject, or a collector who wants to show off your best pieces in a personal, online museum.

After you've decided the kind of Web page or Web site you want to produce, you should consider the question of content. Stagnant sites will not draw repeat visitors, and if you want to generate traffic, you will have to update the material on a regular basis. Do you intend to generate all this content on your own, or will you be recruiting other people to produce the content? Content creation is usually the most overlooked aspect of Web design, but unless your ambition is limited to producing something such as an online family log, with photos of family and pets, birth dates, and a list of everyone's hobbies and interests, creating content might constitute your single greatest challenge.

Attracting and growing a vibrant base of visitors to your **Web site** or **Web page** requires you to have a good idea of who will make up your audience. You need to consider issues of demographics—who is interested in your Web site, how old are they, and so on. Are you aiming at surfers with a casual interest in your subject matter, or are you focusing on the expert audience?

After you've dealt with these important matters, you need to decide whether you intend to work from a **template** or create your site from scratch using the New task pane. All but the most experienced users should begin with one of the templates provided with FrontPage. These templates offer a satisfying variety of formats representing the most popular Web site styles. You can also customize a template to your specific needs by replacing the headers, textual arrangements, or graphic elements.

New Task Pane

Command	Description
Blank Page	Opens a new, blank Web page in Design view.
Text File	Opens a new, empty text file in Code view.
From Existing Page	Opens a new copy of an existing Web page.
More Page Templates	Displays the Page Templates dialog box that lists available templates.
One Page Web Site	Displays the Web Site Templates dialog box with the One Page Web Site template selected.
SharePoint Team	Displays the Web Site Templates dialog box with the SharePoint Team Site template selected.
Web Package Solutions	Displays the Web Site Templates dialog box with the Packages tab. A **package** is a complete Web site compressed into a single file.
More Web Site Templates	Displays the Web Site Templates dialog box.

Creating a One Page Web Site

When you start FrontPage, a blank Web page opens based on a default blank template. The default blank template defines the page margins, default font, and other settings. The blank Web page doesn't become a Web site until you save it. Instead of starting FrontPage and saving the new page, you can use the New task pane to quickly create a one page blank Web site, which you can fill in. You can then add new pages easily and link them together to create a connected Web site.

Create a One Page Web Site

1. Click the File menu, and then click New.

2. Click One Page Web Site on the task pane.

   The Web Site Templates dialog box opens.

3. Click the One Page Web Site icon.

4. Specify the location where you want to store the Web site (click Browse, if necessary).

5. Click OK.

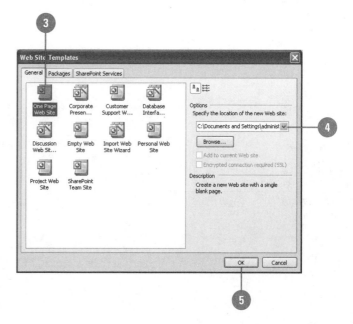

Creating a Web Site Using a Template

FrontPage comes with templates and wizards that make it easy to create a Web site. A **template** opens a Web site with predefined headings, links, and placeholder text that specifies what information you should enter (such as your address). A Web site template includes a set of related Web pages with established links ready for you to customize the content. You can use the Web Site Templates dialog box to create a Web site using templates, which include One Page Web Site, Empty Web Site, Personal Web Site, Customer Support Web Site, Project Web Site, and SharePoint Team Site.

Create a Web Site Using a Template

1. Click the File menu, and then click New.

   TIMESAVER *Click the New button list arrow on the Standard toolbar, and then click Web Site to open the Web Site Templates dialog box.*

2. Click More Web Site Templates on the task pane.

   The Web Site Templates dialog box opens.

3. Click the template icon you want to use.

4. Specify the location where you want to store the Web site (click Browse, if necessary).

5. Click OK.

> ### See Also
>
> *See Chapter 13, "Working Together on a SharePoint Team Site" on page 323 for information on creating and working with SharePoint.*

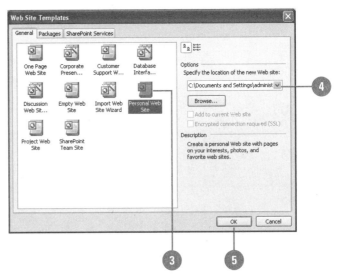

Creating a Web Site Using a Wizard

FrontPage comes with templates and wizards that make it easy to create a Web site. A **wizard** walks you through the steps to create a finished Web page tailored to your preferences. The choices that appear as you progress through a Web site wizard depend on the kind of information the Web site is designed to present and manage. First the wizard asks you for information, and then when you click Finish, the wizard creates a completely formatted Web page based on the options and content you entered. You can use the Web Site Templates dialog box to create a Web site using templates, which include Corporate Presence, Database Interface, Import Web Site, and Discussion Web Site.

Create a Web Site Using a Wizard

1. Click the File menu, and then click New.

2. Click More Web Site Templates on the task pane.

   The Web Site Templates dialog box opens.

3. Click the wizard icon you want to use.

4. Specify the location where you want to store the Web site (click Browse, if necessary).

5. Click OK.

6. Step through the wizard, entering the necessary information.

7. When you're done, click Finish.

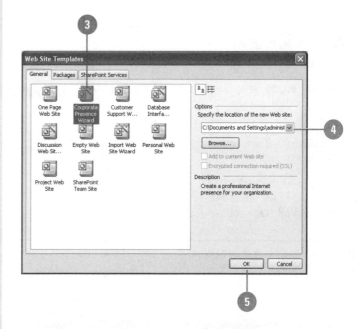

Opening an Existing Web Site

If you need to update an existing Web site, FrontPage gives you ways to open the site. You can use the Open button list arrow on the Standard toolbar, the Recent Sites command on the File menu, and the open links on the Getting Started task pane. You can open a Web site from your local hard drive, a network drive, or a Web server using a Web address, known as a **Uniform Resource Locator (URL)**. If you type a file name in the File Name box, FrontPage opens that file using the Windows file system. If you type a Web address, such as *www.myhomepage.com*, FrontPage retrieves all the files from that location just like a browser. When you open several pages at the same time, they all appear in the same window. However, if you open a new site while another site is still open, the new site opens in a new FrontPage window.

Open a Web Site from a Local Computer

1. Click the Open button list arrow on the Standard toolbar, and then click Open Site.

2. Click an icon on the Places bar to open a frequently used folder.

3. If necessary, click the Look In list arrow, and then select the folder location of the Web page you want to open.

4. Select the Web folder with the site you want to open.

5. Click Open.

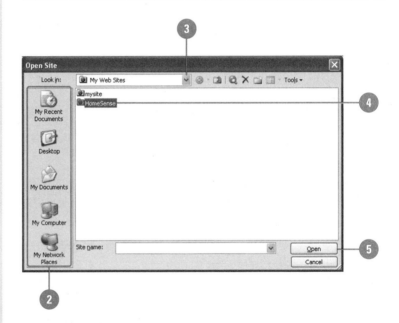

Did You Know?

You can open a recently opened Web site. If you've recently accessed a Web site, you can use the File menu to quickly open it again. Click the File menu, click Recent Sites, and then click the site you want.

For Your Information

Internet URLs

A URL (Uniform Resource Locator) is like a postal address, each part of the address helps indicate where it's supposed to go. The entire address includes the Hypertext Transfer Protocol (HTTP), a colon, two forward slashes, and the site type (usually www for World Wide Web). This is followed by the domain address (the site's name), a period, and the domain name (refers to the type of site, such as .com for commercial). A sample URL is *http://www.quepublishing.com*.

Open a Web Site from a Web Server

1. Click the Open button list arrow on the Standard toolbar, and then click Open Site.

2. Type the URL of the page you want.

   TROUBLE? *If the URL doesn't connect, create a network connection, and then use My Network Places on the Places bar. On the Windows desktop, click the Start button, click My Network Places, click Add Network Place, and then follow the wizard instructions to create a shortcut to a Web or network folder.*

3. Click Open.

4. Type the user name and password for the Web server.

5. Select the Remember My Password check box if you don't want to type your user name and password in the future.

6. Click OK.

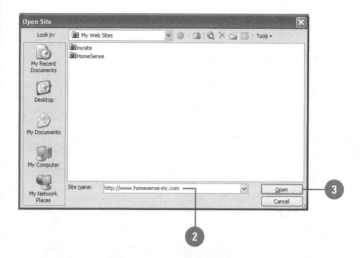

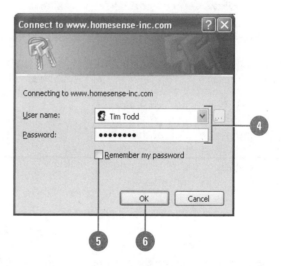

Changing Views

FrontPage displays the contents of a Web site and Web page in different ways to help you work efficiently with your content. When you click the Web Site tab, FrontPage displays six views at the bottom of the window, which you can also access from the View menu.

Folders view displays a list of files in the Web site, organized by folder. From this view, you can manage files and folders, and open files with the corresponding editor.

Remote Web Site view displays a comparison of files in the current local Web site and the remote site. From this view, you can copy a working version of a site to the live site on a service provider's Web server.

Reports view displays a list of information and links to help manage the site.

Navigation view structures the pages of a web in a flowchart. The web is displayed in a hierarchical format, with the home page at the top of the chart. The pages that branch off directly from the home page (Parent page) are considered Child pages of the home page.

Hyperlinks view displays files in a site, organized by hyperlink reference.

Tasks view displays a list of reminders relating to pages.

When you click a document tab, FrontPage enters **Page** view and displays as many as five views at the bottom of the window.

Design view displays Web pages in WYSIWYG (What You See Is What You Get) view for editing.

Split view displays the screen in half horizontally. The top half displays the current page in Code view and the bottom half displays the current page in Design view.

No Frames view displays the current page as a browser that doesn't support frames. This view is available only when the page is a frameset.

Code view displays the HTML and any embedded code for a page.

Preview view starts Microsoft Internet Explorer and displays the current page.

Folders view

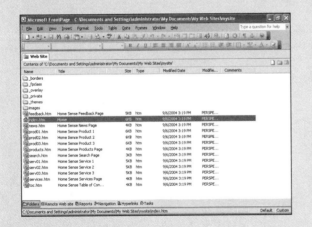

Reports view

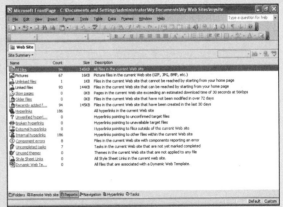

Navigation view

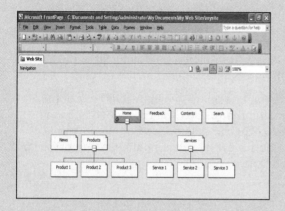

Hyperlinks view

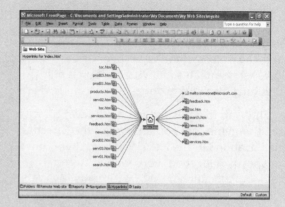

Tasks view

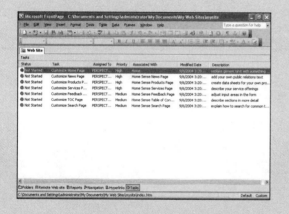

Page view

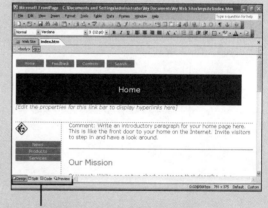

Design, Split, Code, and Preview views

Working with Folders View

The Folders view displays all files and folders currently under construction. To access this view, click the Web Site tab or click Folders on the View menu. Two main folders (Private and Images) are created for all new template-based sites, regardless of the wizard you used. However, templates and wizards do create additional files and folders.

The Web folder is tagged by the web's location, the name that you entered in the Specify The Location Of The New Web box. If you did not specify a location, your web is stored in the default location C:\My Documents\My Web

Sites\folder. The Private folder contains any information obtained from special forms or any other data input objects on the site and cannot be accessed by a visitor. Finally, the Images folder enables you to store any images, from digital photos to clip art, which are part of this web.

You can open files in this view by double-clicking them. Files will be opened in Page view. You can delete files from your web in Folders view by selecting the file and pressing the Delete key.

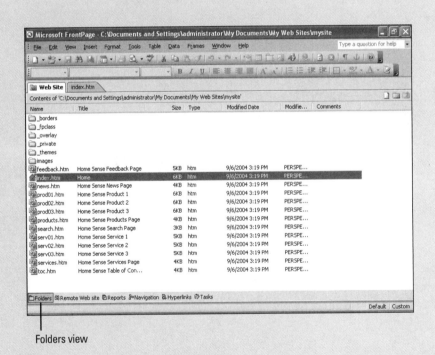

Folders view

36

Viewing the Folder List

FrontPage offers a useful feature for managing files and folders, called the **Folder list**. The Folder list displays the window in two panes, or frames, which allows you to view information from two different locations. The left pane of the Folder list displays the file hierarchy of all the folders and files in your Web site, and the right pane displays Web site files and folders, or individual Web pages. This arrangement enables you to view the file hierarchy of your Web site and the contents of a folder simultaneously, making it easy to copy, move, delete, and rename files and folders. Using the plus sign (+) and the minus sign (-) to the left of an icon in the Folder list allows you to display different levels of folders in your Web site without opening and displaying the contents of each folder. You can open folders and files by double-clicking them.

View the Folder List

1. Open the Web site in which you want to view.

2. Click the View menu, and then click Folder List.

3. Perform the commands you want to display folder structure and contents:

   ◆ To show the file and folder structure, click the plus sign (+).

   ◆ To hide the file and folder structure, click the minus sign (-).

   ◆ To display the contents of a folder, click the folder icon.

   ◆ To open a file, double-click the file.

4. When you're done, click the Close button on the Folder list.

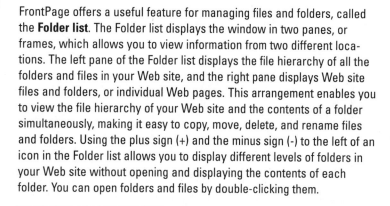

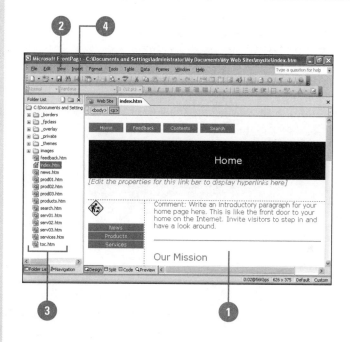

> **Did You Know?**
>
> *You can quickly determine if a folder contains folders.* When neither plus sign (+) nor minus sign (-) appears next to an icon in the Folder list, the item has no folders in it.

2

Working with Navigation View

The Navigation view structures the pages of a web in the form of a flowchart. The web is displayed in a hierarchical format, with the home page, or **Mother page**, at the top of the chart. The pages that branch off directly from the home page (**Parent page**) are considered **Child pages** of the home page.

Any page that links directly to the home page is a Child page, but it can also be a Parent page if it, in turn, produces Child pages that link to it. Each page that opens one tier below the page it is linked to is a Child page. The terms Parent and Child page are therefore relational in nature. The higher page in the hierarchy will always be the parent to any linked lower page, which will always be the child. Therefore, a second-level page can be both the Child of a page and the Parent page of a lower-level Child page.

Navigation view provides an easy way to view your pages. Using the plus sign (+) and the minus sign (-) in the icon in the Navigation view allows you to display different levels of pages in your Web site. It also provides the easiest method for re-arranging the order of your pages, or creating new Parent pages. You can reposition a page in your web by dragging a page.

Navigation view also includes the Navigation View toolbar, which contains the following buttons: New Page, Add Existing Pages, New Custom Link Bar, Included In Link Bars, View Subtree Only, Portrait/Landscape, and Zoom. You can use these buttons to add pages, create Web site navigation, and change the display in Navigation view.

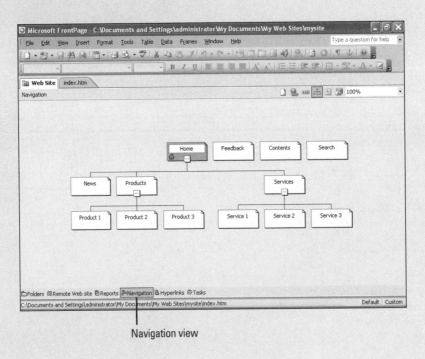

Navigation view

Creating a Web Site in Navigation View

If you want to create a Web site from scratch and prefer a visual approach, you can do it in Navigation view. Navigation view allows you to design a Web site in a storyboard approach, where you can see the big picture. You can build a Web site in Navigation view by creating an empty Web site, adding a home page, and then inserting new blank pages. Each new page appears in Navigation view as a child of whatever page you select before inserting it.

Create a Web Site in Navigation View

1 Click the New button list arrow on the Standard toolbar, and then click Web Site.

2 Click the Empty Web icon, and then click OK.

3 Click the Navigation button.

4 Right-click anywhere inside Navigation view, point to New, and then click Top Page.

5 Click the Home page icon title, and then type title (this name will appear at the top of the Web page).

6 Click the Home page, and then click the New Page button on the Navigation View toolbar.

7 To add more pages, repeat Step 6. Each new page appears as a child of the page you select.

8 Click the Folders button to create the physical pages.

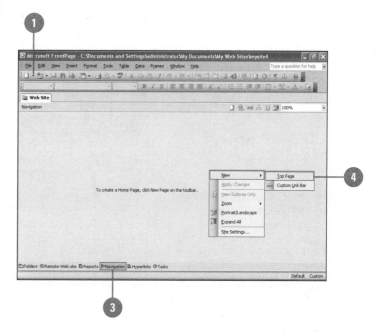

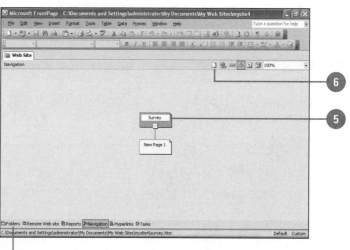

Did You Know?

You can display the Navigation view in the Folder list. Click the View menu, click Folder List, click a Web page tab, and then click Navigation at the bottom of the Folder list.

Importing Web Content

When you're working on a Web site, you might want to import a page file (or even an entire folder) that was created in another Microsoft program. Or you might want to download a site that you admire from the Web so that you can analyze its structure closely before preparing your own. FrontPage makes it easy to import a file, folder, or a Web site. When you import a Web site, FrontPage uses the Import Web Site Wizard to step you through the process. The wizards helps you transfer files using FrontPage Server Extensions or SharePoint Services, WebDAV (Distributed Authoring and Versioning), FTP (File Transfer Protocol), Windows file system, and HTTP (directly from a Web site on the Internet).

Import Web Content

① Open the Web site in which you want to import Web content.

② Click the View menu, and then click Folder List.

③ Select the folder you want to import the file or folder to (if you're importing a picture, for example, target it to the Images folder).

④ Click the File menu, and then click Import.

⑤ Click Add File or Add Folder.

⑥ Click the Look In list arrow, and then select the location with the file, folder, or URL you want to import.

⑦ Click the file or folder, and then click Open to add it to the Import dialog box.

⑧ When you have selected all the files that you want to import, click OK.

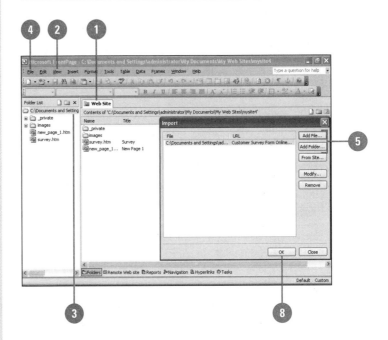

Import Web Content from a Web Site

1. Open the Web site in which you want to import Web content.

2. Click the View menu, and then click Folder List.

3. Select the folder you want to import the file or folder to (if you're importing a picture, for example, target it to the Images folder).

4. Click the File menu, and then click Import.

5. Click From Site.

   The Import Web Site Wizard dialog box opens.

6. Click the option indicating how you want to get the files. For the HTTP option, type a Web address.

7. Click Next, and then follow the wizard instructions to complete the task. Each option asks you to support different information.

8. When you're done, click Finish.

   The wizards imports the Web files into corresponding folders in your site.

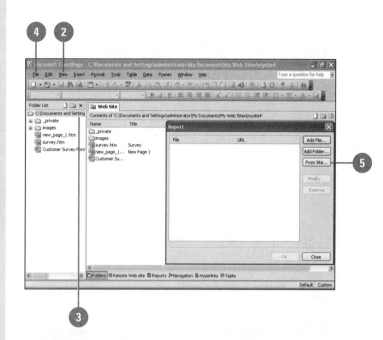

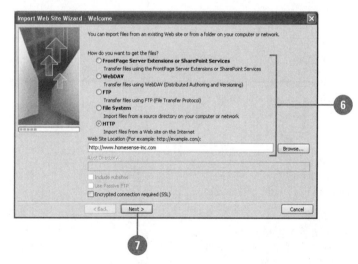

Adding Pages to Your Web Site

Whether you have the basic Web site created via a wizard, or are beginning from scratch, you will eventually need to add new pages to the site. New pages can be blank or template based, so it is also possible to integrate template pages with your own pages that you created from scratch. The Page Templates dialog box contains an extensive selection of single-page templates. After you create the new page, you need to create a hyperlink to the existing Web.

Add Pages to a Web Site

1. Click the Web Site tab for the site in which you want to add a new page, and then click the Folders button.

2. If necessary, click the View menu, and then click Folder List to display the Folder list.

3. Right-click a blank area of the Folders window, point to New, and then click Blank Page.

   A new file appears in the Folder List, and is assigned a default name which is highlighted and framed in a box.

4. Type a new name (including .htm at the end) for the page, and then press Enter.

5. Click the Navigation button at the bottom of the window.

6. Drag the file name icon for the page from the Folder list into the Navigation view.

   Expanding and contracting perforated lines appear any place where your page can be positioned.

7. When the new page is where you want it, release the mouse button to position the page.

8. Double-click the new page to open it for editing.

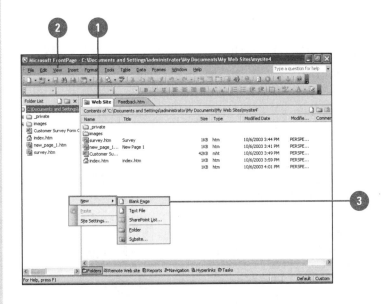

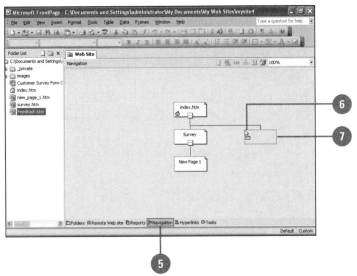

Add Pages to a Web Site Using Templates

1 Click the New button list arrow on the Standard toolbar, and then click Page.

2 Click the tab with the page template you want to use.

◆ **General.** Provides typical page templates.

◆ **My Templates.** Custom templates saved in the current Web site. If there are no templates, this tab doesn't appear.

◆ **Web Parts.** Page arrangements to display Web parts for Web site on a Web server with SharePoint. If Web site doesn't reside on a Web server, this tab doesn't appear.

◆ **Frames Pages.** Provides frame page templates.

◆ **Style Sheets**. Initializes a cascading style sheet (CSS) file to standardize the appearance of Web pages.

3 Click the template icon you want to use.

4 Click OK.

5 Click the Save button on the Standard toolbar, type a name for the page, and then click Save.

6 Click the Web Site tab, and then click the Navigation button at the bottom of the window.

7 Drag the file name icon for the page from the Folder list into the Navigation view.

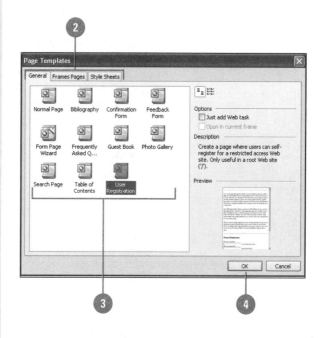

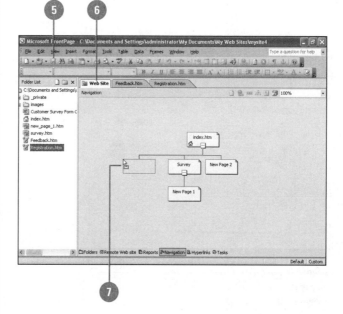

Applying a Theme to a Web Page

While the templates provide a nice structure and underpinning for your site, they can sometimes look a little generic. Using **Themes**, motifs that visually unify your site, you can personalize your web with the use of color, banners, buttons, and bullets. Initially, a site made from a template will probably be adequate for your needs, but as you visit more sites and become more familiar with the Internet, you will notice tell tail indications of template-based sites. Themes are crucial in building an original, distinctive site. When your needs become more sophisticated, no template will suit all your needs. Using themes is the most accessible and user-friendly method to enhance your web.

Format a Web Page Using a Theme

1. Click the Format menu, and then click Theme.

2. Select the pages in which you want to apply the theme.

3. Select a theme on the task pane.

4. Select the check boxes you want to further modify the theme.

   ◆ **Vivid Colors.** Sharpens colors within the theme.

   ◆ **Active Graphics.** Adds a semi-3-D quality that cause the buttons and text to stand out.

   ◆ **Background Picture.** Places either a shade or an image as the background.

5. When you're done, click the Close button on the task pane.

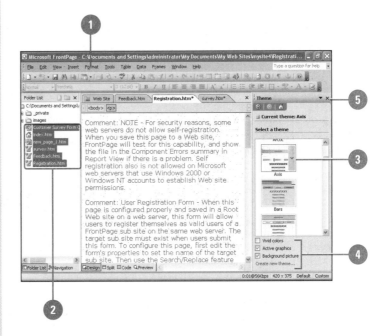

Did You Know?

You can distribute themes. FrontPage themes can be used in other Office programs. A theme consists of a folder and three files which is stored at C:\Program Files\Common Files\Microsoft Shared\ Theme*theme name.* You can copy these files to other computers.

Customize a Theme

1. Click the Format menu, and then click Theme.

2. Point to the theme you want to customize on the task pane.

3. Click the list arrow, and then click Customize.

4. Click Colors.

5. Click a color scheme on the Color Schemes tab or use the Color Wheel and Custom tabs to select your own set of colors.

6. Click OK.

7. Click Graphics.

8. Click the Item list arrow, and then click a graphic type.

9. Select the options you want from the Picture and Fonts tab to customize the graphic.

10. Click the Normal Graphics or Active Graphics option to make graphics more or less vivid.

11. Click OK.

12. Click Text, change the fonts used in the theme, and then click OK.

13. Click Save As, type a theme name, and then click OK.

14. Click OK to close the Customize Theme dialog box.

15. When you're done, click the Close button on the task pane.

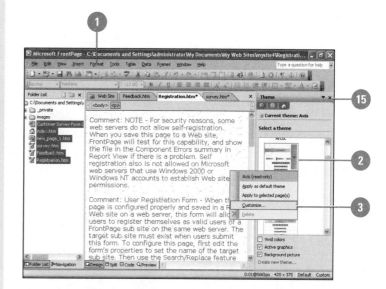

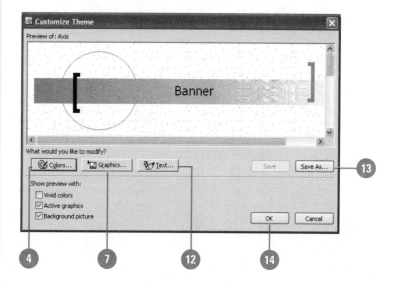

Saving a Web Site

After you finish working with a Web site, you need to save the material. When you add a new Web page or change an existing page in a Web site, the icon changes (adding a pencil) to make easier to identify the modified files. When you save a Web site, you save each Web page and any related, or embedded, files, such as graphics, included with the pages. You can use the Save All command on the File menu to quickly save all modified files. If graphics on a Web page need to be saved, the Save Embedded Files dialog box appears, asking you to select any options you want and save the files.

Save a Web Site

1. Click the File menu, and then click Save All.

2. If necessary, specify which image files you want to save with the Web page or pages, and where to save them.

   ◆ **Rename.** Rename the embedded file name.

   ◆ **Change Folder.** Change the embedded folder location.

   ◆ **Set Action.** Set option to save or not save an embedded file.

   ◆ **Picture File Type.** Change the graphic type and quality.

3. Click OK.

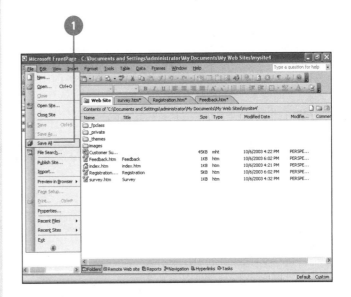

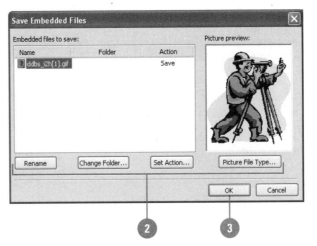

Renaming a Web Site

When you create a Web site using a template or wizard, FrontPage automatically give the site a general name (mysite1, mysite2, etc.) and saves it. You can rename the site to something more meaningful to you. You can right-click the Web site folder or use the Site Settings command on the Tools menu.

Rename a Web Site

1. Click the Tools menu, and then click Site Settings.

2. Click the General tab.

3. Type a new site name.

4. Click OK.

Did You Know?

You can rename the Web folder.
Right-click the Web folder in Folders view or the Folder list, click Rename, type a new name, and the press Enter. You can also rename a Web folder in Windows Explorer.

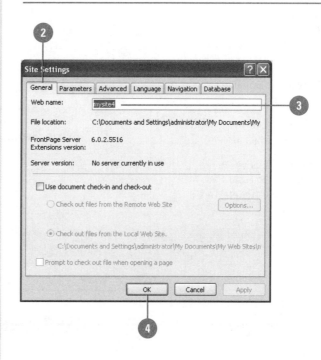

Deleting a Web Site

If you no longer want or need a Web site you can delete it. When you delete a Web site, FrontPage deletes everything it contains, including Web pages, pictures, text files, FrontPage files, and all folders. If you want to save any files in the Web site folder, you need to back them up before deleting the site.

Delete a Web Site

1. Open the Web site you want to delete.

2. Click the View menu, and then click Folder List.

3. Right-click the Web site you want to remove, and then click Delete.

4. Click the option to Remove FrontPage Information From This Web Site Only or click Delete This Web Site Entirely.

5. Click OK.

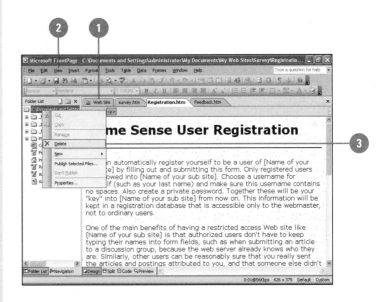

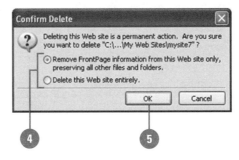

Managing and Linking Web Pages

Introduction

Once on the Web, you can open other Web pages in the Folders or Navigation views, or you can even open up another page in FrontPage using the Windows menu. Microsoft Office FrontPage 2003 provides several ways to navigate between pages. After you open a Web page, you can use the document tabs at the top of the editing window in Design view, choose the Web page's name from the Window menu, or press Ctrl+Tab until the page you want appears in the window to navigate between pages.

One of the most user-friendly components of FrontPage is its capability to automatically convert text and images into HTML format. When you save a Web or Web page, it is actually being saved in HTML format. After you create a Web site, you can use Navigation view to quickly and easily manage individual Web pages. When you are surfing the Web, a bookmark in your browser is a shortcut to a Web site or page, a placeholder so that you can quickly access a favorite location in cyberspace.

Hyperlinks connect you to information in other documents. Rather than duplicating the information stored in other documents, you can create hyperlinks to the relevant material. Web sites are continually changing as new content and hyperlinks provide greater functionality and ease of use for visitors. If a link becomes outdated or unnecessary, you can easily revise or remove it. You can also test the hyperlinks to make sure that they are pointing you to the right direction and the correct information.

You can preview your Web pages in a browser, or in Design view. Because each browser can display your site differently, you will want to examine your site using several of the most popular browser formats. You can also create your own template, instead of using one of the built-in page templates that comes with FrontPage.

What You'll Do

Open Web Pages from Within a Web

Navigate Web Pages

Display Web Pages in the HTML Format

Manage Web Pages in Navigation View

Create Bookmarks

Create Hyperlinks to Files, Web Pages, and E-Mail Addresses

Edit Hyperlinks

Add Shared Borders

Work with Hyperlinks View

Verify Hyperlinks

Preview Web Pages

Preview and Print Web Pages

Export Web Content

Create a Page Template

Use a Dynamic Page Template

Save a Web Page with Different Formats

Opening Web Pages from Within a Web

FrontPage allows you to multi-task, which means you can have more than one Web page open at the same time. After you open a Web site, you can quickly open Web pages in Folders or Navigation views, or from the Folder list instead of using the Open button on the Standard toolbar or the Open command on the File menu. If you want to view open Web pages in a separate FrontPage window, you can choose New Window from the Window menu, and then open the pages or sites you want. You can press Alt+Tab to switch between the separate windows. Instead of starting from scratch to create a new page, you can open a copy of an existing page with the default new Web page title of New_Page_1.htm.

Open a Web Page in Folders or Navigation View

1. Open the Web site with the Web page you want to open.

2. Click the Web Site tab.

3. Click the Folders or Navigation button.

4. Double-click the icon or file name representing the page you want to access.

Did You Know?

You can open a linked page from Design view. Press and hold Ctrl and click a hyperlink in the page, or right-click a hyperlink in a page that's already open, and then click Follow Hyperlink.

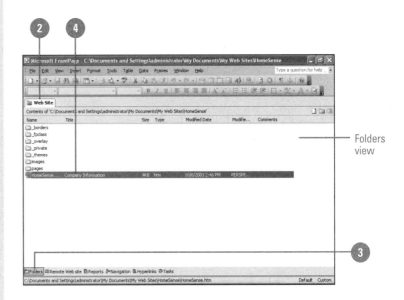

Folders view

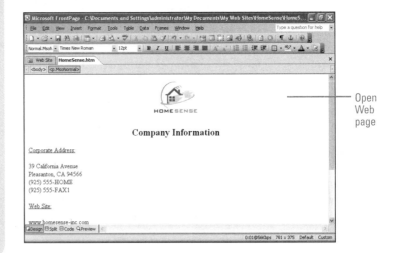

Open Web page

Open a Web Page Using the Folder List

1. Open the Web site with the Web page you want to open.

2. Click the View menu, and then click Folder List.

3. Double-click the page you want to open.

4. Click the Close button on the Folder List.

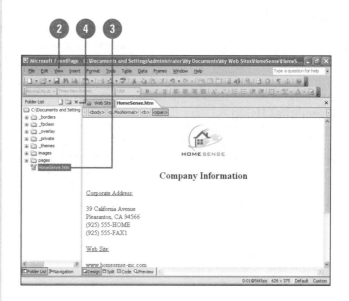

Open a Copy of a Web Page Using the Folder List

1. Open the Web site with the Web page you want to open.

2. Click the View menu, and then click Folder List.

3. Right-click the page you want to copy, and then click New From Existing Page.

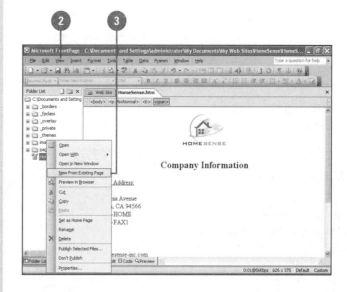

Navigating Web Pages

FrontPage provides several ways to navigate between pages. After you open a Web page, you can use the document tabs at the top of the editing window in Design view, choose the Web page's name from the Window menu, or press Ctrl+Tab until the page you want appears in the window to navigate between pages.

Navigate Web Pages Using Document Tabs

1. Click the View menu, and then click Page.

2. Click the document tab with the page you want to display.

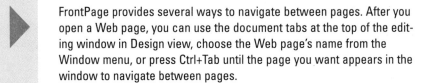

Navigate Web Pages Using the Windows Menu

1. Click the Window menu.

   This displays a list of up to nine open Web pages.

2. Click the page you want to open. The Web page opens in Page view.

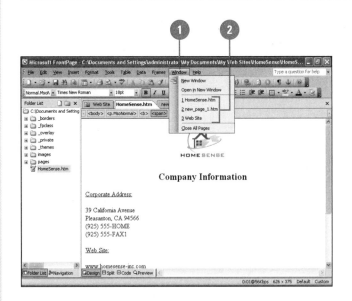

Displaying Web Pages in the HTML Format

One of the most user-friendly components of FrontPage is its capability to automatically convert text and images into HTML format. If you're familiar with HTML, you might be comfortable enough to work in this mode. HTML adds a series of format instructions to your content using tags, such as <i>, that indicate how to format the text for display on the Web. Use the Quick Tag Selector to select any tag in your Web page. Use the Quick Tag Editor to insert, wrap, and edit HTML tags. FrontPage uses colored text to distinguish between elements when working in HTML format.

Display a Web Page in HTML

1. Open the Web page you want to display in the HTML format.

2. Click the Split or Code button at the bottom of the window.

   The Web page appears in HTML coded form.

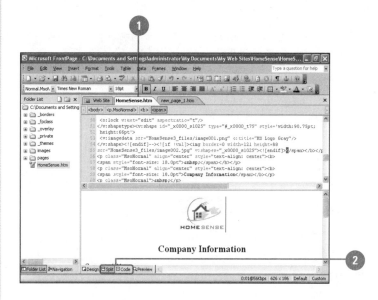

Display HTML Tags in Design View

1. Open the Web page you want to display HTML tags.

2. Click the View menu, and then click Reveal Tags.

   HTML tags appear in capsule-size, six-sided frames within the text.

3. To turn off HTML tags, click the View menu, and then click Reveal Tags again.

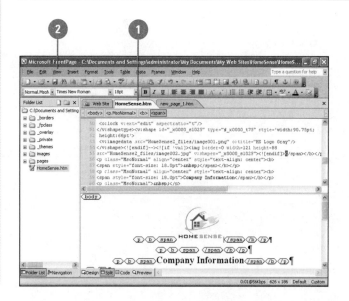

Managing Web Pages in Navigation View

After you create a Web site, you can use Navigation view to quickly and easily manage individual Web pages. You can add pages to a Web or move pages to a different location by simply dragging the page in Navigation view. If a page name is not exactly what you want, you can quickly rename it. If you no longer need or want a Web page, you can remove it. You can determine whether you want the page deleted from your hard drive or just from the Web.

Add an Existing Web Page to a Web Site

1. Open the Web site with the Web page you want to open, and then click the Web Site tab.

2. Click the Navigation button.

3. Click the page icon to which you want to connect the page.

4. Click the Add Existing Page button on the Navigation View toolbar.

5. If necessary, click the Existing File Or Web Page button, and then click one of the Look In buttons.

6. Click the page you want to add.

7. Click OK.

Did You Know?

You can rename a Web page. In Navigation view, click the page icon with the title you want to rename, click the text, type a new name, and then press Enter. This doesn't change the name of the Web page file, which you can do in the Folder list.

See Also

See "Adding Pages to Your Web Site" on page 42 for information on adding and renaming pages.

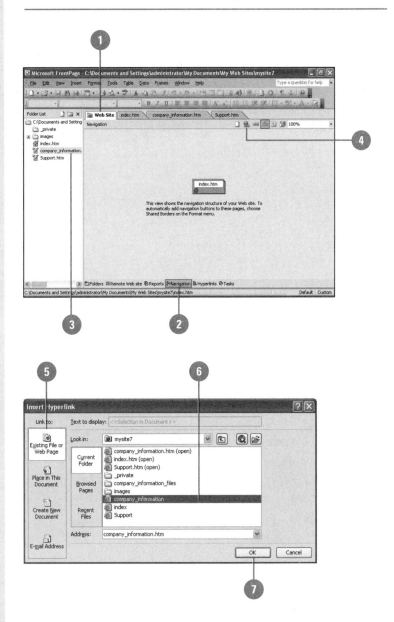

Move a Web Page

1. Open the Web site with the Web page you want to open, and then click the Web Site tab.

2. Click the Navigation button.

3. Drag the page icon to the position where you want it to occupy on your site.

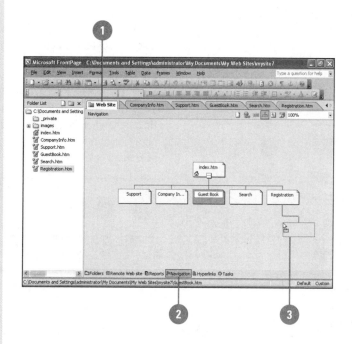

Delete a Web Page

1. Open the Web site with the Web page you want to open, and then click the Web Site tab.

2. Click the Navigation or Folders button.

3. Click the page icon you want to delete.

4. Press Delete.

5. Click the delete option you want to remove the page from the structure in Navigation view or the entire Web site.

6. Click OK.

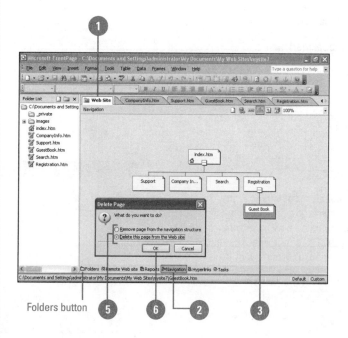

Folders button

Creating Bookmarks

When you are surfing the Web, a bookmark in your browser is a shortcut to a Web site or page, a placeholder so that you can quickly access a favorite location in cyberspace. In FrontPage, the term bookmark is used to denote a link that helps the reader navigate a long Web page quickly, rather than having to scroll through it. After you have placed one or more bookmarks, they are available to navigate to in the Bookmark dialog box. If you no longer need a bookmark, you can delete it. However, when you delete a bookmark, any hyperlinks that are connected to the deleted destination are not automatically adjusted and are now dead links that you need to locate and repair.

Create a Bookmark

1. Click the View menu, click Page, and then open the Web page you want to use.

2. Select the text or graphic element within the page that you want to bookmark. If you have broken the page into sections, section headers make excellent bookmarks.

3. Click the Insert menu, and then click Bookmark.

4. Type a bookmark name.

5. Click OK.

   In Design view, the bookmark appears with a perforated underline.

Did You Know?

You can rename a bookmark. Right-click the bookmark, click Bookmark Properties, type the new name, and then click OK. FrontPage does the rest, reconfiguring any relevant hyperlinks.

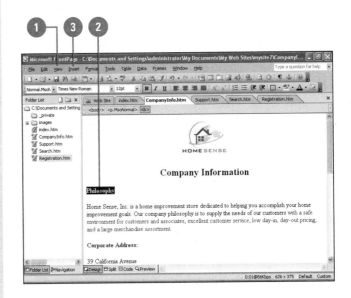

Navigate to Bookmarks

1. Click the Insert menu, and then click Bookmark.

2. Click the bookmark in which you want to navigate.

3. Click Go To.

4. Click OK.

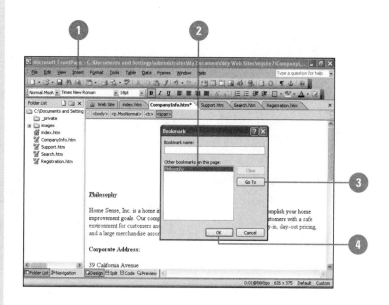

Delete Bookmarks

1. Click the Insert menu, and then click Bookmark.

2. Click the bookmark you want to remove.

3. Click Go To.

4. Click Clear.

See Also

See "Verifying Hyperlinks" on page 65 for information on verifying hyperlinks after you delete a bookmark.

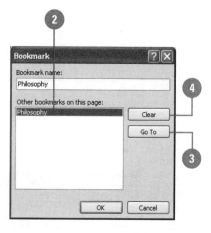

Creating Hyperlinks to Files, Web Pages, and E-Mail Addresses

Hyperlinks connect you to information in other documents. Rather than duplicating the important information stored in other documents, you can create hyperlinks to the relevant material. You can create hyperlinks to external files and pages from a local or Internet location. Linking to external sites cannot be accomplished through the Navigation view; instead you use the Insert Hyperlink button on the Standard toolbar. You can also create hyperlinks to e-mail addresses. Creating a link to an e-mail address allows users of your Web page to contact you, or any other e-mail recipient that you specify.

Create a Hyperlink to an External Web Page or File

1. Click the View menu, and then click Page.

2. Open a page of your site.

3. Select the word or words you want to link from.

4. Click the Insert Hyperlink button on the Standard toolbar.

5. Click the Existing File Or Web Page button on the Link To bar.

   The words you entered as the link on your Web page appear in the Text To Display box.

6. Click Current Folder, Browsed Pages, or Recent Files to locate a file or Web page.

7. Select the file or Web page to which you want to link, or type a URL to access an Internet location in the Address box.

8. Click OK.

   Page view appears, where the link opens in blue.

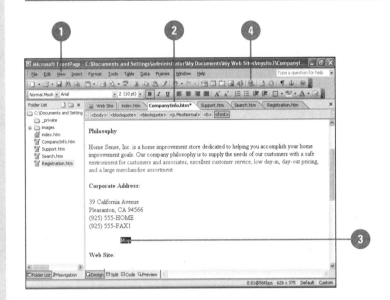

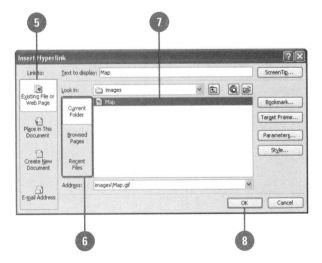

Create a Hyperlink to an E-mail Address

1. Click the View menu, and then click Page.

2. Open a page of your site in Page view.

3. Select the word or words you want to link from.

4. Click the Insert Hyperlink button on the Standard toolbar.

5. Click the E-mail Address button on the Link To bar.

   The words you entered as the link on your Web page appear in the Text To Display box.

6. Type the e-mail address you want to link to and the text you would like to automatically appear in the Subject line (optional).

7. Click OK to complete the link.

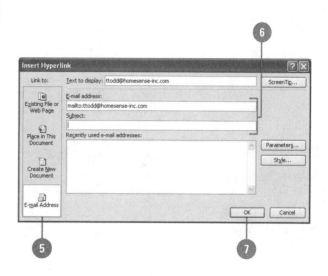

Did You Know?

You can change other options in the Insert Hyperlink dialog box. Other options available through the Insert Hyperlink dialog box are Bookmark, Target Frame (when you click a hyperlink on a page displayed in one frame on a Frames Page, the page the hyperlink points to usually opens another frame, designated the Target Frame), Parameters (access to additional hyperlink parameters), and Style (additional formatting options).

For Your Information

Hyperlinking to Adobe Acrobat and Other Files

In addition to Web pages, you can create hyperlinks to Adobe Acrobat (PDF) files, Microsoft Office documents, and ZIP files to name a few. When a visitor clicks a hyperlink to a file, the related program starts and opens the file directly from the Web page. If the visitor's computer doesn't have the program, the file doesn't open. To avoid this problem, you need to inform visitors what software they need to view the file. In many cases, you can provide a link to obtain the software.

3

Editing Hyperlinks

Web site are continually changing as new content and hyperlinks provide greater functionality and ease of use for visitors. If a link becomes outdated or unnecessary, you can easily revise or remove it. When you click a hyperlink for the first time (during a session), the color of the hyperlink changes, indicating that you have accessed the hyperlink. If you prefer a different color, you can change the color of the hyperlink in different states.

Change a Hyperlink

1. Right-click the hyperlink, and then click Hyperlink Properties.

2. Change the address for the link (use the Browse For Web or Browse For File buttons if necessary).

3. Click OK.

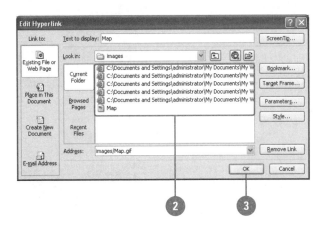

Remove a Hyperlink

1. Right-click the hyperlink, and then click Hyperlink Properties.

2. Click Remove Link.

Change Hyperlink Colors

1. Right-click a blank area in a Web page, and then click Page Properties.

2. Click the Formatting tab.

3. Click the list arrow next to the corresponding hyperlink option, and then click a color.

   ◆ **Hyperlink.** The color used for a hyperlink that hasn't been used yet.

   ◆ **Visited Hyperlink.** The color used after a hyperlink has been used.

   ◆ **Active Hyperlink.** The color used while the user is actually clicking the hyperlink.

4. Click OK.

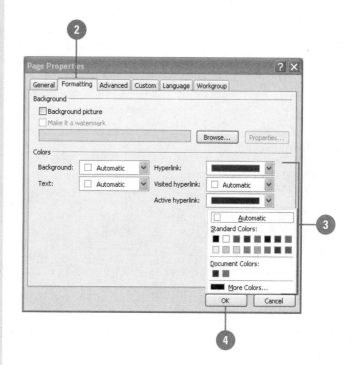

Adding Shared Borders

Shared borders provide a consistent and easy way to add navigation to a Web site. Whatever you put in a shared border, such as buttons, hyperlinks, or text, appears on every page in the site. You can add up to four shared borders located at the top, left, right, or bottom edge of each page in the site. You can also add Web components—such as Page Banner, Link Bar, or Date And Time—to a shared border to provide added functionality and output based on different events.

Add a Shared Border

1. Open the Web site in which you want to add a shared border.

2. Click the Format menu, and then click Shared Borders.

   TROUBLE? *If the Shared Borders command is dimmed, click the Tools menu, click Page Options, click the Authoring tab, select the Shared Borders check box, and then click OK.*

3. Click the All Pages or Current Page option.

4. Select one or more of the check boxes for each border you want to use.

5. Select the Include Navigation Buttons check box for the borders you want to use.

   If you select the check box under Top, FrontPage adds a Page Banner and a Link Bar component. If you select the check box under Left or Right, FrontPage add a Link Bar component to the border.

6. Click OK.

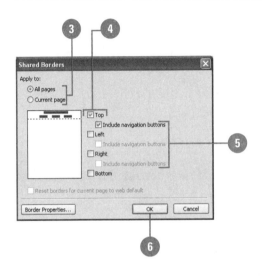

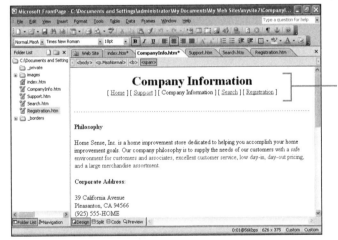

Shared border

Change Shared Border Text

1. Open a Web page with the shared border.

2. Click the existing text in the shared border to select it.

3. Type the new text.

Modify a Web Component in a Shared Border

1. Open a Web page with the shared border.

2. Double-click the Web component you want to change.

3. Change the options you want.

4. Click OK.

Did You Know?

You can insert a Web component later. Place the insertion point in the shared border, click the Insert menu, and then click Page Banner, Date And Time, or Web Component, respectively, to insert a page banner, the date and time, or a link bar.

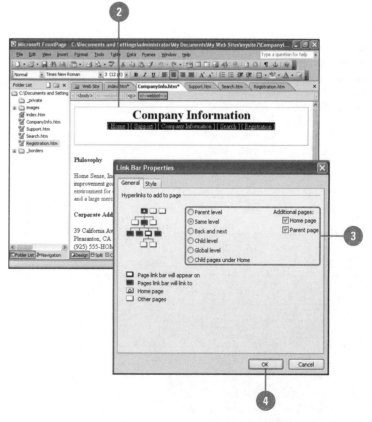

Working with Hyperlinks View

The Hyperlinks view offers a simplified presentation of the source and destination of internal and external hyperlinks that appear on a given page. These links are displayed in a flowchart fashion. Clicking the plus sign (+) box for any page displays that page's links. This provides a quick, easy method to expand or shrink the link view to display the entire link structure of the pages, or only those that link directly to the home page. Double-clicking a page automatically displays that page in Page view and moves it to the center of the hyperlink display when you revert to Hyperlinks view.

Display Hyperlinks View

1 Open the Web site in which you want to display hyperlinks.

2 Click the Web Site tab.

3 Click the Hyperlinks button at the bottom of the window.

4 Click a plus sign (+) to display the entire link structure of a page.

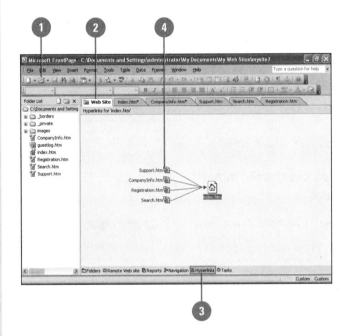

Did You Know?

Links are displayed using a variety of buttons. In Hyperlinks view, a page containing a globe button represents the presence of a link to the Web. A page featuring a picture button signifies a link to a visual element, and an envelope button indicates the hyperlink leads to a piece of e-mail.

Verifying Hyperlinks

When you have a layout of your hyperlinks, you'll want to confirm that they're accurately linked. Because sites are purchased, re-started, and even shut down on a regular basis, URLs to external links can change. The Hyperlinks view displays your links, but it doesn't assure that they are correct. To verify links, use the Reports view.

Verify Hyperlinks in Reports View

1. Click the View menu, point to Reports, point to Problems, and then click Hyperlinks.

2. Click the Verify Hyperlinks button on the Reporting toolbar.

3. Click the Verify All Hyperlinks option.

4. Click Start.

5. If prompted to connect to the Web, click Yes.

   FrontPage 2003 automatically checks any links that haven't been confirmed as correct and generates a report. Scan the Status column and make sure you don't have any broken links. If there are none, the process is over.

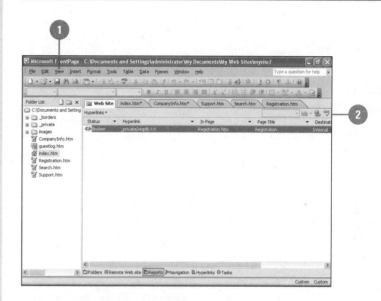

Did You Know?

You can re-connect a broken link. If you do have a broken link, right-click it, and then click Edit Hyperlink. The Edit Hyperlink dialog box opens with the link of the page in question, and a blank space for you to enter the correct address. There are also two boxes so that you can choose to apply the change to all pages where the link appears, or only in selected places.

Previewing Web Pages

The Preview view displays how the Web will appear to a visitor who is browsing with Microsoft's Internet Explorer. Because each browser can display your site differently, you will want to examine your site using several of the most popular browser formats. When you are ready to see how your page will look to visitors, click the Preview button in Page view. You can also simulate the page size of a browser as you work in Design view. If the Design view window is wider than the width you specify, gray areas appear on either side. If Design view is narrower than the width you specify, you'll need to scroll the Design view window right or left. A dotted line across the page indicates the bottom of the browser window.

Preview a Web Page Using the Preview Button

1. Open the Web page you want to preview.

2. Click the Preview button at the bottom of the window.

Preview a Web Page in Design View

1. Open the Web page you want to preview in Design view.

2. Click the View menu, and then point to Page Size.

3. Click the browser page size you want.

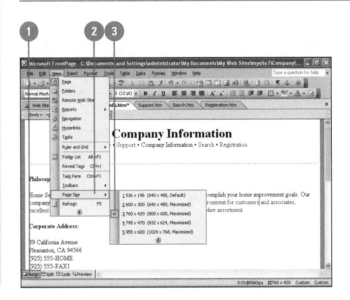

Preview a Web Page Using a Browser

1. Open the Web page you want to preview.

2. Click the File menu, and then point to Preview In Browser.

3. Click the browser you want to use to preview your site or page.

   This option determines the size of the window in which the Web will be previewed. If your computer monitor's resolution is 800 x 600 or higher, click the 640 x 480 option to get a preview of how your site will appear on a monitor with lower resolution capabilities. Otherwise, click the Default option.

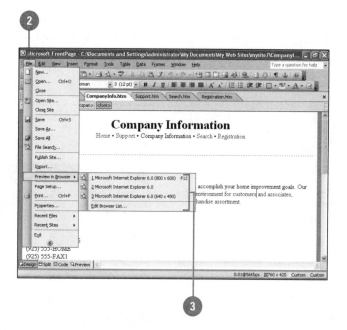

Did You Know?

You need to install other browsers before you can preview your pages. You must have previously installed the full version of other browsers like Netscape Navigator if you want to preview how your pages will appear to users of those browsers.

You need to save your pages before you can preview them. To be sure that you have saved the page you want to preview, click the Automatically Save Page check box to select it in the Preview in Browser dialog box.

For Your Information

Adding a Browser in FrontPage

If you want to add additional browsers in FrontPage after it is installed, click the File menu, point to Preview In Browser, click Edit Browser List, and then click Add to open the Add Browser dialog box. You can then type the browser's name and the command you want to use to open it. You can also click the Browse button to access the browser directly from a Windows File dialog box. Other options on the Preview In Browser dialog box enable you to edit or delete existing browser entries, and set window sizes.

Previewing and Printing Web Pages

Printed pages are helpful when you are working in Preview view. Rather than toggling between a page in progress and a Browser Preview of that page, for example, you can print the Preview so that you have it in hard copy format. Printouts are also helpful when editing your pages. Before printing, you can preview the page to determine that there are no obvious errors.

Preview Web Pages

1 Open and display the Web page you want to preview.

2 Click the File menu, and then click Print Preview. This opens a scaled-down image of the page you want to print and a series of buttons. The button choices are:

◆ **Print button.** Engages the printing process. The preview closes and the Print dialog box opens.

◆ **Next Page button.** Displays the next page in the sequence for multiple-page printing.

◆ **Previous Page button.** Takes you to the previous page in a sequence.

◆ **Two Page button.** Toggles between a single-page and a two-page spread in Preview mode.

◆ **Zoom In button.** Magnifies the preview image.

◆ **Zoom Out button.** Reduces the size of the characters to show more of the page preview.

◆ **Close button.** Closes the Preview mode.

3 When you're done, click the Close button.

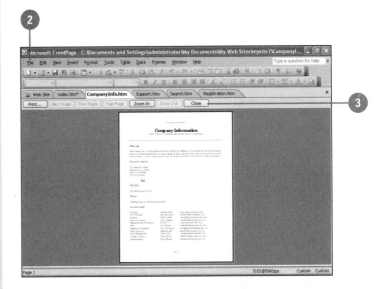

Print Web Pages

1. Open and display the Web page you want to print.

2. Click the File menu, and then click Print.

3. Select the print options you want.

4. Click OK.

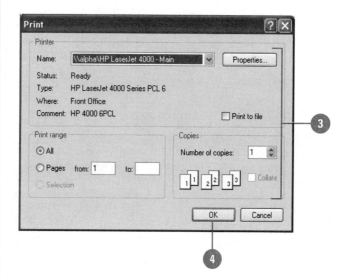

Exporting Web Content

Export Web Content

① Select the files or folders you want to export.

② Click the File menu, and then click Export.

③ Click the Save In list arrow, and then select the folder location where you want to export the Web content.

④ Click the Save As Type list arrow, and then click the file type you want.

   ◆ HTML (.htm, .html)

   ◆ GIF and JPEF (.gif, .jpg)

   ◆ Microsoft Office Files (.doc, .xls, .ppt)

⑤ Click Save.

When you export Web content, you save the information in a new format so that it can be opened in an entirely different program. You can export one or more files from FrontPage to a location outside your Web using the Export command or Copy and Paste commands. This process can be executed using the Folder List, Folders view, or Navigation view.

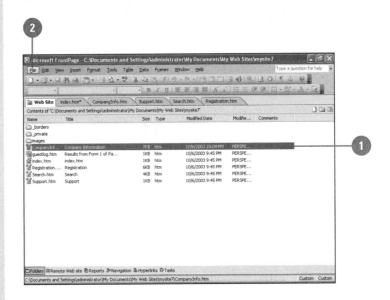

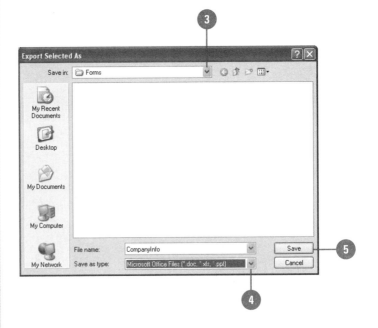

Export Web Content Using Copy and Paste

1. Select the information you want to copy.

2. Click the Copy button on the Standard toolbar.

3. Display the location in which you want to move the content.

4. Click the area where you want to place the content.

5. Click the Paste button on the Standard toolbar.

   The source files or folders are copied into their new location.

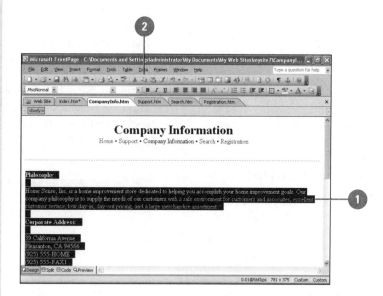

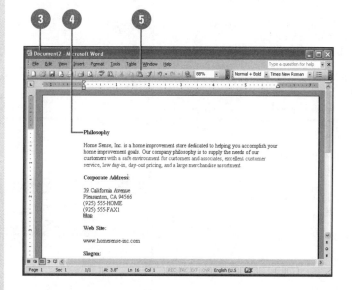

Creating a Page Template

Instead of using one of the built-in page templates that comes with FrontPage, you can create your own. There are two kinds of page templates: static and dynamic. A **static template** is a Web page you create and design, which is completely editable. After you save a static page template, you can access it in the My Templates tab of the Page Templates dialog box. A **dynamic template** is a Web page with editable areas like a static template, yet also contains non-editable areas with content that changes based on circumstances, such as actions taken by a user or the date.

Create a Static Template

1. Design and display the Web page you want to create into a static template.

2. Click the File menu, and then click Save As.

3. Type a name for the template.

4. Click the Save As Type list arrow, and then click FrontPage Template.

   The folder location changes to the Pages folder, where FrontPage stores page templates.

5. Click Save.

6. Type the title you want for the template.

7. Type a description for the template.

8. Click OK.

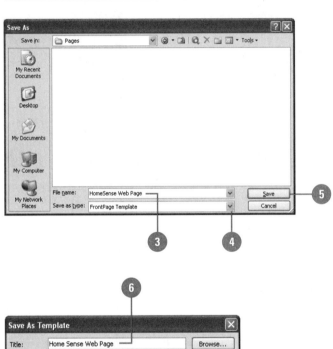

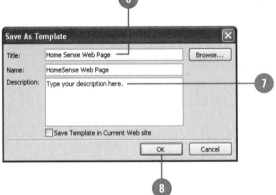

Create a Dynamic Template

1. Design and display the Web page you want to create into a dynamic template. Be sure to leave areas open to create editable regions.

2. Click the File menu, and then click Save As.

3. Type a name for the template.

4. Click the Save As Type list arrow, and then click Dynamic Web Template.

    The folder location changes to the Pages folder, where FrontPage stores page templates.

5. Click Save.

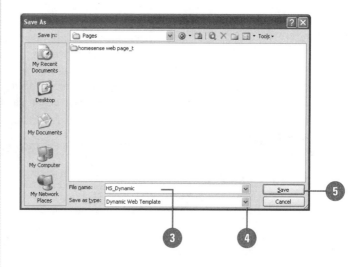

Create Editable Regions for a Dynamic Template

1. Display the Dynamic Web Template in Page view.

2. Select the page area you want to vary from page to page.

3. Click the Format menu, point to Dynamic Web Template, and then click Manage Editable Regions.

4. Type a name for the area you selected.

5. Click Add.

6. Click Close.

    You can repeat Steps 2 through 6 to designate other dynamic areas.

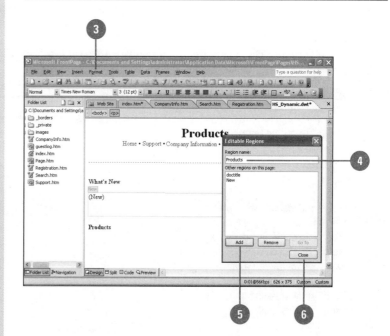

3

Using a Dynamic Page Template

After you create a dynamic Web template, you can apply, or attach, the template to an open Web page. When you attach a dynamic Web template to a Web page, FrontPage tries to map regions on the ordinary Web page to editable regions in the template. If you don't like the initial mapping, you can modify or skip it. After you attach a dynamic Web template to an ordinary Web page, you can modify non-editable regions in Code view, or any editor other than Design view to create updatable content.

Attach a Dynamic Template

1. Display the Web page in which you want to apply a dynamic page template.

2. Click the Format menu, point to Dynamic Web Template, and then click Attach Dynamic Web Template.

3. Locate and select the dynamic Web template you want to apply.

4. Click Open.

5. Select which regions in the new page will receive content/regions from the old page.

6. Click Modify, select a new mapping, and then click OK.

7. Click OK to attach the template.

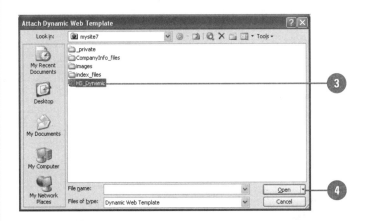

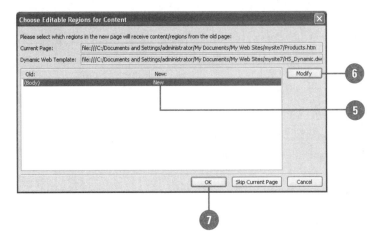

> ## Did You Know?
>
> **You can update a dynamic Web template.** When you make changes to a dynamic Web template in Design view, you can use the Update Selected Page, Update All Pages, or Update Attached Pages commands on the Dynamic Web Templates submenu (on the Format menu) to update the template.

Saving a Web Page with Different Formats

A file type specifies the file format (for example, a template) as well as the program and version in which the file was created (for example, Office FrontPage 2003). You might want to change the type if you're creating a custom template or sharing files with someone who needs them for use in another program. You use the Save As dialog box to change the file type for a page. The Save As Type list arrow displays a list of the available formats for the program or current selection.

Save a Web Page as a Different Type

1. Click the File menu, and then click Save As.

2. Click the Save In list arrow, and then click the drive where you want to save the Web page.

3. Click the Save As Type list arrow.

4. Click the file format you want.

5. Click Save.

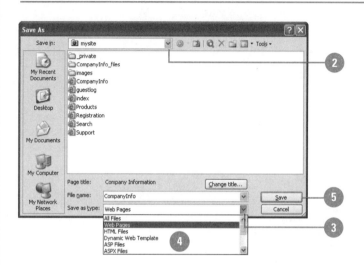

Common Formats

Format	Format
All Files	Saves the complete Web site
Web Pages	Saves the selected Web page (.htm)
HTML Files	Saves the selected Web page as a HTML file
Dynamic Web Template	Saves the selected Web page as a changeable FrontPage template
ASP Files	Saves the selected Web page as an Active Server Page
CSS Files	Saves the selected Web page as a cascading style sheet
XML	Saves the selected Web page as an XML file
Text	Saves the selected Web page as a text file
FrontPage Template	Saves the selected Web page as a static FrontPage template

Working with Web Page Text

4

Introduction

As you build your Web pages, you'll find that entering, selecting, correcting, moving, and copying will become commonplace. You can use all of the text functions as you do in any other Office program. With Microsoft Office FrontPage 2003, you can use all the common moving, deleting, and copying functions that you have already grown accustom to. The Office Clipboard is there to help as it holds up to 24 sections of material. You can also find and replace and format text just as you would in Word or Excel.

When entering text, you might find it necessary to add a bulleted or numbered list. You can also create sublists and collapsible lists to use on your pages. Choosing the alignment of your text, your line spacing, and paragraph tabs all work the same way as other Office 2003 programs.

It may become necessary to apply a style to your Web pages as you develop them. A **style** is a collection of formatting settings saved with a Web site or template that you can apply to text, graphics, and tables at any time. If you modify a style, you make the change once, but all text tagged with that style changes to reflect the new format. You can also create a **Cascading Style Sheet** (CSS), which is style information that can be referenced by individual or multiple Web pages.

Of course, while working with all of this text, using FrontPage's spell checker is a must. You can spell check, add familiar or custom words to your dictionary, check for common grammatical errors, or use the Thesaurus to enhance your Web pages. International Microsoft Office FrontPage users can change the language that appears on their screens by changing the default language settings.

Entering Text in a Web Page

There are two methods of entering text on a Web page: as part of a template or from scratch. When starting out, we strongly recommend that you work from a template. If you are working with templates, you can begin by editing the boilerplate text that opens as part of the template.

Select the template text that you wish to replace and begin typing. The boilerplate text disappears and your text begins flowing into that section of the template. Be sure to constrain your text to the original area provided in the template and, if necessary, edit what you wish to say to make the copy fit within the allotted space.

The other way to enter text is on a blank page. Create a new Web page, and then start typing.

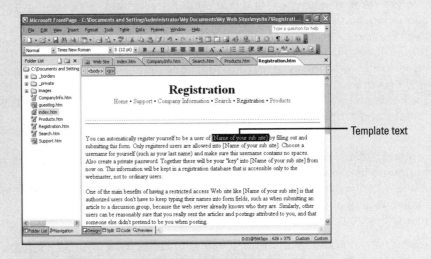

Template text

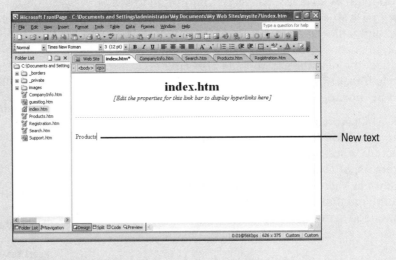

New text

Selecting Text in a Page

The first step in working with text is to highlight, or **select**, the text you want. Once you've selected it, you can format, replace, delete, copy, and move (cut) words, sentences, and paragraphs within one Web page or between Web pages. When you finish with or decide not to use a selection, you can click anywhere in the page to **deselect** the text.

Select Text

1 Position the pointer in the word, paragraph, line, or part of the page you want to select.

2 Choose the method that accomplishes the task you want to complete in the easiest way.

Refer to the table for methods to select text.

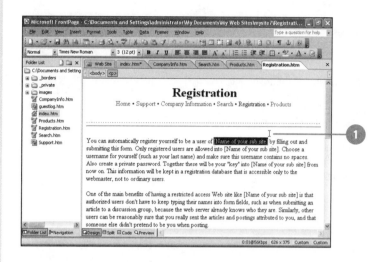

Selecting Text	
To Select	**Do This**
A single word	Double-click the word.
A single paragraph	Triple-click a word within the paragraph.
A single line	Click in the left margin next to the line.
Any part of a page	Click at the beginning of the text you want to highlight, and then drag to the end of the section you want to highlight.
A large selection	Click at the beginning of the text you want to highlight, and then press and hold Shift while you click at the end of the text that you want to highlight.
An outline heading or subheading in Outline view	Click the bullet, plus sign, or minus sign.

4

Editing Text

You can edit text in FrontPage several ways. First, you can select the text you want to edit, and then type text to replace it or press the Delete key to remove it. Another way to edit text is to place the insertion point in the text, and then type to insert text or press the Backspace or Delete keys to remove it. The Backspace key deletes text to the left, while the Delete key deletes text to the right.

Select and Edit Text

1. Select the text you want to edit.

2. Perform one of the following editing commands:

   ◆ To replace text, type your text.

   ◆ To delete text, press the Backspace key or the Delete key.

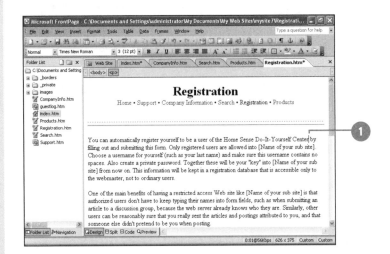

Insert and Edit Text

1. Click in the page to place the insertion point where you want to make the change.

   ◆ To insert text, type your text.

   ◆ To delete text, press the Backspace key or the Delete key.

TIMESAVER *Press Ctrl+ Backspace or Ctrl+Delete to delete one word at a time left or right.*

Making Corrections

Everyone makes mistakes and changes their mind at some point, especially when creating or revising a document. With FrontPage, you can instantly correct typing errors by pressing a key. You can also reverse more complicated actions, such as typing an entire word, formatting a paragraph, or creating a chart. With the Undo button, if you change your mind, you can just as easily click the Redo button to restore the action you reversed.

Undo or Redo an Action

◆ Click the Undo button to reverse your most recent action, such as typing a word, formatting a paragraph, or creating a chart.

TIMESAVER *Press Ctrl+Z to undo.*

◆ Click the Redo button to restore the last action you reversed.

TIMESAVER *Press Ctrl+Y to redo your undo.*

◆ Click the Undo button list arrow, and then select the consecutive actions you want to reverse.

◆ Click the Redo button list arrow, and then select the consecutive actions you want to restore.

Undo button ┐ ┌ Undo button list arrow

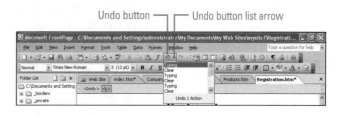

Redo button ┐ ┌ Redo button list arrow

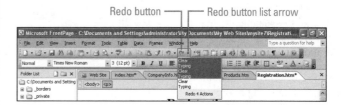

4

Moving and Copying Text

Text can be moved and copied in FrontPage just like in other word processing software. You can move or copy text within a Web page, between Web pages, or to another program. When you cut (for a move) or copy text or graphics, FrontPage places it on the Clipboard. To complete the copy or move, you paste the data stored on the Clipboard in another location. When you paste an item, a button, known as a smart tag, allows you to immediately adjust how information is pasted or how automatic changes occur. To copy or move text or graphics without using the Clipboard, you can use a technique called **drag-and-drop**. Drag-and-drop makes it easy to copy or move text or graphics short distances on your Web page.

Move or Copy Text Using Drag-and-Drop

1 Select the text you want to move or copy.

2 To move the text from its current location, drag the selection to the new location, and then release the mouse button.

3 To copy the text to a new location, hold down Ctrl and drag the selection to the new location, and then release the mouse button.

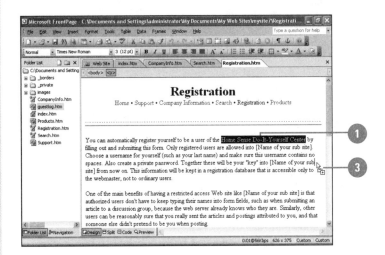

Did You Know?

You can copy and paste between documents. You can cut or copy text between pages and even between FrontPage and other Microsoft programs. Switch between programs on the system taskbar at the bottom of the screen.

Move or Copy Text

1. Select the text you want to move or copy.

2. To move the text from its current location, click the Cut button on the Standard toolbar. The text is removed from its current location and placed on the Clipboard.

3. To copy the text to a new location, click the Copy button on the Standard toolbar. A copy of the text is placed on the Clipboard.

4. Click to position the insertion point where you want to place the cut or copied text.

5. Click the Paste button on the Standard toolbar.

   The text is copied from the Clipboard to the new location, but also remains on the Clipboard for future placements.

6. If necessary, click the Paste Options button, and then click an option to adjust the pasted information.

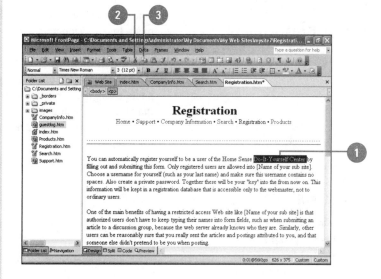

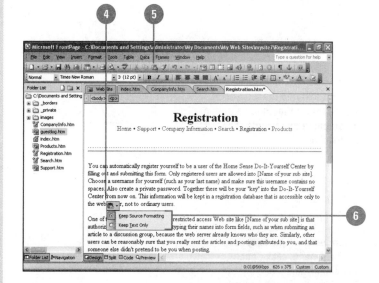

Working with the Office Clipboard

The **Office Clipboard** is available from within any Office program and holds up to 24 pieces of copied information, any or all of which you can paste to a new location. As you cut or copy information, Office collects it in the Office Clipboard. You can use the Office Clipboard task pane to manage the information and use it in documents. The Office Clipboard allows you to collect multiple items and paste them quickly. When you paste an item, the Paste Options button appears below it. When you click the button, a menu appears with options to specify how Office pastes the information. The available options differ depending on the content you are pasting.

Paste Items from the Office Clipboard

1. Click the Edit menu, and then click Office Clipboard.

   TIMESAVER *Press Ctrl+C twice to access the Office Clipboard.*

2. Click where you want to insert the text.

3. Click any icon on the Clipboard task pane to paste that selection. If there is more than one selection, you can paste all the selections at once by clicking Paste All.

4. When you're done, click the Close button on the task pane.

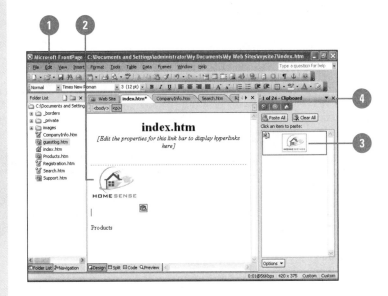

Did You Know?

You can turn on or off paste options. Click the Tools menu, click Options, click the Edit tab, select or clear the Show Paste Options Buttons check box, and then click OK.

You can paste information in a different format. Select the object or text, click the Copy button on the Standard toolbar, click to indicate where you want to paste the object, click the Edit menu, click Paste Special, click the object type you want, and then click OK.

Delete Items from the Office Clipboard

1. Click the Edit menu, and then click Office Clipboard.

2. Click the list arrow of the item you want to paste, and then click Delete.

3. To erase all items in the Office Clipboard, click Clear All.

4. When you're done, click the Close button on the task pane.

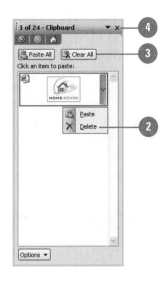

Change Clipboard Options

1. Click the Edit menu, and then click Office Clipboard.

2. Click Options, and then click any of the following options:

   ◆ Show Office Clipboard Automatically

   ◆ Show Office Clipboard When Ctrl+C Pressed Twice

   ◆ Collect Without Showing Office Clipboard

   ◆ Show Office Clipboard Icon On Taskbar

   ◆ Show Status Near Taskbar When Copying

3. When you're done, click the Close button on the task pane.

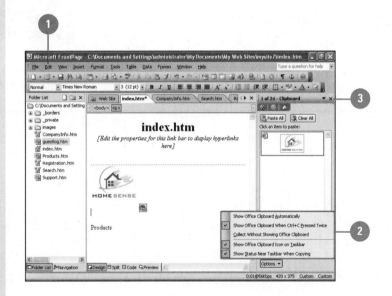

4

Creating Bulleted and Numbered Lists

The best way to draw attention to a list is to format the items with bullets or numbers. For different emphasis, you can change any bullet or number style to one of the predefined formats. You can also customize the list style or insert a picture as a bullet. If you move, insert, or delete items in a numbered list, FrontPage sequentially renumbers the list for you. Every time you press Enter, a new bullet will appear. To end a list, press Enter twice. The capability to generate bulleted and numbered lists is essential to the creation of most webs. Both types of these lists are generated in Page view.

Create Bulleted and Numbered Lists

1. Click the View menu, click Page, and then open the Web page you want to use.

2. Select the text you want to change into a bulleted or numbered list, or click where you want to start a list.

3. Click the Bullets or Numbering button on the Formatting toolbar.

4. If you're starting a list, type the first entry, and then press Enter.

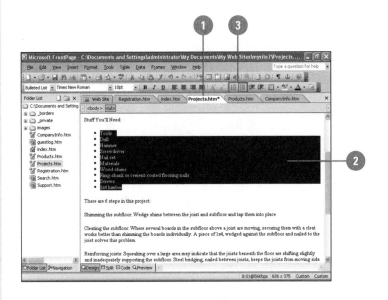

Change Bulleted and Numbered Lists

1. Click the View menu, click Page, and then open the Web page you want to use.

2. Select the list you want to format.

3. Click the Format menu, and then click Bullets And Numbering.

4. Click the tab (Picture Bullets, Plain Bullets, or Numbers) for the type of change you want to make.

   If you are using a Theme, the Plain Bullets tab is unavailable. Picture Bullets is the default setting and the dialog box will use the design of those specified by the Theme.

5. Click the style change you want.

6. Click OK.

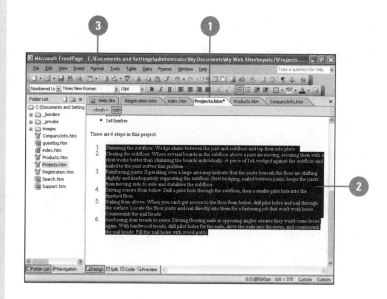

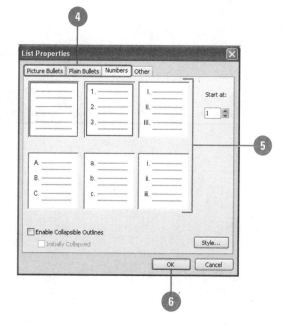

Did You Know?

You can insert a custom bullet.
Produce a custom bullet, and then save it, preferably in either GIF (.gif) or JPEG (.jpg) format. In FrontPage, place the insertion point at the place where you want to start the list. Click the Format menu, click Bullets And Numbering, click the Picture Bullets tab, click the Specify Picture option button, click Browse to locate your creation, double-click a picture, and then click OK. You can proceed as you would with any other bullet style.

Creating Sublists and Collapsible Lists

In addition to the standard bulleted and numbered lists, you can also create indented lists, or sublists. A sublist creates multilevels in a list. You can create a sublist with a bulleted or numbered list. You use the Increase Indent button on the Formatting toolbar to create the multilevels. FrontPage can make multilevel lists collapsible, which means you can hide and show sublists. When you click the parent of the sublist (the non-indented line above the sublist), the sublist collapses or expands.

Create a Sublist List

1. Click the View menu, click Page, and then open the Web page you want to use.

2. Select the text you want to change into a sublist, or click where you want to start the sublist (press Enter to create a new line).

3. Click the Increase Indent button on the Formatting toolbar twice.

    The first click creates a Normal style paragraph and the second click creates a sublist bullet.

4. If you're starting a sublist, type the first entry, and then press Enter.

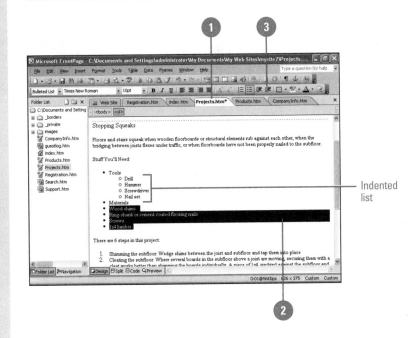

Indented list

Create a Collapsible List

1. Click the View menu, click Page, and then open the Web page you want to use.

2. Select the list in which you want to create a collapsible list.

3. Click the Format menu, and then click Bullets And Numbering.

4. Select the Enable Collapsible Outlines check box.

5. Select or clear the Initially Collapsed check box.

6. Click OK.

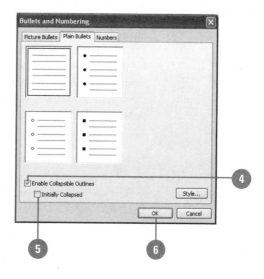

Preview a Collapsible List

1. Click the View menu, click Page, and then display the Web page with the collapsible list.

2. Click the Preview button.

3. Click the parent of the sublist to collapse or expand the sublist.

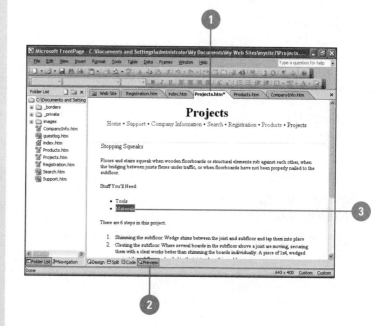

4

Finding and Replacing Text

Suppose that you discover you have misspelled or want to change a word throughout an entire Web page. You do not need to read through the document to find every instance of the word and manually change it. The Find and Replace commands can do that for you. If the word you want to change extends across fifty pages, you can still make the change without having to edit fifty individual pages. FrontPage can find every instance for you, and walk you through the Web site from page to page until all the corrections have been made.

Find and Replace Text on a Web Page

1. Click the Edit menu, and then click Find.

2. Enter the text for which you are searching, and then click the Replace tab.

3. Enter the replacement text.

4. Click the Current Page option.

5. Select the search parameters you want (Match Case, Find Whole Word Only, etc.).

6. Select one of the following buttons:

   ◆ **Replace All button.** Replaces all instances of the text.

   ◆ **Replace button.** Replaces the selected instance of the text.

   ◆ **Find Next button.** Locates the next instance of the text.

7. When you're done, click Close.

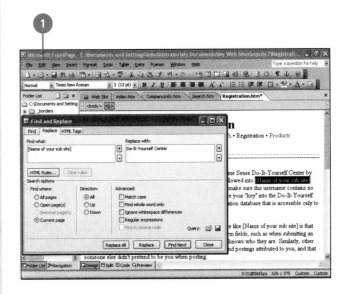

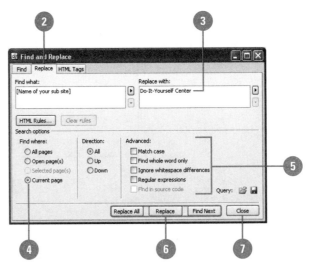

Find and Replace Text on a Web Site

1 Click the Folders button on the Views bar.

2 Click the Edit menu, and then click Find.

3 Enter the text for which you are searching, and then click the Replace tab.

4 Enter the replacement text.

5 Click the Selected Pages option or the All Pages option.

6 Click Find In Site.

The list of pages containing the selected word(s) opens.

7 Press and hold Ctrl, and then click the specific pages you want searched.

8 When FrontPage lists the pages in which the text you're seeking was found (step four), you can open any of these pages in Page view by double-clicking the page from the list. The first instance of the text you're looking for is highlighted. This text can be replaced via the Replace command.

9 When you're done, you are prompted to close the current document before moving on to the next. If changes were made, your page will be automatically saved.

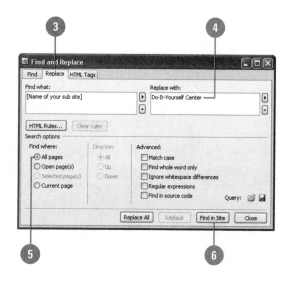

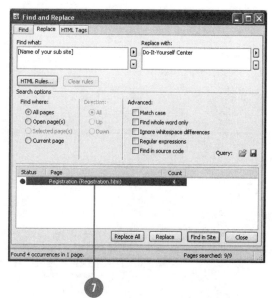

Formatting Text

You'll often want to format, or change the style of text to add emphasis to part of a Web page. **Boldface**, *italics*, <u>underlines</u>, and other text effects are toggle switches, which means you simply click to turn them on and off. For special emphasis, you can apply multiple formats, such as bold and italics. You can also change the font typeface and size. Using one font typeface for headings and another for main text adds a professional look to your Web page.

Format Text Quickly

1. Click the View menu, click Page, and then open the Web page you want to use.

2. Select the text you want to format.

3. Click a formatting button on the Formatting toolbar to apply the attribute you want.

   ◆ Bold button.

   ◆ Italic button.

   ◆ Underline button.

   ◆ Font Color button list arrow.

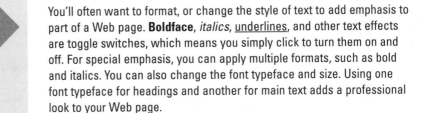

Font Color button list arrow

Change the Font Quickly

1. Click the View menu, click Page, and then open the Web page you want to use.

2. Select the text you want to format.

3. Click the Font list arrow, and then click a font typeface.

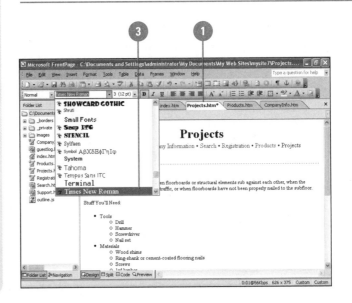

Change the Font Size of Text Quickly

1. Click the View menu, click Page, and then open the Web page you want to use.

2. Select the text you want to format.

3. Select the font sizing option you want.

   ◆ Click the Font Size list arrow on the Formatting toolbar, and then click a font typeface.

   ◆ Click the Increase Font Size or Decrease Font Size button on the Formatting toolbar.

Format Text Using the Font Dialog Box

1. Click the View menu, click Page, and then open the Web page you want to use.

2. Select the text you want to format.

3. Click the Format menu, and then click Font.

4. Select the formatting options you want.

   ◆ Select a font.

   ◆ Select a font style.

   ◆ Select a font size.

   ◆ Select a font color on the Color list.

   ◆ Under Effects, select the effect of your choice, if any.

5. Click OK.

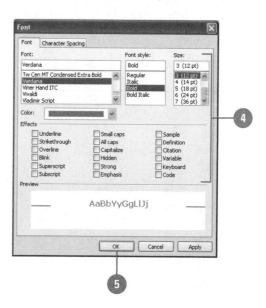

Setting Text Alignment and Spacing

Text alignments vary the look of a Web page and help lead the user through the text. You can align text along the left or right margin, in the center, or equally across the page. You can quickly change text alignment using alignment buttons on the Formatting toolbar. Line spacing is another way to vary the look of a Web page. The lines in a Web page are single-spaced by default, but you can easily change line spacing to double or 1.5 lines to allow extra space between every line. Sometimes, you'll want to add space above and below certain paragraphs, such as for headlines or indented quotations to help set off the text.

Change Text Alignment

1 Click the View menu, click Page, and then open the Web page you want to use.

2 Select the text you want to align.

3 Click an alignment button on the Formatting toolbar to apply the attribute that you want the selected text.

- ◆ **Align Left button.** Aligns text along the left margin. The text is uneven along the right margin.

- ◆ **Center button.** Aligns text in the middle of the page.

- ◆ **Align Right button.** Aligns text along the right margin. The text is uneven along the left margin.

- ◆ **Justify button.** Aligns text evenly between the two margins.

> ### Did You Know?
>
> *You can change character spacing.*
> Select the text you want to change, click the Format menu, click Font, click the Character Spacing tab, click the Spacing list arrow, click Normal, Expanded, or Condensed, click the Position list arrow, click a vertical position option, and then click OK.

Change Line Spacing

1. Click the View menu, click Page, and then open the Web page you want to use.

2. Select the paragraph you want to change.

3. Click the Format menu, and then click Paragraph.

4. Click the Line Spacing list arrow, and then click the spacing you want.

5. Type the space you want to add above each selected paragraph (in points).

6. Type the space you want to add below each selected paragraph (in points).

7. Click OK.

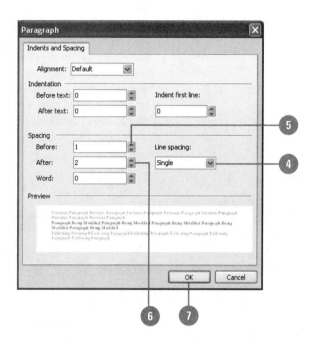

Change Paragraph Indents

1. Click the View menu, click Page, and then open the Web page you want to use.

2. Select the paragraph you want to change.

3. Click the Format menu, and then click Paragraph.

4. Type the space you want before the selected paragraph (in points).

5. Type the space you want after the selected paragraph (in points).

6. Type the space you want before the first line of the selected paragraph (in points).

7. Click OK.

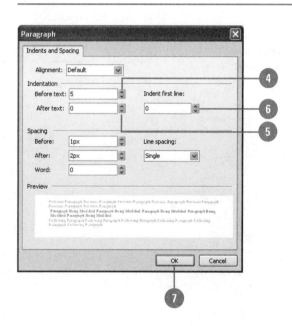

4

Applying and Creating Styles

A **style** is a collection of formatting settings saved with a Web site or template that you can apply to text, graphics, and tables at any time. If you modify a style, you make the change once, but all text tagged with that style changes to reflect the new format. FrontPage provides you with **Built-In Styles**, or you can create your own **User-Defined Styles**. Both built-in and user-defined styles are available from the same style list while you edit a page. When you create a user-defined style, you can also create an embedded Cascading Style Sheet (CSS), which is style information that is applied to the open Web page.

Apply a Style to Text

1. Click the View menu, click Page, and then open the Web page you want to use.

2. Select the text you want to change into a heading or subheading.

3. Click the Style list arrow on the Formatting toolbar.

4. Click a style (such as Heading 1, Heading 2, etc.) from the drop-down list.

See Also

See "Creating a Cascading Style Sheet" on page 98 for information on creating an external cascading style sheet.

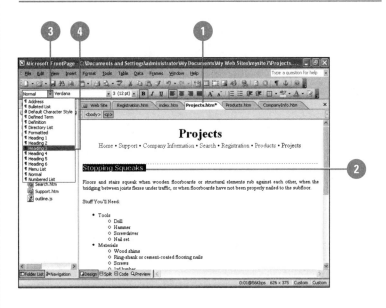

Create a Style and Embedded Cascading Style Sheet

1. Click the View menu, click Page, and then open the Web page you want to use.

2. Click the Format menu, and then click Style.

3. Click New.

4. Type a name for the style.

5. Click the Style Type list arrow, and then click Paragraph to include the selected text's line spacing and margins in the style, or click Character to include only formatting, such as font, size, and bold, in the style.

6. Click Format, click a formatting command to include additional formatting to the style, and then click OK.

7. Click OK, and then click OK again.

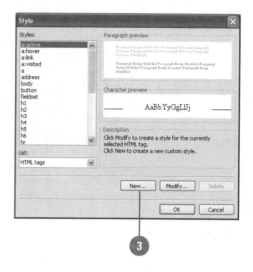

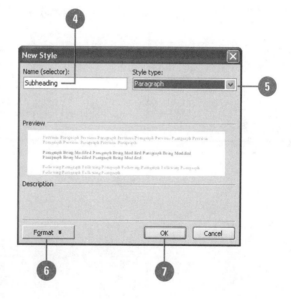

Did You Know?

You can modify a style. Open the Web page or .css file with the style you want to change, click the Format menu, click Style, click the List list arrow, click User-Defined Styles, select the style, click Modify, make changes to the style, click OK, and then click OK again.

4

Creating a Cascading Style Sheet

Cascading Style Sheets are becoming the predominant method of formatting a Web site. A **Cascading Style Sheet (CSS)** is style information that can be referenced by individual or multiple Web pages. A CSS contains style definitions, called Selectors, which are the HTML components linked to a specialized list of style properties and values. A selector is followed by those properties and values. For example, H1 {font-size: x-large; color: green}, H2 {font-size: large; color: blue}. H1 and H2 are selectors that modify the formatting properties of standard HTML tags. There are three types of Cascading Style Sheets in FrontPage: **embedded** (for a individual Web pages), **external** (for multiple pages in the same file), and the rarely-used **inline**, which you create when you apply a style directly to an item using the Style button on its Properties dialog box. An external CSS file uses a .css file extension.

Create an External Cascading Style Sheet

1. Click the New button list arrow on the Standard toolbar, and then click Page.

2. Click the Style Sheets tab.

3. Click the type of CSS you want to create.

   ◆ **Normal Style Sheet.** The basic style to which you can add your own styles.

4. Click OK.

5. Click the Save button on the Standard toolbar, type a name, select the CSS Files format, and then click Save.

6. To add styles, use the Style Toolbar.

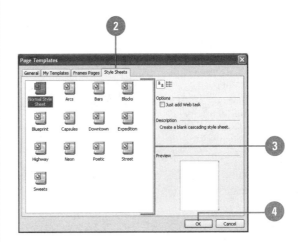

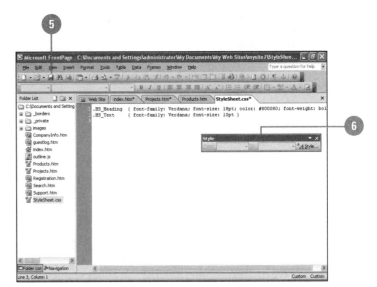

> ### See Also
>
> See "Applying and Creating Styles" on page 96 for information on creating an embedded cascading style sheet.

Link a Cascading Style Sheet to Web Pages

1. In the Folder list, select the Web pages in which you want to link to a CSS.

2. Click the Format menu, and then click Style Sheet Links.

3. Click the Selected Page(s) option.

4. Click Add.

5. Locate and select the cascading style sheet (.css) file.

6. Click OK.

7. To the order of use of multiple styles for a page, click the Move Down or Move Up buttons.

8. To remove a style sheet, select it, and then click Remove.

9. When you're done, click OK.

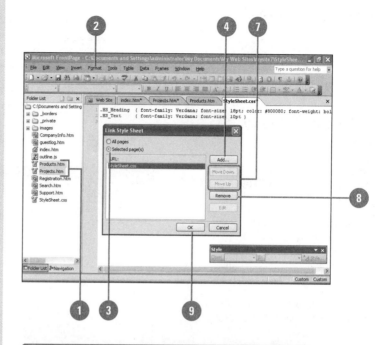

Did You Know?

You can delete a style. Open the Web page or .css file with the style you want to delete, click the Format menu, click Style, click the List list arrow, click User-Defined Styles, select the style, click Delete, and then click OK.

You can enable or disable CSS. Click the Tools menu, click Page Options, click the Authoring tab, select or clear the CSS 1.0 (formatting) check box, select or clear the CSS 2.0 (positioning) check box, and then click OK.

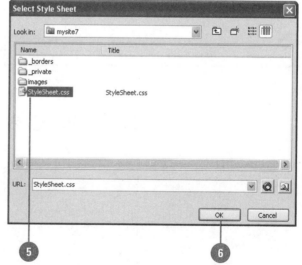

4

Inserting Symbols

FrontPage comes with a host of symbols and special characters for every need. Insert just the right one to keep from compromising a Web page's professional appearance with a hand-drawn arrow («) or missing mathematical symbol (å). Before you insert a symbol, be aware that not all browsers support all symbols. Be sure to test your pages on several browsers.

Insert Symbols and Special Characters

1. Click the View menu, click Page, and then open the Web page you want to use.

2. Click where you want to insert a symbol or character.

3. Click the Insert menu, and then click Symbol.

4. To see other symbols, click the Font list arrow, and then click a new font.

5. Click a symbol or character.

6. Click Insert.

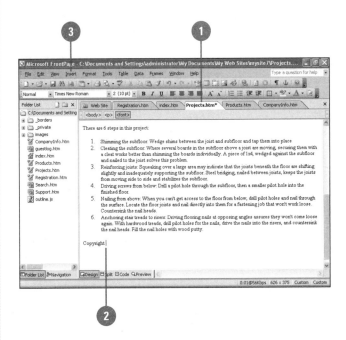

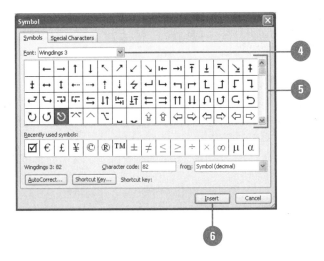

Inserting Comments

Comments are useful when you want to leave a note for yourself or a team member about a Web page or the site. Perhaps a particular part of the site needs to be clarified, or the formatting of an item is inconsistent. FrontPage comments display text in Design view, but don't appear when visitors display the site. In Design view, FrontPage comments appear as purple text.

Insert and Delete a Comment

1 Click the View menu, click Page, and then open the Web page you want to use.

2 Click where you want to insert a comment.

3 Click the Insert menu, and then click Comment.

4 Type your comment in the comment box.

5 Click OK.

6 To delete a comment, click the comment, and then press Delete.

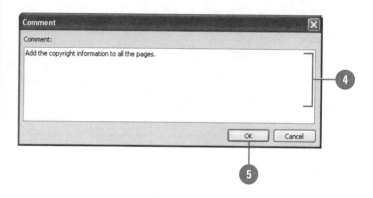

Edit a Comment

1 Click the View menu, click Page, and then open the Web page you want to use.

2 Double-click the comment.

3 Modify the comment text in the comment box.

4 Click OK.

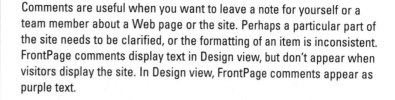
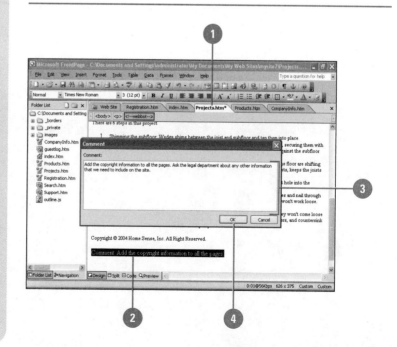

Inserting Horizontal Lines

Horizontal lines have a variety of uses in the construction of a web. Whether they're used to separate sections of a page or to underline an important piece of text, you have several decisions to make. Lines have a variety of properties that you can modify, including width, height, alignment, and color. If a theme has already been applied to the page, the line is changed by the theme's properties.

Insert a Horizontal Line

1. Click the View menu, click Page, and then open the Web page you want to use.

2. Click where you want to insert a horizontal line.

3. Click the Insert menu, and then click Horizontal Line.

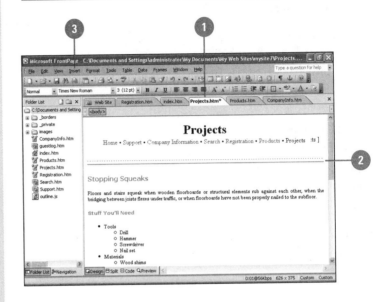

Modify a Horizontal Line

1. Click the View menu, click Page, and then open the Web page with the horizontal line you want to change.

2. Double-click the horizontal line you want to modify.

3. Select the formatting options you want.

   ◆ **Width.** Width of the line. Specified in pixels or as a percentage of the window width.

   ◆ **Height.** Height of the line in pixels.

   ◆ **Alignment.** Alignment of the line on the page.

   ◆ **Color.** Color of the line, unless you want it shaded. If you select a color, shading is no longer an option.

   ◆ **Solid Line.** Select the check box to create a solid line. Clear it to create a shaded line.

4. Click OK.

Did You Know?

The formatting options for lines in themes are limited. If a theme has been applied to a page, you can only change the line's alignment.

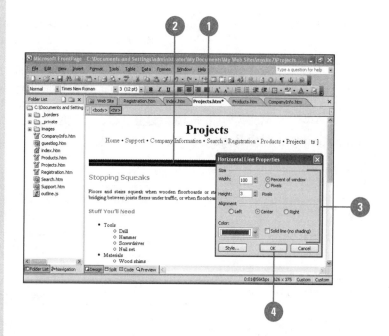

4

Checking Spelling

Using FrontPage, you can correct spelling errors on a Web site immediately, or create a task for each page with an error and correct them later. Begin by opening the page whose spelling you want to examine. If you commonly use words unique to a hobby or profession that would not appear in a normal dictionary, or are unlikely to be part of the common vernacular, consider adding them to your dictionary so that they will not repeatedly be called into question during spell checks.

Check Spelling in a Web Page

1. Click the View menu, click Page, open the Web page you want to check, and then click where you want to start checking.

2. Click the Tools menu, and then click Spelling.

   The program begins scanning the pages for words that aren't in its dictionary.

3. Click the suggested word or type the correct word, and then click Change. Click Change All to correct all instances of the word.

4. If the unrecognized word is correctly spelled but the program doesn't know it (as with a name, for example), click Ignore to ignore this instance of the word, or click Ignore All to ignore all instances of this word.

5. Click Add to add this word to your custom dictionary.

6. When the spell checker reaches the end of the document, if it hasn't searched the beginning, a prompt will ask if you want it to resume the search at the start of the document.

7. When you're done, click OK.

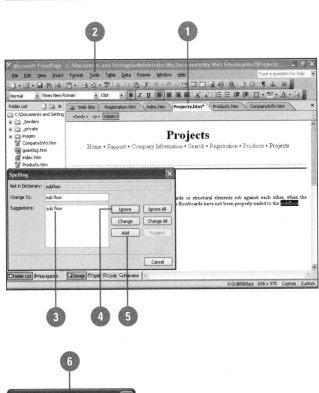

Spell Checking in a Web Site

1. Click the View menu, and then click Folder List.

2. Select the pages in the Web site you want to check. Click the first page to check, and then press and hold down Ctrl while clicking the other pages you want examined for spelling.

3. Click the Tools menu, and then click Spelling.

4. Click the Entire Web Site option or the Selected Page(s) option.

5. Click Start.

6. Double-click the first misspelled word in the list. If a misspelled word needs to be corrected, the Spelling dialog box opens. Otherwise, the Continue With The Next Page? dialog box opens.

7. To correct a misspelled word, use the buttons in the Spelling dialog to change or ignore the misspelled word. To continue spell checking the next page, click Next Page.

8. If you want to stop the spell check or it is done checking all the pages, click Back To List.

9. Click Cancel to close the Spelling dialog box.

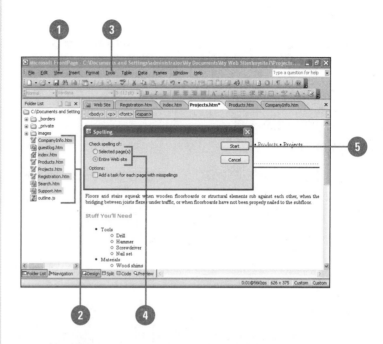

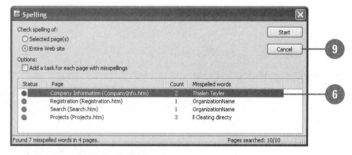

Did You Know?

You can add a task for misspelled words. By assigning spelling corrections to Tasks, you can come back and correct them at your convenience. Click the Add a Task for Each Page With Misspellings check box to select it in the Spelling dialog box.

4

Checking Spelling as You Type

As you type, a red wavy line appears under words not listed in FrontPage's dictionary (such as misspellings or names) or duplicated words (such as *the the*). You can correct these errors as they arise. When FrontPage learns the spellings of words you use regularly, it even automatically corrects some errors as you type. If the unrecognized work is correct, you can add it to the dictionary.

Enable Check Spelling and Grammar Options

1. Click the Tools menu, and then click Page Options.

2. Click the General tab.

3. Select the Check Spelling As You Type check box.

4. Click OK.

Correct Spelling and Grammar as You Type

1. In a Web page, right-click a word with a red wavy underline.

2. Click a substitution, or click Ignore All to skip any other instances of the word.

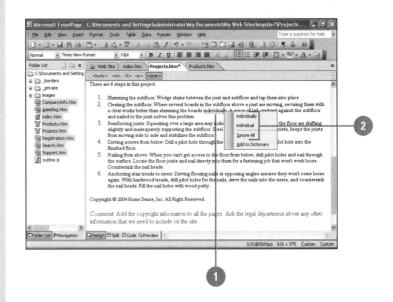

Did You Know?

You can add a familiar word to your dictionary. Right-click the red wavy line under the word in question, and then click Add To Dictionary.

You can remove the red wavy line. Click the Tools menu, click Page Options, select the Hide Spelling Errors In All Documents check box, and then click OK.

Finding the Right Words

Repeating the same word in a Web page can reduce a message's effectiveness. Instead, replace some words with synonyms, words with similar meanings, or find antonyms, words with opposite meanings. If you need help finding exactly the right word, you can use the Thesaurus.

Use the Thesaurus

1. Click the View menu, click Page, and then open the Web page you want to use.

2. Select the word you want to look up.

3. Click the Tools menu, and then click Thesaurus.

4. Click a word to display its synonyms and antonyms.

5. Click the word you want to use.

6. Click Replace.

7. Click Cancel.

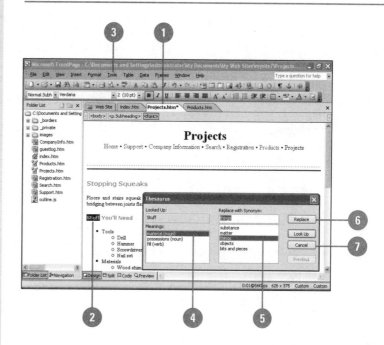

Using Multiple Languages

International Microsoft Office FrontPage users can change the language that appears on their screens by changing the default language settings. Users around the world can enter, display, and edit text in all supported languages, including European languages, Japanese, Chinese, Korean, Hebrew, and Arabic, just to name a few. You'll probably be able to use Office programs in your native language. If the text in your Web page is written in more than one language, you can designate the language of selected text so the spelling checker uses the right dictionary.

Add a Language to Office Programs

1 Click Start on the taskbar, point to All Programs, point to Microsoft Office, point to Microsoft Office Tools, and then click Microsoft Office 2003 Language Settings.

2 Click to select the languages you want to use.

3 Click Add.

4 Click OK, and then click Yes to quit and restart Office.

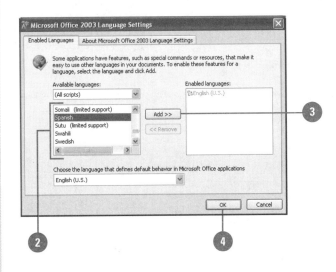

Did You Know?

You can check your keyboard layout.
After you enable editing for another language, such as Hebrew, Cyrillic, or Greek, you might need to install the correct keyboard layout so you can enter characters for that language. In the Control Panel (Classic view), double-click the Regional And Language icon, click the Language tab, and then click Details to check your keyboard.

Mark Text as a Language

1. Click the View menu, click Page, and then open the Web page you want to use.

2. Select the text you want to mark.

3. Click the Tools menu, and then click Set Language.

4. Click the language you want to assign to the selected text.

5. Click OK.

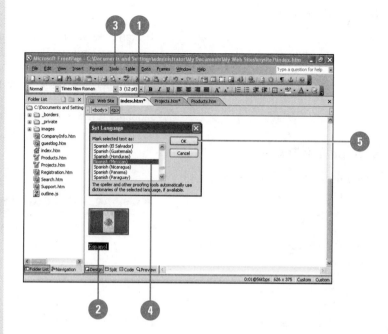

Changing Default Text

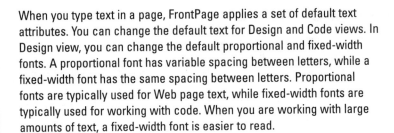

When you type text in a page, FrontPage applies a set of default text attributes. You can change the default text for Design and Code views. In Design view, you can change the default proportional and fixed-width fonts. A proportional font has variable spacing between letters, while a fixed-width font has the same spacing between letters. Proportional fonts are typically used for Web page text, while fixed-width fonts are typically used for working with code. When you are working with large amounts of text, a fixed-width font is easier to read.

Change Default Text

1. Click the Tools menu, and then click Page Options.

2. Click the Default Fonts tab.

3. Click the language you want as the default.

4. Select the defaults fonts you want for Design view.

5. Select the default font and size you want for Code view.

6. Click OK.

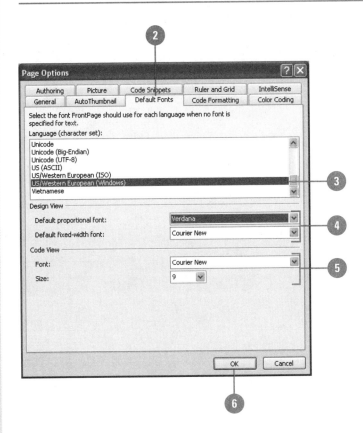

Inserting Text from a File

If you have a word processing document that you want to use as a Web page, you can insert the entire file. You use the File command on the Insert menu to select the file and insert the contents. The Select File dialog box works just like the Open dialog box. FrontPage allows you to insert files in several formats, including Rich Text Format (.rtf), Text Files (.txt), Word 97-2003 (.doc), and HTML (.htm, .html).

Insert a File

1. Click the View menu, click Page, and then open the Web page you want to use.

2. Click where you want to insert the content of the file.

3. Click the Insert menu, and then click File.

4. Click the Files Of Type list arrow, and then select the type of file you want to insert.

5. Locate and select the file.

6. Click Open.

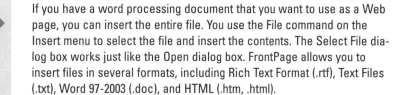

Working with Web Page Graphics

Introduction

As you begin to include graphics into your Web pages, it's important to understand all the different types of graphics and how they can be used in Microsoft Office FrontPage 2003. There are company logos for business sites, banner graphics, special bullets, link bars with navigation buttons, and so forth. The most common formats for graphics are GIF and JPEG.

When it comes time to start inserting graphics, the most common type is probably Microsoft Office's clip art located in each Office program. You can also add pictures from digital cameras or scanned images. There are additional resources on the Web, where you can check regularly for new and exciting clips. Microsoft provides a Clip Organizer where you can store and organize all your favorite clips.

Once you get the clip into your Web page, you can move it to the location you want. You might need to manipulate the graphic by rotating or flipping it for the perfect fit and angle. Most likely, you'll also need to crop or resize the graphic to be the size you need. You can position graphics and text elements on the page in different ways. Use absolute positioning to place an element at an exact location on the page, or relative positioning to place an element inline with text, where it can move depending on the changes you make the page.

Other graphic elements such as working with layers, wrapping text, changing a graphic's contrast and brightness, changing colors, and other graphical formatting can be done in FrontPage. More technical elements such as changing a graphic's format, changing the way a graphic is displayed, and creating a low resolution graphic can also be done. If there have been too many changes to a graphic, FrontPage let's you start over by restoring the graphic and it's original properties.

Understanding Graphics

Graphics can be used to provide visual interest, supplemental information, or even to support a theme. Whether it's the company logo on a business site or a special photo on your personal site, graphics brighten up a Web. Graphics can be used in a variety of ways in FrontPage. For example, you can use a graphic element as a background. There are company logos for business sites, banner graphics, special bullets, link bars with navigation buttons, and so forth. The most common formats for graphics are GIF (up to 256 colors) and JPEG (more than 256 colors). Both formats have specific strengths and weaknesses. With GIF format graphics, for example, you can designate one of your 256 or fewer colors as transparent, while JPEG is better suited to pictures containing thousands, or even millions of colors. You can also determine the level of file compression by resetting the graphic quality. The lower you set the quality, the higher the file compression and the smaller the file size.

There are several other graphic formats, including:

- ◆ BMP (Bitmap Format, the native Microsoft Windows format supports graphics up to 24-bits)

- ◆ TIFF (Tagged Image File Format, a high-resolution, tag-based file format)

- ◆ TGA (Truevision Targa Graphics Adaptor, which supports 1-bit to 32-bit graphics and boasts several professional-level features)

- ◆ RAS (Raster format, lightly compressed, it supports graphics up to 36-bit)

- ◆ EPS (Encapsulated PostScript file format, it enables PostScript graphics files to be integrated into other documents)

- ◆ PNG (Portable Network Graphics, a GIF alternative that supports transparency for multiple colors)

- ◆ WMF (Microsoft Windows Metafile, which supports bitmapped vector and EPS data; for example, clip art from the Microsoft Clip Organizer is WMF).

When you save a graphic in a file format other than GIF or JPEG, FrontPage converts the file to GIF format if it has 256 colors or less, or to JPEG if it has more than 256 colors. You can change the default file type settings and the default file type conversion and paste setting by using the Pictures tab in the Page Options dialog box. To change graphic default settings, click the Tools menu, click Page Options, click Picture tab, specify the settings you want, and then click OK.

Click to change default file type settings.

Inserting Clip Art

You can insert clips from the Clip Art task pane or your own files. **Clips**—copyright-free images or pictures, sounds, and motion clips—enhance any Web page. For example, you can insert clip art graphics of scenic backgrounds, maps, buildings, or people. A motion clip is an animated picture—also known as an animated GIF—frequently used in Web pages or videos. You can also insert your own files you scanned or created in a drawing program, and you can organize clip art in various collections using the Clip Organizer.

Insert Clip Art

1 Click the View menu, click Page, and then click where you want to insert clip art.

2 Click the Insert menu, point to Picture, and then click Clip Art.

3 Type the word(s) that describes the clip art you want to find.

4 Click the Search In list arrow, and then select the check boxes with the collection in which you want to search.

Use the plus (+) and minus (-) signs to navigate the list.

5 Click the Results Should Be list arrow, and then select the check boxes with the type of media you want to search.

6 Click the Go button.

7 Click the clip art image you want to insert.

8 When you're done, click the Close button on the task pane.

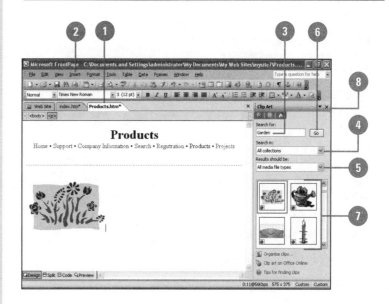

5

Adding and Removing Clips

You might want to add pictures and categories to the Clip Organizer for easy access in the future. You can import your own clips (pictures, photographs, sounds, and videos) into the Clip Organizer. For example, if you have a company logo that you plan to include in more than one presentation, add it to the Clip Organizer. You can also add groups of clips to the Clip Organizer. If you no longer need a picture in the Clip Organizer, you can remove it, which also saves space on your computer.

Add a Clip

1. Click the File menu, point to Picture, click Clip Art, and then click Organize Clips on the Clip Art task pane.

2. Click the File menu, point to Add Clips To Organizer, and then click On My Own.

3. Click the Look In list arrow, and then select the drive and folder that contains the clip you want to import.

4. Click the Files Of Type list arrow, and then select the file type.

5. Click the clip you want to import.

6. Click Add.

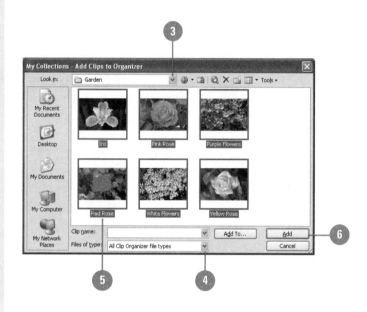

Remove a Clip

1. Click the File menu, point to Picture, click Clip Art, and then click Organize Clips on the Clip Art task pane.

2. Point to the clip you want to remove, and then click the list arrow.

3. To delete the clip from all Clip Organizer categories, click Delete From Clip Organizer.

   To remove the clip from just one category, click Delete From the listed category.

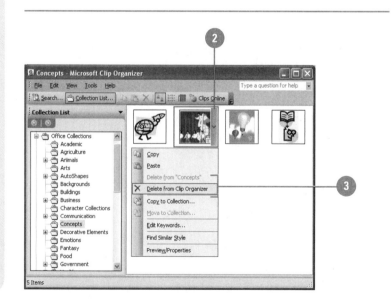

Organizing Clips

The clips that come with the Clip Organizer are already organized, but if you've added clips without organizing them, it's probably hard to find what you need in a hurry. The Microsoft Clip Organizer sorts clip art images, pictures, sounds, and motion clips into categories. The Clip Organizer allows you to organize and select clips from Microsoft Office, from the Web, and from your personal collection of clips. To help you locate a clip quickly, you can place it in one or more categories. You can also assign one or more keywords to a clip and modify the description of a clip. When you add media files, Clip Organizer automatically creates new sub-collections under My Collections. These files are named after the corresponding folders on your hard disk. To help you find clips later on, Clip Organizer also creates search keywords based on the file's extension and folder name.

Organize Clips

1. Click the File menu, point to Picture, click Clip Art, and then click Organize Clips on the Clip Art task pane.

2. Find and point to the clip you want to categorize or change the properties of, click the list arrow, and then click one of the following:

    ◆ Click Copy To Collection to place a copy of the clip in another category.

    ◆ Click Move To Collection to move the clip to another category.

    ◆ Click Edit Keywords to edit the caption of the clip and to edit keywords used to find the clip.

3. Click the Close button to close the Clip Organizer dialog box.

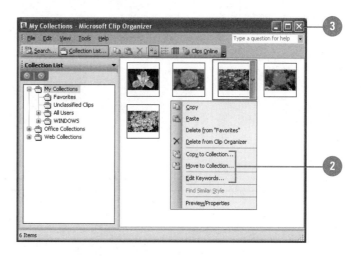

Did You Know?

You can create a new collection. In the Clip Organizer, click the File menu, click New Collection, type a new collection name, and then click OK.

5

Accessing Clips on the Web

If you can't find the image that you want in the Clip Organizer, you can search for additional images in Clip Art On Office Online, a clip gallery that Microsoft maintains on its Web site. To access Clip Art On Office Online, you can click the link at the bottom of the Clip Art task pane or click the Clips Online button on the Clip Organizer toolbar. This launches your Web browser and navigates you directly to the Office Online Web site, where you can access thousands of free clip art images.

Open Clips Online

1 Click the Insert menu, point to Picture, and then click Clip Art.

2 Click Clip Art On Office Online on the task pane.

3 Establish a connection to the Internet.

Your Web browser displays the Microsoft Office Online Clip Art And Media Home Web page.

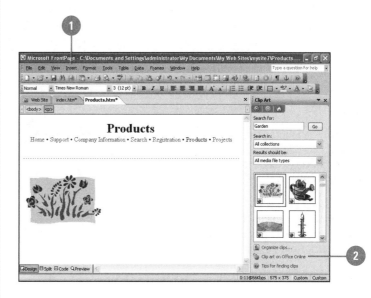

View Clips in a Category

1 Click Clip Art On Office Online on the task pane to open the Microsoft Office Online Clip Art And Media Home Web page.

2 If necessary, click the Accept button on the Clips Online Web page.

3 Scroll down to the Browse Clip Art And Media section, and then click the name of the category you want.

Search for a Clip

1. Click the Search list arrow on the Office Online Web page, and then select the media type you want: Clip Art, Photos, Animations, or Sounds.

2. Click the Search For box.

3. Type a keyword.

4. Click the green Click To Search arrow.

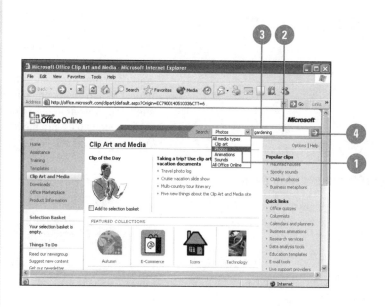

Download a Clip

1. Once you have displayed a list of clips on the Office Online Web page, select the check box below a clip to add it to your selection basket.

    You can select as many as you want. Clear the check box to deselect a clip.

2. Click Download 1 Item (will vary depending on the number of items you are downloading), review the Terms of Use, and then click Accept.

3. If a security virus warning dialog box appears, click Yes, and then click Continue.

4. Click Download Now, and then click Open.

    The clip is stored on your hard disk and shown in your Clip Organizer where you can categorize it.

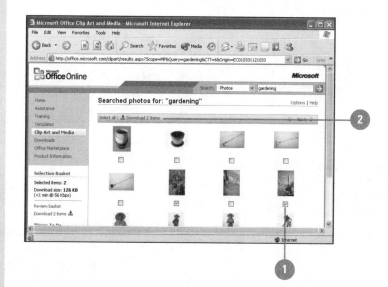

Inserting Graphics

FrontPage makes it possible for you to insert graphics, pictures, scanned photographs, or artwork you scanned or created in a drawing program. You can use the Insert menu to insert files or you can drag and drop files from the Folder List. All files associated with a Web site are stored on your computer (typically in the My Webs folder within the My Documents folder). When you open your Web site, the files and folders in the Web site folder appear in the Folders List. You can use Windows Explorer to copy or move files into the Web site folder and then drag files onto your Web pages from the Folder List.

Insert Graphics from a File

1. Click the View menu, click Page, and then open the Web page you want to use.

2. Position the insertion point where you want to insert a graphic.

3. Click the Insert menu, point to Picture, and then click From File.

4. Click the Look In list arrow, and then select the folder location of the file you want to insert.

5. Click the file(s) you want to insert.

6. Click Insert.

> ### Did You Know?
>
> **You can display thumbnail images in the Picture dialog box.** In the Picture dialog box, click the View button list arrow, and then click Thumbnails.

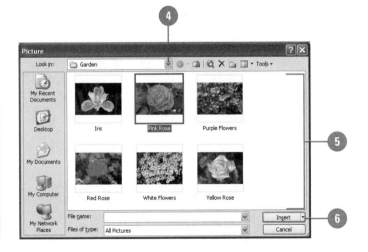

120

Insert Graphics from the Folder List

1. Use Windows Explorer to copy or move the graphic files you want to use into the Web site folder.

2. Open the Web site in which you want to insert graphics.

3. Click the View menu, and then click Folder List.

4. Click the View menu, click Page, and then display the Web page you want to use.

5. If necessary, double-click the folder with the graphics you want to use.

6. Drag a graphic file to a location on the Web page.

7. When you're done, click the Close button on the Folder list.

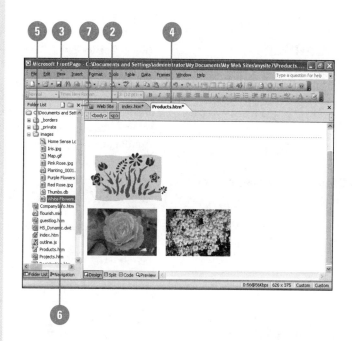

See Also

See "Cropping and Resizing Graphics" on page 126 for information on resizing a graphic.

For Your Information

Tracing Graphics

If you have a scanned image of a Web page layout or an existing document that you want to use on a Web page, you can use Trace Image to make it easier for you to re-create. Trace Image sets a copy of the image as a background picture in Design view. Open the Web page in which you want to trace an image, click the View menu, point to Trace Image, click Configure, click Browse and locate the image you want to use, set the x and y (distance from the left (x) and top (y) edge of Design view to the left and top edge of the tracing image), set the Opacity, and then click OK. After you specify a tracing image, you can use Show Image on the Trace Image submenu to display and hide the image.

5

Inserting a Graphic from a Scanner or Camera

If you have a scanner or digital camera connected to your computer, you can scan or download a picture into a Web page and you have the choice of storing it in the Clip Organizer. You can use a digital still or video camera, or a live Web camera. For a video or Web camera, you can capture an image and use it in a Web page. When you scan an image, you can use default or custom settings to scan and insert the image. Check the instructions that come with your digital camera or scanner to make sure it is set up correctly and is compatible with FrontPage.

Insert a Graphic from a Scanner or Camera

1. Click the View menu, click Page, and then open the Web page you want to use.

2. Click to place the insertion point where you want to insert the graphic.

3. Click the Insert menu, point to Picture, and then click From Scanner Or Camera.

4. Click the Device list arrow, and then select the device connected to your computer.

5. Select the resolution (the visual quality of the image).

6. Select or clear the Add Pictures To Clip Organizer check box.

7. To use default settings, click Insert.

8. To specify your own settings to scan a picture or capture and select a camera image, click Custom Insert, and then follow the device instructions.

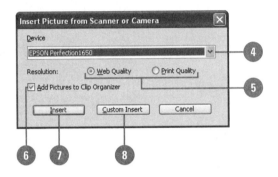

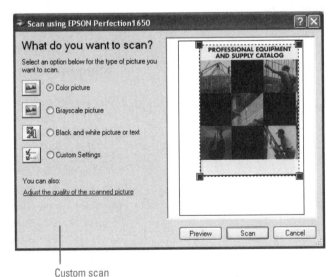

Custom scan

Copying and Pasting Graphics from the Web

Copying and pasting objects is another integral part of Web design. In a Web page, you can copy and paste graphics in the same way in which you copy and paste text. When you want to copy a graphic from the Web, the process is slightly different in a Web browser; you use the right-click method. When you copy material from the Web, you need to get permission from the owner to use it. In many cases, the Web site provides conditions of use.

Copy and Paste Graphics from the Web

1. Open your Web browser, and then search the Web for a graphic as you normally would using your browser.

2. Right-click the graphic, and then click Copy. Depending on your browser, you command might differ.

3. Close your browser and switch back to FrontPage.

4. Click the View menu, and then click Page.

5. Click where you want to insert the graphic.

6. Click the Paste button on the Standard toolbar.

   This inserts a reference on your page to the graphic on the Web site.

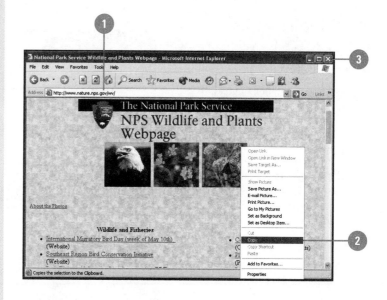

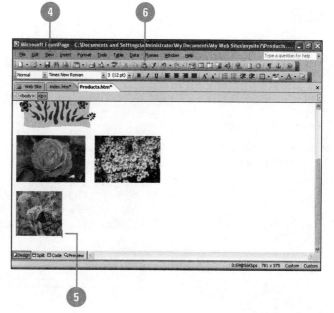

Selecting and Moving Graphics ▶

As you learn more about and use FrontPage, you'll want to enhance your Web pages with more than just text. To do so, you can insert an object. An **object** is a picture or graphic image you create with a drawing program or insert from an existing file of another program. For example, you can insert a company logo that you have drawn yourself, or you can insert clip art. To work with an object, you need to select it first. Then you can resize or move it with its selection handles, the little circles that appear on the edges of the selected object.

Select and Deselect an Object

◆ In Page view, click an object to display its handles.

　To select more than one object at a time, hold down Shift as you click each object.

◆ In Page view, click elsewhere within the document window to deselect a selected object.

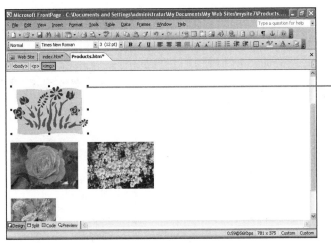

Selection handles

Move an Object

① Click the View menu, click Page, and then open the Web page you want to use.

② Click an object to select it.

③ Drag the object to a new location.

④ Release the mouse button to drop the object in the new location.

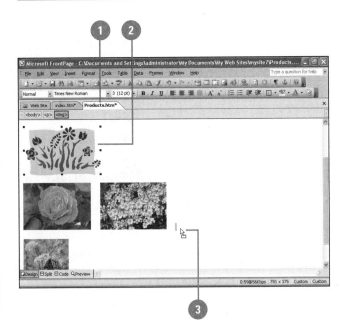

Rotating and Flipping Graphics

After you insert a graphic or create an object, you can change its orientation on the page by rotating or flipping it. Rotating a graphic keeps the original front to back positioning and rotates the graphic clockwise or counter-clockwise to achieve the desired affect, while flipping a graphic creates a mirror graphic of a graphic, oriented either horizontally or vertically. Rotating turns an object 90 degrees to the right or left; flipping turns an object 180 degrees horizontally or vertically.

Rotate and Flip Graphics

1. Click the View menu, click Page, and then open the Web page you want to use.

2. Select the Picture, Clip Art, Autoshape, or WordArt you want to flip or rotate.

3. If necessary, right-click any toolbar, and then click Picture to display the Picture toolbar.

4. To rotate the graphic, click either the Rotate Right 90 button or the Rotate Left 90 button on the Pictures toolbar.

5. To flip the graphic, click either the Flip Horizontal button or the Flip Vertical button on the Pictures toolbar.

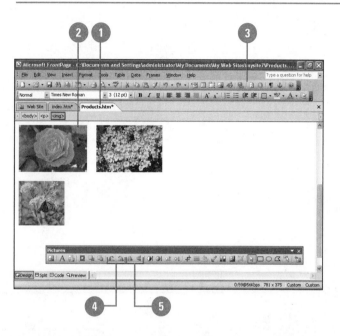

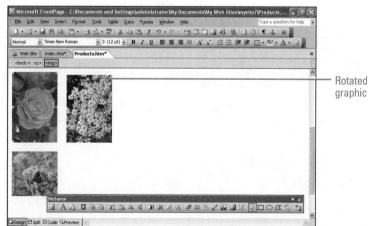

Rotated graphic

5

Cropping and Resizing Graphics

Cropping is the process of framing a portion of a photo and eliminating any unnecessary visual elements. If, for example, you have a photo that is not centered properly, you can crop out the side to center it. You can also resize graphics, using both numerical and graphic-direct techniques. However, if you enlarge a graphic to much, you lose image details. After you resize a graphic, the Picture Actions button appears, where you have the option to retain the picture file's original size, but tell the browser to use the new size, or to change the picture's physical size to the new size, known as resampling. The next time you save the page, FrontPage prompts you to save the picture at the new size.

Crop a Graphic

1. Click the View menu, click Page, and then open the Web page you want to use.

2. Select the graphic you want to crop.

   Resize handles appear on the graphic and the Pictures toolbar opens.

3. Click the Crop button on the Pictures toolbar.

   A cropping box appears inside the graphic.

4. Drag a resize handle on the cropping box to include the part of the graphic that you want to keep.

5. Click the Crop button on the Pictures toolbar again to eliminate the area outside of the cropping box.

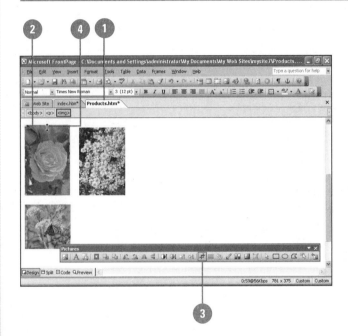

Resize Graphics Directly

1. Click the View menu, click Page, and then open the Web page you want to use.

2. Select the graphic you want to resize. Resize handles appear on the graphic and the Pictures toolbar opens.

3. Drag a resize handle (small squares) to the size you want. To resize a graphic while preserving its proportions (that is, its aspect ratio), drag a handle located in the graphic's corners diagonally.

4. Click the Picture Actions button, and then click an option to resample or not.

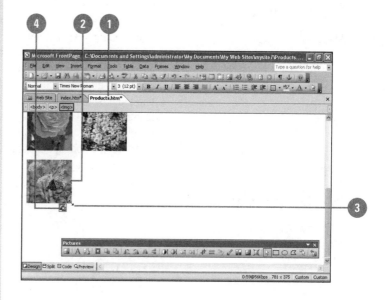

Resize Graphics Numerically

1. Click the View menu, click Page, and then open the Web page you want to use.

2. Right-click the graphic, and then click Picture Properties.

3. Click the Appearance tab.

4. Select the Specify Size check box.

5. If you want to preserve the height-to-width proportions of the picture, select the Keep Aspect Ratio check box. The aspect ratio refers to the proportions of a graphic. If you select this option, you only need to change the width or height, not both.

6. Decide whether you want to change the size in pixels or in percentage, and then enter values in the Width and Height boxes.

7. Click OK.

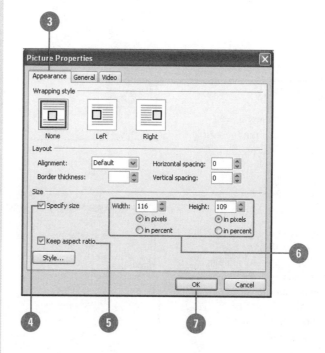

Changing Graphic Positioning

FrontPage gives you the control you need to place graphics and text on the page in exactly the place where you want them. You can position graphics and text elements on the page in different ways. You can use absolute positioning to place an element at an exact location on the page, or relative positioning to place an element inline with text, where it can move depending on the changes you make on the page. When you change positioning, FrontPage creates a separate layer (identified by a blue border and a name tag in the upper-left corner) for the element, which you can resize, move, and name. An element placed using absolute positioning appears in a fixed location relative to the top-left corner of the page.

Change Graphic Positioning

1. Click the View menu, click Page, and then open the Web page you want to use.

2. Select the graphic you want to change positioning.

3. Click the Format menu, and then click Position.

4. Click the Absolute or Relative box.

5. Click OK.

   A blue layer appears with the graphic.

6. To move or resize the positioning layer, click the edge of the layer (if necessary), and then drag the edge or a handle.

Did You Know?

You can use the Positioning or Pictures toolbar to set absolute positioning options. Right-click any toolbar, and then click Positioning or Pictures. Select the Web page elements you want, click the Position Absolutely button, and then drag the handles to resize the positioning layer.

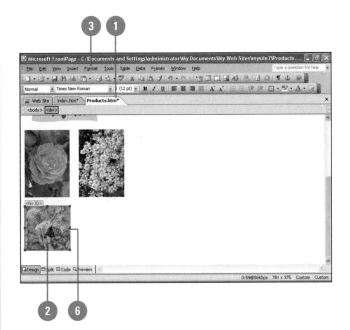

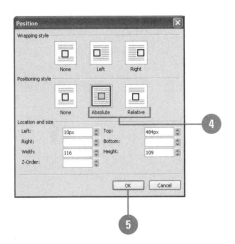

Changing Graphic Stacking Order

Absolute positioning allows you to position graphics in a stacking order relative to each other. Stacking is the placement of objects one on top of another to overlay each other. You can create overlapping graphics by applying absolute positioning to each graphic you want to arrange, selecting individual graphics, and using the Bring Forward and Send Backward buttons on the Pictures toolbar. The stacking position is indicated by the z-value in the Position dialog box or the Layers task pane, where you can change it. A higher z-value appears on top. You can set positioned graphics in front of or behind both regular page content and each other. However, at different solutions, absolute elements might not appear exactly where you intended. Be sure to test the page.

Change Graphic Stacking Order

1. Click the View menu, click Page, and then open the Web page you want to use.

2. Select the object or objects you want to arrange.

3. Click the Position Absolutely button on the Pictures toolbar.

4. Click the Bring Forward or Send Backward button on the Pictures toolbar.

Did You Know?

You can move or resize the positioning layer. Click the edge of the layer (if necessary) to select it, and then drag the layer edge to move it or a handle to resize it.

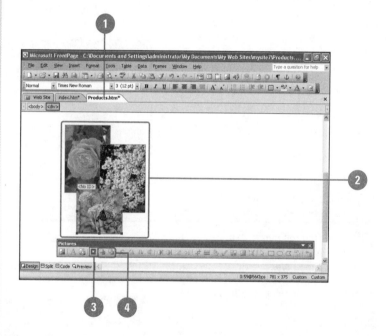

Working with Layers

FrontPage provides the Layers task pane to make it easy to work with layers. You can use the Layers task pane to create, name, and control the display of layered elements. In addition to creating a layer when you apply positioning, you can also insert or draw empty layers and then insert graphics and text. In the task pane, you can click the Eye icon to toggle between visible (eye open), hidden (eye closed), and inherit (no icon). The inherit state takes its visibility from the positioned element. The z-value in the task pane identifies the overlap (where the higher z-value appears on top). The ID value is the layer name referred to by scripts and style sheets.

Create and Name a Layer

1. Click the View menu, click Page, and then open the Web page you want to use.

2. Click the New Layer button on the Standard toolbar.

3. Click the Format menu, and then click Layers.

4. Double-click the layer name you want to change.

5. Type a new name (no spaces), and then press Enter.

6. To insert a graphic or text, drag a graphic in the layer or click in the layer, and then type.

7. When you're done, click the Close button on the task pane.

Did You Know?

You can delete a layer quickly. Click the layer edge or ID value, and then press Delete.

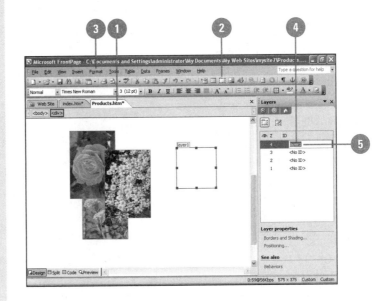

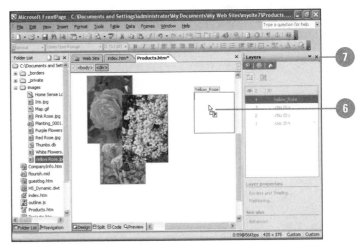

Create an Attached Layer

1. Click the View menu, click Page, and then open the Web page you want to use.

2. Click the layer to which you want to attach another one.

3. Click the New Layer button on the Standard toolbar.

4. Drag to position the new layer where you want it relative to the other layer.

   When you move the initial layer, the attached layer moves too.

5. To collapse the attached layer in the task pane, click the plus sign (+).

6. When you're done, click the Close button on the task pane.

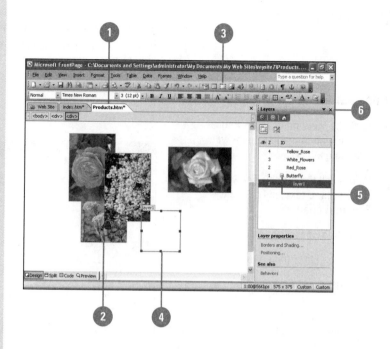

Change the Layer Display

1. Click the View menu, click Page, and then open the Web page you want to use.

2. Click the Format menu, and then click Layers.

3. Click the Eye icon to toggle between visible (eye open), hidden (eye closed), and inherit (no icon).

4. Click another layer on the task pane to apply the change.

5. When you're done, click the Close button on the task pane.

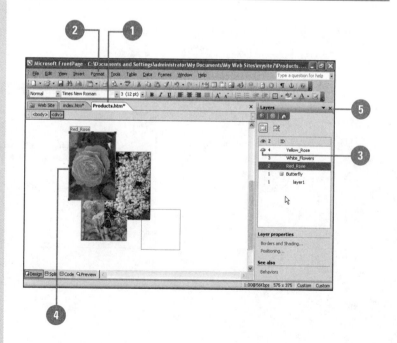

5

Wrapping Text

You can wrap text around a graphic to attractively integrate text and graphics in a Web page. You can use the Wrapping Style options in the Pictures Properties dialog box to have text flow around the right or left side of a graphic.

Wrap Text Around a Graphic

1. Click the View menu, click Page, and then open the Web page you want to use.

2. Right-click the graphic you want to wrap around text, and then click Picture Properties.

3. Click the Appearance tab.

4. Click the Left or Right box.

5. Click OK.

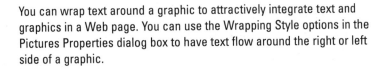

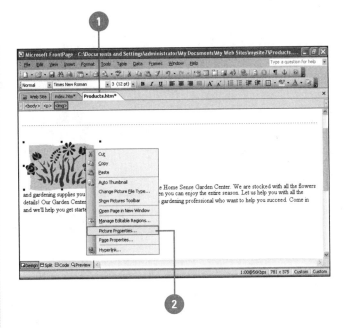

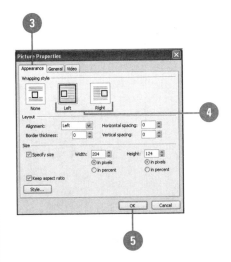

Adding Text to a Graphic

You can add additional interest to a graphic by adding text to it. The Text button on the Pictures toolbar make it easy to add the text box. If your graphic is not a GIF, FrontPage asks you to covert the graphic. An empty text box appears on the graphic with an insertion point, ready for you to type your text. You can drag the handles to resize the text box as necessary or drag the text box edge to move the text box. You can select the text or text box, and then format the text using the Formatting toolbar.

Add Text to a Graphic

1. Click the View menu, click Page, and then open the Web page you want to use.

2. Select the graphic in which you want to add text.

   Resize handles appear on the graphic and the Pictures toolbar opens.

3. Click the Text button on the Pictures toolbar, and then click OK to convert the graphic to a GIF, if necessary.

4. Enter your text in the box that is displayed on the graphic, and then click outside the text.

5. Use formatting buttons on the Formatting toolbar to modify the font type, size, color, and alignment.

6. To resize or move the text box, select the text box, and then drag one of the resize handles (resize) or the middle of the box (move).

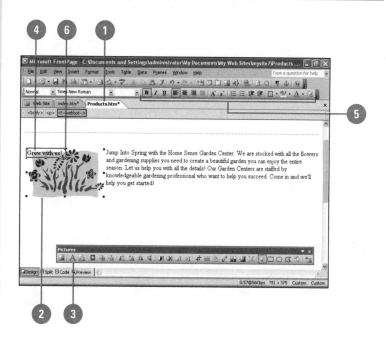

Did You Know?

You can open the Pictures toolbar if it doesn't appear. If the Pictures toolbar doesn't open when you select a graphic, click the View menu, point to Toolbars, and then click Pictures.

5

Adjusting Graphic Contrast and Brightness

Once you have inserted clip art and other objects into a Web page, you can adapt them to meet your needs. Perhaps the clip is too small to be effective, or you don't quite like the colors it uses. You can increase or decrease the brightness of a graphic, as well as the color contrast using the Pictures toolbar. In addition, you can introduce a wash, a gray art effect that increases the brightness but dims the contrast and serves as an excellent background.

Adjust Graphic Contrast and Brightness

1 Click the View menu, click Page, and then open the Web page you want to use.

2 Select the graphic you want to adjust.

Resize handles appear on the graphic and the Pictures toolbar opens.

3 To alter the color contrast, click the More Contrast button or the Less Contrast button on the Pictures toolbar.

4 To change the brightness, click the More Brightness button or the Less Brightness button on the Pictures toolbar.

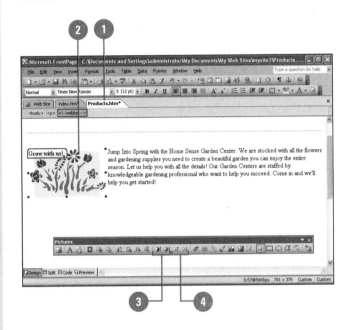

Wash Out the Color in a Graphic

1. Click the View menu, click Page, and then open the Web page you want to use.

2. Select the graphic you want to change. Resize handles appear on the graphic and the Pictures toolbar opens.

3. Click the Color button on the Pictures toolbar.

   A list menu opens.

4. Click Wash Out.

   The picture has now been faded, or washed out.

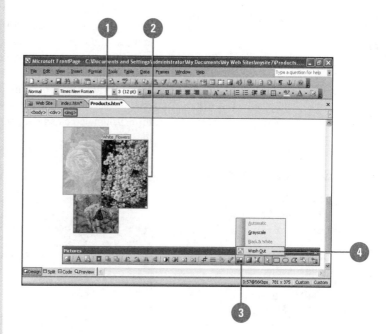

5

Converting Graphic Color

You can also convert color graphic to grayscale. Grayscale applies black and white shading values to color graphics, using a variety of gray tones in place of the different colors. When a color is designated as transparent, whenever that color appears in the graphic, the background is visible through it. Graphics can have only one transparent color, and if you select a transparent color for a graphic that already has a transparent color selected, the original transparent color will revert to its original form. When you close the page, FrontPage prompts you to save the page in GIF format.

Convert a Graphic to Grayscale

① Click the View menu, click Page, and then open the Web page you want to use.

② Select the graphic you want to convert to grayscale.

Resize handles appear on the graphic and the Pictures toolbar opens.

③ Click the Color button on the Pictures toolbar.

A list menu opens.

④ Click Grayscale.

The picture is now in black and white.

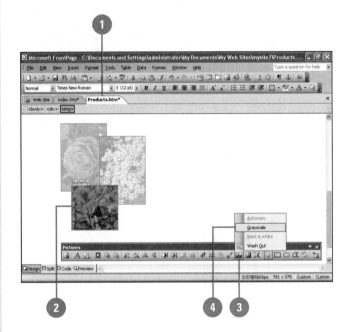

Make Colors in a Graphic Transparent

1. Click the View menu, click Page, and then open the Web page you want to use.

2. Select the graphic you want to change.

   Resize handles appear on the graphic and the Pictures toolbar opens.

3. Click the Set Transparent Color button on the Pictures toolbar.

   When you move your cursor onto the graphic, it becomes an eye dropper.

4. Click the color within the graphic that you want to make transparent.

   Every pixel of that color is now rendered transparent, creating a speckling effect.

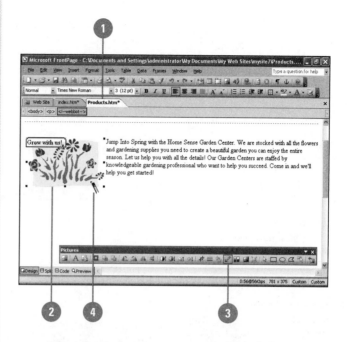

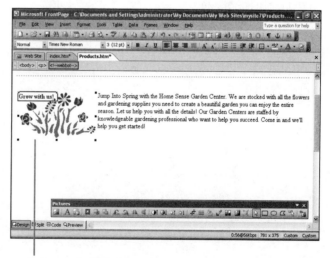

Background color in the graphic was changed to be transparent.

5

Adding Borders

It is also possible to add a one, two, three, or four-sided border. Special effects can be used to bevel the border or create the illusion of dimensionality. In addition to adding a border to a graphic, you can also add a bevel-style frame. When you click the Bevel button on the Pictures toolbar, FrontPage transforms the edge of your graphic into a bevel-style frame. You can continue to click the Bevel button until you are satisfied with the degree of the bevel.

Add Borders to a Graphic

1. Click the View menu, click Page, and then open the Web page you want to use.

2. Right-click the graphic you want to add a border, and then click Picture Properties.

3. Click the Appearance tab.

4. Enter a value for the width and height of the border in pixels. If necessary, experiment to get a sense of how the pixels work. To remove the border, type *0* (zero).

5. Click OK.

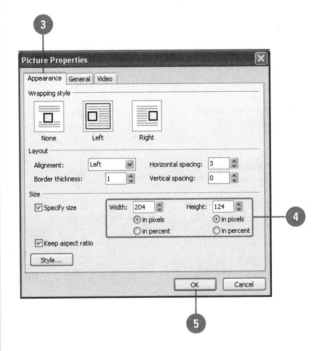

Add a Beveled Edge Around a Graphic

1. Click the View menu, click Page, and then open the Web page you want to use.

2. Click the graphic in which you want to add a beveled edge.

3. Click the Bevel button on the Pictures toolbar.

4. Continue to click the Bevel button until you achieve the look you want.

Did You Know?

You can undo bevel changes. If you don't like a bevel change, you can click the Undo button on the Standard toolbar to reverse the last change or several changes.

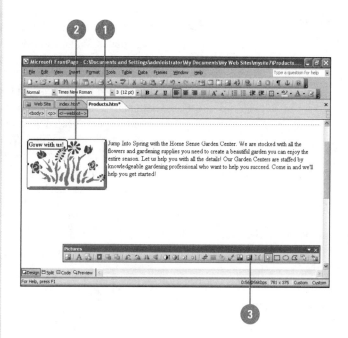

Changing Graphic Formats

When you insert clip art in a Web page, the file arrives in the WMF (Windows Metafile) format, which is not a good format to use on the Web pages. When you save a Web page with WMF files or any other non Web graphic, FrontPage prompts you to save the graphics on that page, and set the file format to JPEG, GIF, or PNG through the Save Embedded Files dialog box. This dialog box automatically opens any time you attempt to save a page containing a graphic element. If you want more control over the formats and settings, you can convert individual graphics yourself to one of four Web friendly formats: GIF, JPEG, PNG-8, and PNG-24. If you change the graphic format to GIF or JPEG, you can set additional options.

Change a Graphic File Format

1. Click the View menu, click Page, and then open the Web page you want to use.

2. Right-click the graphic you want to change, and then click Change Picture File Type.

3. Click the file type option you want.

4. For GIF or JPEG, select the applicable additional settings.

   ◆ **Interlaced.** Displays a coarse version of a picture until the full version is downloaded.

   ◆ **Transparent.** Displays one color (typically the background) of the picture as transparent.

   ◆ **Quality.** Specifies a degree of compression. Typical values are 70 through 90.

   ◆ **Progressive Passes.** Specifies the number of coarse versions of a picture before the full version appears. Specify 0 to display the picture at full resolution as it arrives.

5. Click OK.

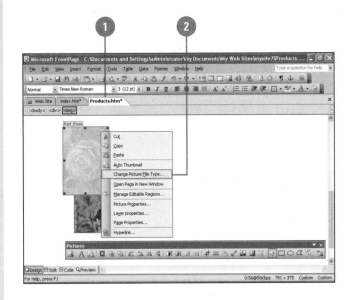

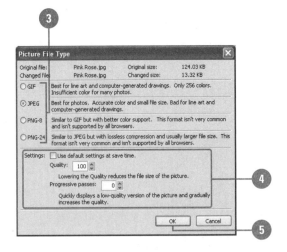

Change Graphic Format During a Web Page Save

1. Click the View menu, click Page, and then open the Web page with the graphics you want to change.

2. Click the Save button on the Standard toolbar to save the page with the graphic on which you want to change the properties.

3. Click the name of the graphic whose properties you want to reset.

4. Click Picture File Type.

5. For GIF or JPEG, select the applicable additional settings.

   ◆ **Interlaced.** Displays a coarse version of a picture until the full version is downloaded.

   ◆ **Transparent.** Displays one color (typically the background) of the picture as transparent.

   ◆ **Quality.** Specifies a degree of compression. Typical values are 70 through 90.

   ◆ **Progressive Passes.** Specifies the number of coarse versions of a picture before the full version appears. Specify 0 to display the picture at full resolution as it arrives.

6. Click OK.

7. Click OK.

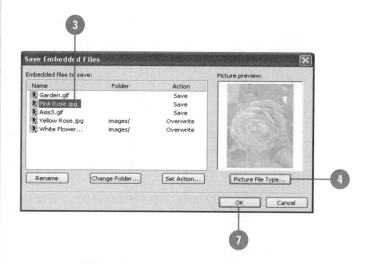

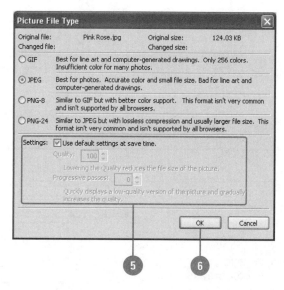

5

Changing the Way Graphics are Displayed

For a variety of reasons, the quality of the graphics you display on your Web site or page will have a major impact on the experience visitors have on your Web site. High quality graphics, for example, take much longer to load than lower resolution graphics, so you will lose some visitors before they even finish loading. Concurrently, very low quality graphics give a less than professional appearance to your Web site. Good designs strive for balance between these two considerations. For that reason, you will sometimes want to change the way graphics are displayed. To create a low resolution version of a graphic by editing it in a third party graphics editor program, you must first configure the editor that you want to use in conjunction with graphic files. You only need to perform this operation once. After you configure you graphic's editor program, you are ready to create a low resolution version of the graphic. Be aware that some Web browsers do not support low resolution graphics.

Configure a Graphics Editor Program

① Click the Tools menu, and then click Options.

② Click the Configure Editors tab.

③ Add a new extension or change an existing one.

   ◆ **Add an extension.** Click the New Extension button, and then type an extension.

   ◆ **Change an extension.** Click the extension you want to change, and then click the New Editor button.

④ Click a program from the list to associate with GIF or click Browse For More to locate the one you want.

⑤ Click OK.

   The file association is added to the list.

⑥ Click OK.

New Editor button

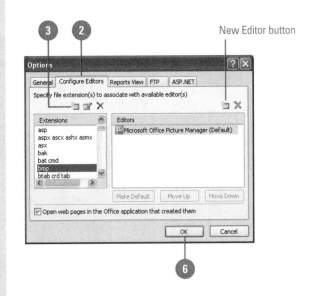

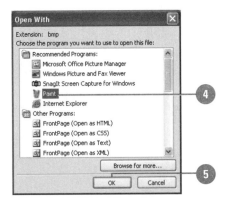

142

Create Low Resolution Graphics

1. Click the View menu, click Page, and then open the Web page you want to use.

2. Right-click the graphic you want to change, point to Open With, and then click the program you want to use.

   The graphic editor program opens.

3. Create a low resolution version of the graphic you want to use by following the instructions that are specific to the graphic editor program that you are using.

4. Returning to FrontPage, right-click the graphic to open the shortcut menu, and then click Picture Properties.

5. Click the General tab.

6. Enter the file name for the alternate low-resolution graphic you created, or click Browse to locate it.

7. Double-click the graphic to associate it.

8. Click OK.

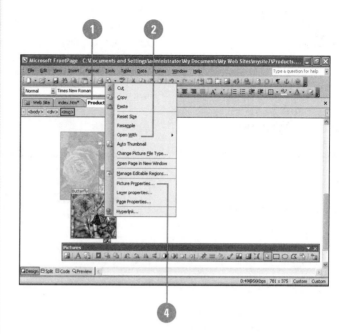

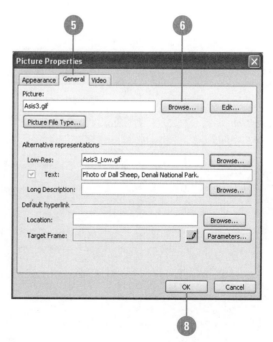

5

Adding Hyperlinks to Graphics

Graphics, like text, can contain hyperlinks. If you set a default hyperlink for a graphic, the Web browser displays the hyperlink destination when the graphic is clicked. When creating a button that is linked to your home page, for example, you can define a default hyperlink that leads to a specific destination, instead of drawing a hotspot around the entire button.

Create a Hyperlink to an Existing Internal Web Page

1. Click the View menu, click Page, and then open the Web page you want to use.

2. Select the graphic you want to use.

3. Click the Insert Hyperlink button on the Standard toolbar.

4. Click Existing File Or Web Page.

5. Browse to select the target page. The URL for the designated page appears in the address box.

6. Click OK.

See Also

See "Creating Hyperlinks to Files, Web Pages, and E-Mail Address" on page 58 for more information on creating hyperlinks.

See "Working with Graphic Hotspots" on page 146 for information on creating hyperlink regions on a graphic.

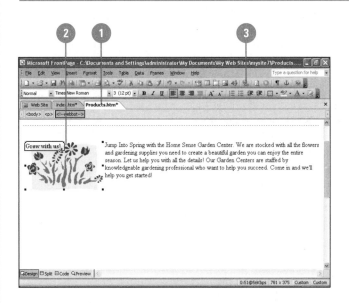

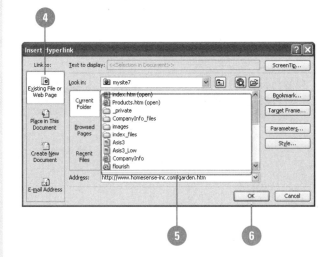

Create a Hyperlink to a New Internal Page

1. Click the View menu, click Page, and then open the Web page you want to use.

2. Select the graphic you want.

3. Click the Insert Hyperlink button on the Standard toolbar.

4. Click Create New Document.

5. Enter the name of the new document.

6. Click the Edit The New Document Later option.

7. Click OK.

8. If you are prompted to save changes to your new blank document, click Yes, specify a location, and then click Save.

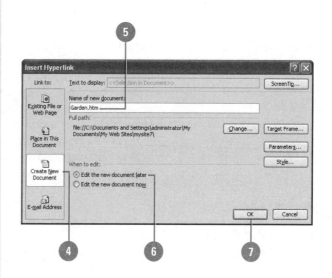

Create a Hyperlink to a Bookmark

1. Click the View menu, click Page, and then open the Web page containing the bookmark.

2. Right-click the page, and then click Hyperlink.

3. Click Bookmark.

4. Click the bookmark you want to use as the destination.

5. Click OK.

6. If you want the destination of the hyperlink to show up in a specific frame, click Target Frame.

7. Specify the frame from the main window, and then click OK.

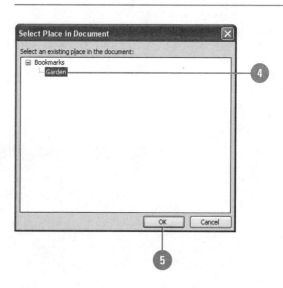

5

Working with Graphic Hotspots

A hotspot is defined as an invisible region on a graphic, text block, or other Web area to which you have assigned a hyperlink. A text hotspot is a word or a string of words that you have integrated into a graphic and that you have assigned to a hyperlink. When a site visitor clicks their cursor over that hyperlink, the link's destination is displayed in the Web browser. In FrontPage, hotspots can be shaped as rectangles, circles, or polygons. A graphic containing one or more hotspots is an Image map. Image maps typically provide clues so that you know where to click. The areas of the graphic that doesn't contain hotspots can be assigned a default hyperlink; when the user clicks anywhere outside a hotspot, they are directed to the destination you set as the graphic's default hyperlink.

Add a Hotspot to a Graphic

1. Click the View menu, click Page, and then open the Web page you want to use.

2. Select the graphic you want to add a hotspot.

3. Click a hotspot button (Rectangular, Circular, or Polygonal) on the Pictures toolbar that conforms to the shape you want.

4. Move the cursor over the picture until it becomes a drawing implement. Drag a hotspot. The shape you designated appears. You can size the hotspot by dragging the sizing handles.

   When you complete the hotspot, the Insert Hyperlink dialog box automatically opens.

5. Enter the URL in which you want to link the hotspot.

6. Click OK.

> **Did You Know?**
>
> **You can return a hotspot to its original position.** Select the hotspot, and then press Esc.

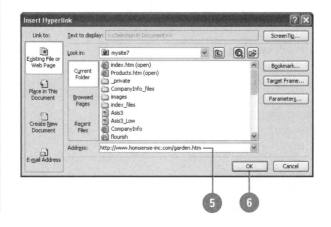

Add a Text-Based Hotspot

1. Click the View menu, click Page, and then open the Web page you want to use.

2. Select the graphic you want to add a text-based hotspot.

3. Click the Text button on the Pictures toolbar.

4. Type your text. To save your entry, click outside the graphic.

5. Double-click an edge of the text box to open the Insert Hyperlink dialog box.

6. Enter the URL you want to link to.

7. Click OK to complete the link.

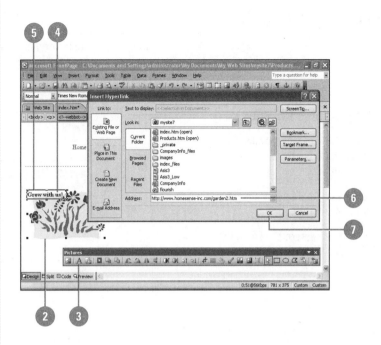

Edit Hotspot Hyperlinks

1. Click the View menu, click Page, and then open the Web page you want to use.

2. Select the graphics that contains the hotspot you want to modify.

3. Perform one or more of the following:

   - **Edit the URL for a hotspot.** Double-click the hotspot, and then alter the destination in the Address box.

   - **Resize the hotspot.** Drag the selection handles.

   - **Delete a hotspot.** Press the Delete key on the keyboard.

   - **Move the hotspot.** Drag it to a new position, or press the arrow keys to move the hotspot in small increments.

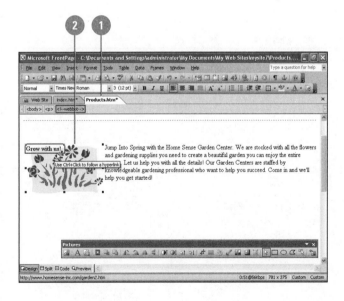

5

Restoring a Graphic

If you make several changes to a graphic that you don't want to keep, you can click the Restore button on the Pictures toolbar to return the graphic back to it's original state since it was last saved. This gives you the ability to try different or interesting effects with a graphic without having to worry about keeping the changes if you don't like the result.

Restore Graphic Changes

 Click the View menu, click Page, and then open the Web page you want to use.

② Click the graphic in which you want to restore.

③ Click the Restore button on the Pictures toolbar.

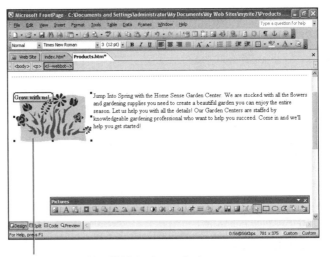

Restored graphic with it's background color

Inserting Multimedia and Special Effects

Introduction

Now that you've worked with some of the introductory graphical elements, it's time to add some additional pizazz to your Web site to really make it stand out. One of the ways to enhance your site is by adding a Flash movie clip. Macromedia Flash movies are vector-based animations and media that you can scale, rotate, and modify without losing any degree of sharpness or quality. Flash movies are especially suited for playback over the Web because they have a small file size, which loads and plays quickly.

When looking at a Web site, there are certain details that can make your Web pages a site that visitors will return to. Microsoft Office FrontPage 2003 helps you generate that type of site. Visitors might notice a washed out background picture called a watermark. Or maybe it's a soothing color or light sound as you pass over certain feature of the page. Having a custom feel will express to your visitors that you've spent time and looked at every detail of your site.

Instead of waiting for a large picture to download, you can use a small preview picture, known as a thumbnail, which downloads much faster. It's common practice to display a small preview picture and give the visitor the choice of whether to view the larger version. You can also have a photo gallery on your Web pages to ensure that your thumbnails are organized. Captions can be added to further help your visitors with the proper photo selection. Other graphical features include adding a marquee to make certain text stand out. You can also add page transitions to your Web site for a custom feel.

Implementing the use of interactive buttons makes moving around a site an easy experience for a visitor. You can customize these buttons, and define hyperlinks for them. You can also apply special effects to your pages using DHTML. These animation effects are triggered by an event, such as clicking on a link.

Inserting Flash Movies

Macromedia Flash movies are vector-based animations and media that you can scale, rotate, and modify without losing any degree of sharpness or quality. Flash movies are especially suited for playback over the Web because they have a small file size, which loads and plays quickly. You can insert Flash movies into your Web page.

Insert a Flash Movie

1. Click the View menu, click Page, and then open the Web page you want to use.

2. Position the insertion point at the location where you want to insert your Flash movie.

3. Click the Insert menu, point to Picture, and then click Movie In Flash Format.

4. Click the Look In list arrow, and then select the folder location containing the Flash movie you want to use.

5. Select the Flash file.

6. Click Insert.

7. Click the Preview button to view the Flash movie.

Did You Know?

You can use other methods to insert a flash movie. You can drag a flash movie file from Windows Explorer to your page (default settings applied to movie), or use the Web Component command on the Insert menu.

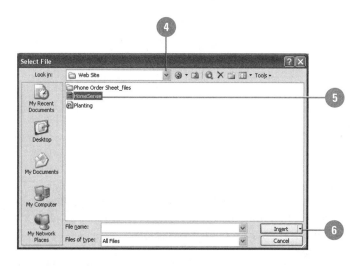

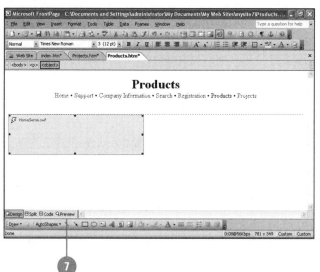

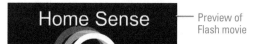

Preview of Flash movie

Change Flash Format Properties

1. Click the View menu, click Page, and then open the Web page you want to use.

2. Double-click the Flash movie.

3. If necessary, click the Appearance tab.

4. Select the appearance options you want. Some of the common options include:

   ◆ **Quality.** The best quality reduces the speed, while low quality plays faster.

   ◆ **Scale.** Specifies display characteristics in the viewing area.

   ◆ **Background Color.** Specifies background color or transparent.

   ◆ **Alignment.** Specifies position in the browser window.

   ◆ **Layout Settings.** Specifies the alignment, border thickness, horizontal spacing, and vertical spacing.

   ◆ **Size Settings.** Specifies the size of the movie.

5. To specify URL locations, playback options, and network locations, click the General tab, and then make the changes you want.

6. Click OK.

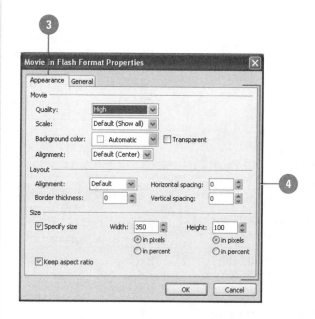

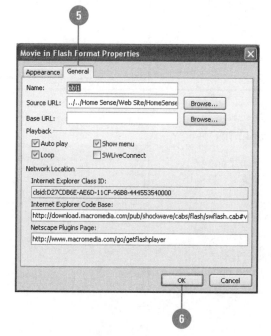

6

Inserting Video Clips

Streaming video clips are becoming more accessible to a broader base of users as high speed internet access using cable modems, DSL and other technologies become more prevalent. FrontPage can insert pre-recorded video clips into your web pages using the Insert menu. The most common video formats are Windows Media Video (WMV), Motion Picture Experts Group (MPEG), QuickTime (MOV), RealVideo (RAM), and Audio Visual Interleaved (AVI).

Insert a Video Clip

1. Click the View menu, click Page, and then open the Web page you want to use.

2. Position the insertion point where you want to insert your video.

3. Click the Insert menu, point to Picture, and then click Video.

4. Click the Look In list arrow, and then select the folder containing the video you want to use.

5. Select the video file.

6. Click Open.

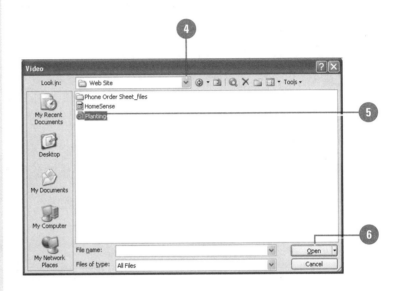

Change Video Clip Properties

1. Click the View menu, click Page, and then open the Web page you want to use.

2. Right-click the video clip, and then click Picture Properties.

3. Click the Video tab, and then select the repeat and start options you want.

4. Click OK.

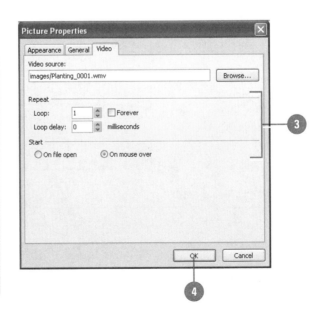

Adding Background Sound

You can introduce background sounds to accompany and enhance your web. There's nothing like hearing a favorite tune when you enter a site or visit a particular page. The sound can be played continuously in a loop, or you can set it for a desired number of plays. Be aware that not all browsers support background sound.

Add a Background Sound to a Web Page

1. Click the View menu, click Page, and then open the Web page you want to use.

2. Right-click the page to which you want to add a background sound, and then click Page Properties.

3. If necessary, click the General tab.

4. Type the sound file name or click Browse, locate and select the sound file you want to use, and then click Open.

5. To set the sound to repeat continuously, clear the Forever check box, and then click the number arrows in the Loop box to set the number of times you want the sound to play.

6. Click OK.

Whenever a visitor opens the page, they will hear the sound effect you chose.

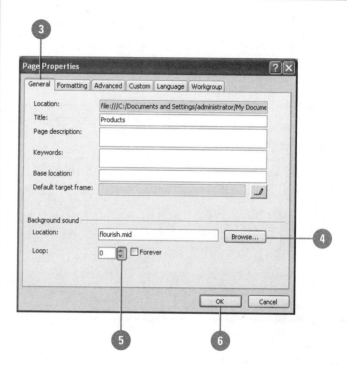

Inserting Background Pictures and Watermarks

You can use a picture as the background for a page. Pictures can be taken from elsewhere on your site, a file, clip art, or the Web. You can also use a background picture in watermark form. A **watermark** is a background effect that displays a graphic in a light shade behind your text on your page. You can use a washed out version of your company logo, or you can add graphical text such as Under Construction. Pictures and watermarks display in the background titled across the page. Be aware that not all web browsers support watermarks.

Insert a Background Picture

1. Click the View menu, click Page, and then open the Web page you want to use.

2. Right-click anywhere on the page to which you want to insert a background picture, and then click Page Properties.

3. Click the Formatting tab.

4. Select the Background Picture check box.

5. Click Browse.

6. Click the Look In list arrow, and then select the folder containing the picture you want to use.

7. Select the picture you want to insert, and then click Open.

   The picture you selected now opens as a background image.

8. Click OK.

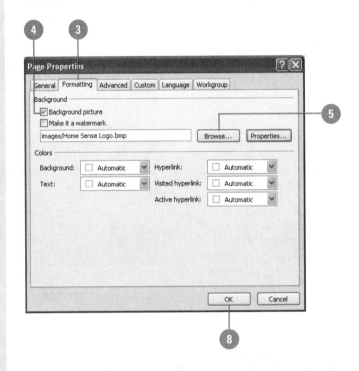

Did You Know?

You can avoid picture background tiling. Make your picture wider than any typical computer screen. You can use a solid background color or make it transparent to achieve the look you want.

Background picture tiled

Insert a Background Picture Watermark

1. Click the View menu, click Page, and then open the Web page you want to use.

2. Right-click anywhere on the page to which you want to insert a background picture, and then click Page Properties.

3. Click the Formatting tab.

4. Select the Background Picture check box.

5. Select the Make It A Watermark check box.

6. Click Browse.

7. Click the Look In list arrow, and then select the folder containing the picture you want to use.

8. Select the picture you want to insert, and then click Open.

   The picture you selected now opens as a background image.

9. Click OK.

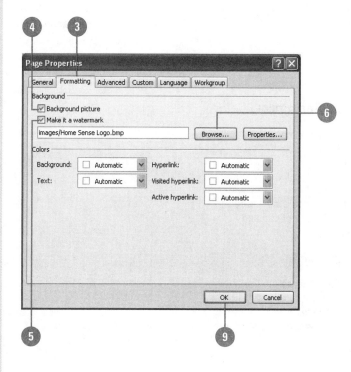

Changing Background Colors

If you'd like to add some interest to your pages, you can add background colors. When selecting background colors, some creative judgment is required. For example, if you choose a dark color for your background, make sure you use a light color for your text (the most commonly used is white) to generate the appropriate contrast required for easy reading.

Change the Background Color

1. Click the View menu, click Page, and then open the Web page you want to use.

2. Right-click the page to which you want to change a background color, and then click Page Properties.

3. Click the Formatting tab.

4. Click the Background list arrow.

5. Click the color you want on the color palette.

6. Click OK.

Did You Know?

You cannot place a background color on a page that is part of a theme. If you're working in a theme, the Background tab will not be available on the Page Properties dialog box. If you want to use a background color, click the Custom tab, select the theme listed under User Variables, and then click Remove. When you reopen the Page Properties dialog box, the Background tab is now available.

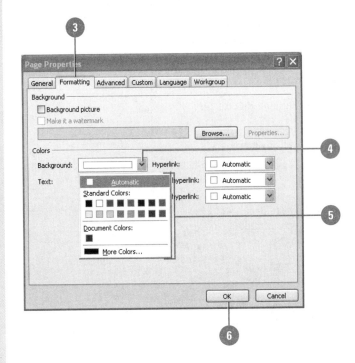

Accessing More Colors

FrontPage comes with a standard set of 16 colors. In addition to the standard colors, FrontPage allows you to add more colors to your page. More Colors are additional colors that you can add to each color menus—the Font Color button menu, for example. More Colors are useful when you want an object or picture to always have the same color. They are also useful when you want to change the color of an object to a specific color, but the standard colors don't not have that color. Colors that you add to a specific color menu appear in all color menus and remain in the menu even if the color scheme changes.

Add a Color to the Menus

1. Click the View menu, click Page, and then open the Web page you want to use.

2. Click any color list arrow (such as Font Color button list arrow) to open a color palette.

3. Click More Colors on the color palette.

4. Do one of the following:

    ◆ Click a color from the expanded palette. Every time you click a color, its corresponding hexadecimal value appears in the Value box.

    ◆ Enter a hexadecimal value in the Value box. An example of such a value would be HEX={99,FF,CC}.

    ◆ To select a color from anywhere on the screen, click Select, and then click any color on the screen.

    ◆ To select a color that represents the color average of an area of the palette, click Select, and then drag the eye dropper cursor to create a box encompassing the colors you want to average.

5. Click OK, and then click OK again.

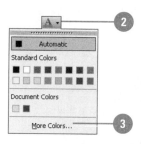

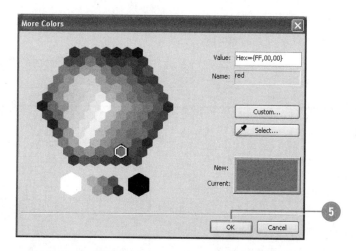

Color Palettes	
Characteristic	**Description**
Standard	Basic 16-color palette
Custom	Palette containing colors you have defined
Document's	Colors being used on the current page
Theme	Colors used as part of the current theme
More	Palette used to define a custom color

6

Creating Custom Colors

RGB (red, green, blue) is a set of color values that describe colors. RGB identifies a color by a set of hexadecimal numbers, an internal computer numbering scheme, that specify the amounts of red, green, and blue needed to create the color. RGB colors appear best over the Web (true color representation without dithers or substitutes) when you use only **browser safe colors**, which is a standard set of 216 color combinations. These RGB values are 0, 51, 102, 153, 204, or 255 in decimal or 00, 33, 66, 99, CC, or FF in hexadecimal. When you use the color dialog boxes, you use decimal values. In Code view, you use hexadecimal values. You can access and create colors using any FrontPage color menu. You can define up to 16 different colors, and then save them to a custom palette. The custom colors become available on all color menus.

Define a Custom Color Palette

1. Click the View menu, click Page, and then open the Web page you want to use.

2. Click any color list arrow (such as Font Color button list arrow) to open a color palette.

3. Click More Colors on the color palette.

4. Click Custom.

5. Click a blank box.

6. Select a color by entering a combination of numerical values, or selecting one of the basic colors in the main palette or a custom color in the color spectrum palette.

7. Click Add To Custom Colors.

8. When you're done, click OK.

9. Click OK again to close the More Colors dialog box.

10. Click OK to close the Page Properties dialog box.

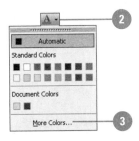

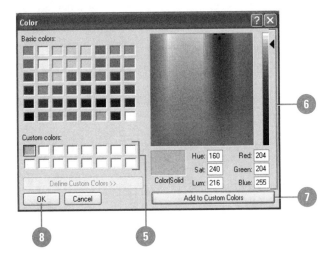

Remove a Custom Color

1. Click the View menu, click Page, and then open the Web page you want to use.

2. Click any color list arrow (such as Font Color button list arrow) to open a color palette.

3. Click More Colors on the color palette.

4. Click Custom.

5. Click the box with the color you want to remove.

6. Click the white color in the standard color palette.

7. Click Add To Custom Colors.

8. When you're done, click OK.

9. Click OK again to close the More Colors dialog box.

10. Click OK to close the Page Properties dialog box.

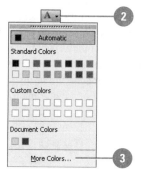

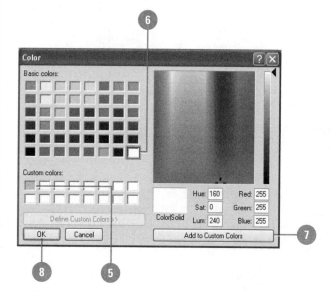

Understanding HSL Colors

Color	Description
Hue	The color itself; every color is identified by a number, determined by the number of colors available on your monitor.
Saturation	The intensity of the color. The higher the number, the more vivid the color.
Luminosity	The brightness of the color, or how close the color is to black or white. The larger the number, the lighter the color.

6

Creating Thumbnails

Create a Thumbnail

1. Click the View menu, click Page, and then open the Web page on which you want to create a thumbnail.

2. Select the graphic image you want to use.

3. Click the Tools menu, and then click Auto Thumbnail.

4. If necessary, drag a handle to resize the thumbnail.

Instead of waiting for a large picture to download, you can use a small preview picture, known as a thumbnail, which downloads much faster. It's common practice to display a small preview picture and give the visitor the choice of whether to view the larger version. FrontPage makes it easy to create a thumbnail using the AutoThumbnail feature. The command removes the large graphic, creates the thumbnail in its place, and then sets up a hyperlink from the thumbnail to the large graphic.

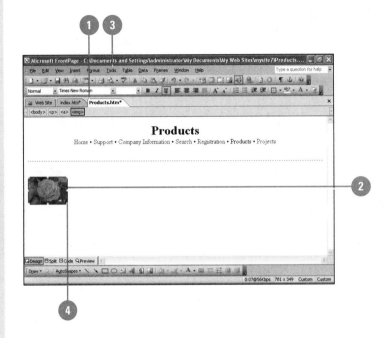

Set AutoThumbnail Properties

1. Click the Tools menu, and then click Page Options.

2. Click the AutoThumbnail tab.

3. Select the general and usage options you want. Some of the common options include:

   ◆ **Set.** Controls the size of the thumbnail picture. You can choose to make all the thumbnail pictures the same width, height, shortest side, or longest side.

   ◆ **Pixels.** Specifies the fixed size applied to the edge.

   ◆ **Border Thickness.** Create borders around each thumbnail picture.

   ◆ **Beveled Edge.** Creates beveled edges for each thumbnail picture.

4. Click OK.

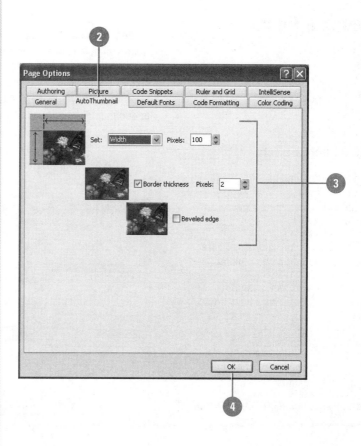

Did You Know?

You can resize a thumbnail that is part of a photo gallery. Click the View menu, click Page, click the Insert menu, and then click Web Component. Double-click Photo Gallery, and then click the thumbnail you want to resize. Under Thumbnail Size, designate the new height and width in terms of pixels.

6

Creating a Photo Gallery

They say a picture is worth a thousand words, but a good caption helps readers to get all the nuances of a picture immediately. The Photo Gallery allows you to insert full-sized pictures and display them as thumbnails. When a visitor clicks one of these thumbnails, the full-sized picture opens. You can display the pictures in the Photo Gallery in the order and size you want and the layout you select. You can also add captions and descriptions for each picture in the gallery.

Create a Photo Gallery

1. Click the View menu, click Page, and then open the Web page you want to use or create a new blank page.

2. Position the insertion point where you want to add a photo gallery.

3. Click the Insert menu, point to Picture, and then click New Photo Gallery.

4. Click the Layout tab.

5. Select the layout you prefer for your photo gallery.

6. Specify the number of pictures you want per row.

7. Click the Pictures tab.

Did You Know?

You can create a Photo Gallery using a template. Click the New button list arrow, click Page, click the General tab, click Photo Gallery, and then click OK. Double-click the photo gallery layout to modify it.

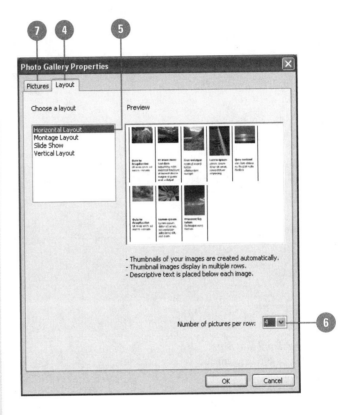

8 Click Add, and then click Pictures From Files.

◆ To insert pictures from a scanner, click Pictures From Scanner Or Camera.

9 Click the Look In list arrow, and then select the folder containing the pictures you want to use.

10 Press and hold Ctrl, select the pictures you want to insert, and then click Open.

11 To arrange the pictures within your gallery, select the name of the graphic, and then click the Move Up button or the Move Down button.

12 To set the width and the height of the thumbnail, enter width and height values in the Width and Height boxes.

13 Click OK.

14 Click the Save button on the Standard toolbar, type a name, and then click Save.

15 If the Save Embedded Files dialog box appears, save the graphic files.

See Also

See "Inserting a Graphic from a Scanner or Camera" on page 122 for information on using a scanner or camera to insert a photograph.

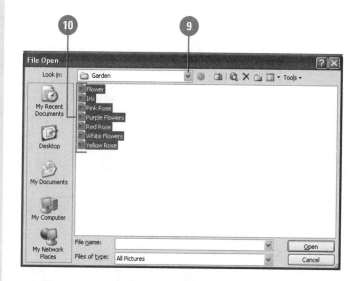

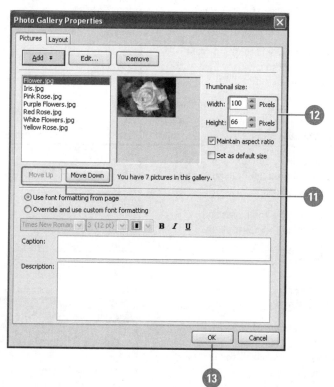

6

Modifying a Photo Gallery

After you create a Photo Gallery, you can make changes to it at any time. You can add or modify captions and ScreenTip descriptions for the pictures, or edit pictures properties. For readers who disable graphic downloads in their browsers, a caption is good way to convey information regarding your pictures. If you need to change a picture, the Photo Gallery allows you to rotate and crop pictures as well as change picture size. If you don't like your changes, you can restore the picture.

Add a Caption to a Picture in the Photo Gallery

1. Click the View menu, click Page, and then open the Web page you want to use.

2. Double-click the photo gallery you want to modify.

3. Select the picture in which you want to add a caption.

4. Click the Use Font Formatting From Page option or the Override And Use Custom Font Formatting option.

5. Type the caption that you want to appear with the picture.

6. Enter the description text you want to appear when a user passes their mouse over the picture.

7. If you want, click the Layout tab, and then select another layout.

8. Click OK.

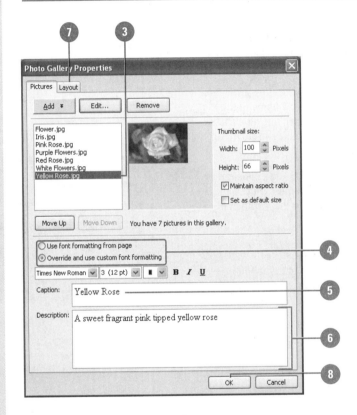

Did You Know?

Captions are not available for all layouts. Text boxes for a Caption or Description are not available in the Montage Layout.

Using SharePoint Services Picture Libraries

If you need more flexibility than the FrontPage Photo Gallery, you can try the Microsoft Windows SharePoint Services picture library. You can store more pictures than the Photo Gallery and you can allow visitors to upload, and modify pictures using the Microsoft Picture Library program included with Microsoft Office 2003. To run SharePoint Services, you need a network server running Windows Server 2003 and SharePoint Services Web server.

Edit Picture Properties in the Photo Gallery

1. Click the View menu, click Page, and then open the Web page you want to use.

2. Double-click the photo gallery you want to modify.

3. Select the picture in which you want to edit.

4. Click Edit.

5. Use the commands to modify the picture.

- ◆ **Picture Size.** Controls the picture width and height, and sets the default size.

- ◆ **Rotate Picture buttons.** Click the buttons to rotate or flip the picture.

- ◆ **Crop Picture button.** Click the button, resize the box, and then click the Crop button again.

- ◆ **Previous and Next button.** Moves backward and forward through all the pictures in the list.

- ◆ **Reset button.** Removes any changes you've made.

6. Click OK.

7. Click OK.

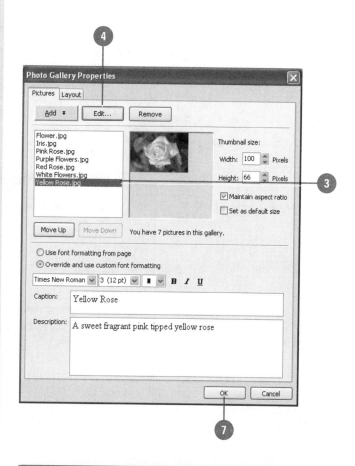

Using Interactive Buttons

An interactive button gives you the the ability to link one page to another page in the current Web site, a site on the World Wide Web, or an e-mail address. You don't have to know HTML code to create, modify, and link an interactive button. You can select a button style from a pre-defined list and then add button text, select button and background colors, and specify the font style, size, and color for all states of the button including the original, hover, and pressed states. After you create the button, you can define a hyperlink for a button.

Create an Interactive Button

1. Click the View menu, click Page, and then open the Web page you want to use.

2. Position the insertion point where you want to insert an interactive button.

3. Click the Insert menu, and then click Interactive Button.

4. Click the button type you want.

5. Type the button title.

6. Type a hyperlink location or use Browse to locate and select it.

7. Click the Font tab.

8. Select the font options you want.

   ◆ **Font, Font Style, and Size.** Specifies the button text font type, style, and size.

   ◆ **Font Color.** Specifies the text font color for the original, hovered, and pressed button.

   ◆ **Alignment.** Specifies the horizontal and vertical alignment of the text.

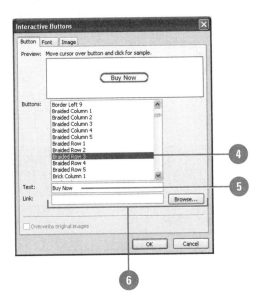

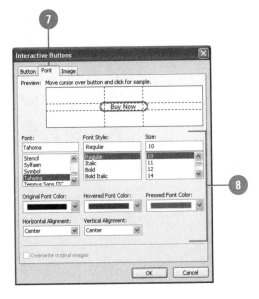

9 Click the Image tab.

10 Specify the image options you want.

◆ **Width and Height.** Controls the width and height of the button.

◆ **Create Hover Image.** Select to change the button when the mouse pointer passes over it.

◆ **Create Pressed Image.** Select to change the button when a visitor clicks it.

◆ **Preload Button Images.** Select to load all the button pictures in memory.

11 Click the JPEG image option to choose a solid background color, or choose the GIF image option to set a transparent background.

12 Click OK.

13 To preview the button, click the Preview button.

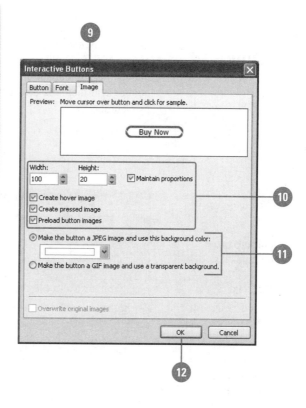

See Also

See "Adding Hyperlinks to Graphics" on page 144 for information on creating a hyperlink to a button graphic.

Did You Know?

Hover buttons are not available in FrontPage 2003. The feature doesn't exist, but if you have existing pages with Hover buttons, they still work and you can double-click them to edit properties.

Adding Special Effects to Hyperlinks

You can add a special rollover effect to hyperlinked text that causes the font to change when a visitor passes their cursor over it. After you enable hyperlink rollover effects, you can specify how you want the text of hyperlinks to appear in the Web page when a site visitor rests the pointer over them. Be aware that hyperlink rollovers are not supported by all browsers.

Add Special Effects to Hyperlinks

1. Click the View menu, click Page, and then open the Web page you want to use.

2. Right-click the hyperlinked text, and then click Page Properties.

3. Click the Advanced tab.

4. Select the Enable Hyperlink Rollover Effects check box.

5. Click Rollover Style.

6. Set the font properties for rollover hyperlinks on the current page.

7. Click OK.

8. Click OK.

9. To preview the effect, click the Preview button.

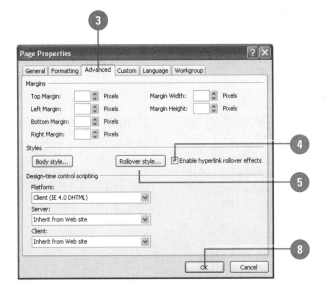

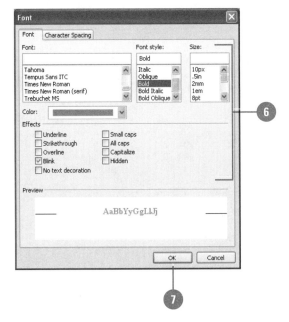

Adding Special Effects to Text

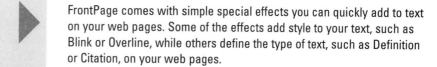

FrontPage comes with simple special effects you can quickly add to text on your web pages. Some of the effects add style to your text, such as Blink or Overline, while others define the type of text, such as Definition or Citation, on your web pages.

Add Font Effects to Text

1. Click the View menu, click Page, and then open the Web page you want to use.

2. Select the text you want to format.

3. Click the Format menu, and then click Font.

4. Select or clear the font special effects check boxes. The unique effects to FrontPage include:

   ◆ **Overline.** Draws a line above the text.

   ◆ **Blink.** Applies blinking animation to the text.

   ◆ **Capitalize.** Capitalizes the first letter in each word.

   ◆ **Strong.** Applies a stronger emphasis to the text.

   ◆ **Emphasis.** Applies a subtle emphasis to the text.

   ◆ **Sample.** Applies a fixed width font to the text.

   ◆ **Definition.** Specifies the text as a definition.

   ◆ **Citation.** Specifies the text as a reference to other sources.

   ◆ **Variable.** Specifies the text as a variable or program argument.

   ◆ **Keyboard.** Specifies the text that is entered by a user.

   ◆ **Code.** Specifies the text as a programming code.

5. Click OK.

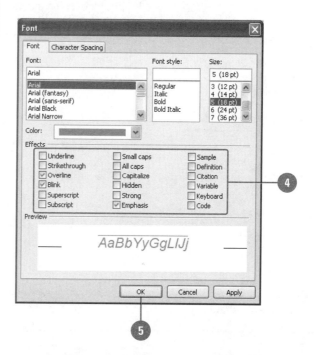

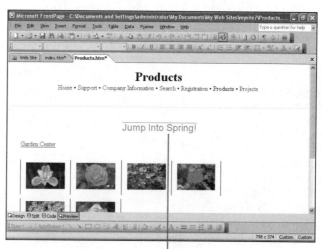

Font effect applied to text

6

Creating Marquees

A marquee is an especially attractive visual special effect. Much as a movie theater marquee shows off what film is playing, a web marquee helps certain Web site elements stand out.

Create a Marquee

1. Click the View menu, click Page, and then open the Web page you want to use.

2. Select the position where you want to place the marquee, or select the existing text that you want to display inside the marquee.

3. Click the Insert menu, and then click Web Component.

4. In the left pane, click Dynamic Effects, and then click Marquee in the right pane.

5. Click Finish.

6. Select the options for the marquee directions, choose the settings for the marquee speed and behavior.

7. Click OK.

8. To preview the marquee, click the Preview button.

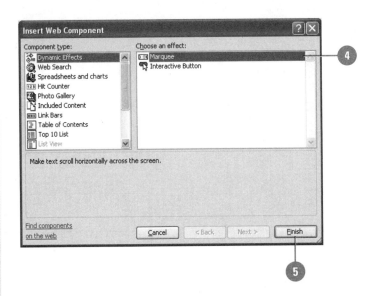

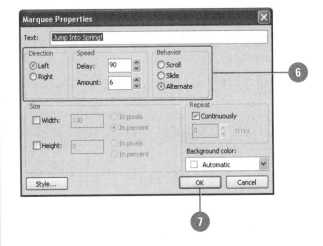

Did You Know?

You can change the spacing between the characters on the Marquee.
To expand or contract the spacing between characters, or to raise or lower the text, click Style in the Marquee Properties dialog box. Click Format, and then click Font. Click the Character Spacing tab, make the changes you want, and then click OK to go back to the Marquee Properties dialog box.

Customize a Marquee

1. Click the View menu, click Page, and then open the Web page you want to use.

2. Right-click the marquee you want to edit, and then click Marquee Properties.

3. Modify these properties to suit the effect you are trying to achieve.

   ◆ **Text.** Text you want to display inside the marquee. There is no limit on length.

   ◆ **Direction.** Determines whether your text within the marquee moves left or right.

   ◆ **Speed.** How fast the text in a marquee moves.

   ◆ **Delay.** Length of the delay, in milliseconds, before the marquee text begins to move.

   ◆ **Amount.** The increment, in pixels, that the text in the marquee moves.

   ◆ **Behavior.** Specifies scroll, slide, and alternate text behaviors.

   ◆ **Size.** Select the Width or Height check box, and then specify width or height settings.

   ◆ **Repeat.** Determines how many times the text effect in a marquee is repeated.

   ◆ **Background Color.** Specifies the color you want displayed behind the marquee's scrolling text.

4. Click OK.

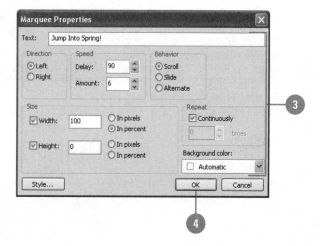

6

Inserting a Dynamic HTML Effect

You can add special effects to your Web pages by using Dynamic HTML (DHTML). With DHTML, you can have animation text fly off the page one word at a time or change a long list of points into a space-saving collapsible outline. An animation effect is tied to a trigger event on the part of the visitor. The trigger event can be anything from clicking a link to entering the site. Formatting alters the look of a specific page element, including changing colors or applying new effects.

Insert a Dynamic HTML Effect

1. Click the View menu, click Page, and then open the Web page you want to use.

2. Select the item you want to animate.

3. Right-click any toolbar, and then click DHTML Effects.

4. Click the On list arrow on the DHTML Effects toolbar, and then select the event (such as Click, Double Click, Mouse Over, and Page Load) that will trigger the animation. The events listed in the On box are determined by the type of page effect you select.

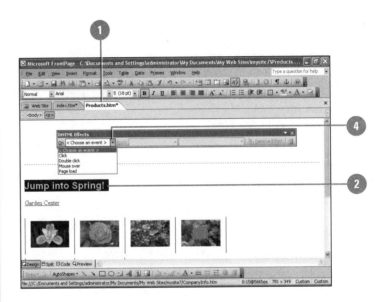

5. Click the Apply list arrow on the DHTML Effects toolbar, and then select the kind of animation effect you want. The main effects include: (Fly Out, Fly In, Drop In By Word, Elastic, Hop, Spiral, Wave, Wipe and Zoom). Other effects include:

   ◆ **Formatting**. Generates an animation that changes the look of a page elements, such as a font changing color.

   ◆ **Swap Picture**. Generates an animation that exchanges pictures.

   ◆ **Choose Settings box**. Click the list arrow, and then select the settings for the effect.

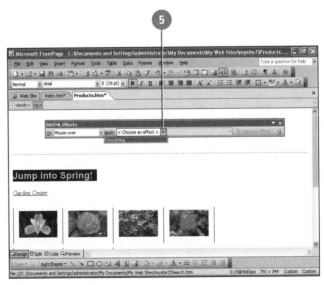

6. Click the Effects list arrow on the DHTML Effects toolbar, and then click a Formatting effect. From this menu, you can select the font style, size, color, effects, and character spacing.

7. After you've selected an animation in the Apply or Effects boxes, you will be given automatic access to a series of options. The settings are:

   ◆ **Choose Font.** (If you assigned a Formatting Animation, you can change the font style, size, color, effects, and character spacing).

   ◆ **Choose Border.** (If you assigned a Formatting Animation, this changes the border or shading).

   ◆ **Choose Picture.** (If you selected a picture and initiated the Swap Picture feature, select this to select the picture you want to swap with the existing picture).

8. When you're done, click the Close button on the DHTML Effects toolbar.

Did You Know?

You can highlight the area with the DHTML effect. Click the Highlight Dynamic HTML Effects button on the DHTML Effects toolbar.

You can remove the DHMTL effect. Click the Remove Effect button on the DHTML Effects toolbar.

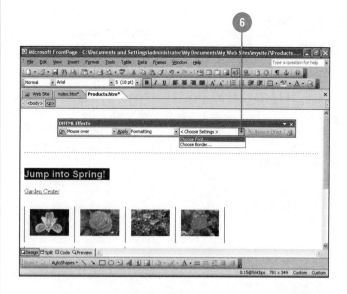

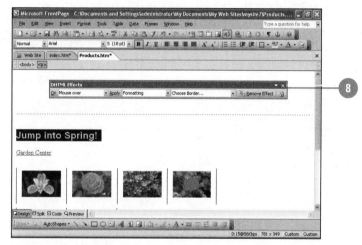

6

Animating Page Transitions

You can use animation in your Web site to provide interest and call attention to important information. When you move from one Web page to another, you can display a transition effect between the two pages. You can select a transition effect, and then specify when the page transition occurs, and how long it lasts. The only disadvantage of page transitions is that the browser must wait for the entire Web page to load before it can apply the transition effect. Be aware that animated page transitions are not supported by all browsers.

Apply a Page Transition

① Click the View menu, click Page, and then open the Web page you want to use.

② Click the Format menu, and then click Page Transition.

③ Click the Event list arrow, and then click an event type: Page Enter, Page Exit, Site Enter, or Site Exit.

④ Click the transition effect you want.

⑤ Set the duration (in seconds) of the transition effect.

⑥ Click OK.

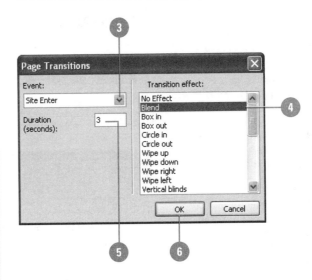

Drawing and Modifying Objects

7

Introduction

In addition to inserting graphics and multimedia, you can also create and insert drawings, AutoShapes, and WordArt to enhance your Web pages. With Microsoft Office FrontPage 2003, you can choose from a set of pre-designed shapes, or you can use tools that allow you to draw and edit your own shapes and forms. FrontPage's drawing tools control how you place objects on your Web page in relation to one another. If you choose to combine objects, you can create sophisticated effects.

When you create drawings, AutoShapes, and WordArt objects in FrontPage, the program stores the elements as a collection of lines, curves, and other shapes instead of a picture. This format is called VML, which stores the information in XML format. Since not all browsers support VML, FrontPage provides an option on the Page Options dialog box to save GIF versions of every drawing, AutoShape, and WordArt object you create to avoid problems.

Once you have the objects on your page, you can apply a number of elements to the graphic. You can color them, apply a fill effect, create a shadow, or even add a 3-D effect to the object. A once drab two dimensional graphic can be enhanced to be the graphic you need for your page. WordArt is an Office component that allows you to add visual enhancements to your text that go beyond changing a font or font size. You can select a WordArt style that stretches your text horizontally, vertically, or diagonally. WordArt is treated like any other graphic in your page development.

After enhancing your graphic, you might need to move it, or change it's alignment. You might find that you need to layer or stack the object a different way to get the affect you're looking for. You can even rotate or flip the object to have it display in the way that works best for your FrontPage document.

Setting VML Options

When you create drawings, AutoShapes, and WordArt objects in FrontPage, the program stores the elements as a collection of lines, curves, and other shapes instead of a picture. This format is called VML, which stores the information in XML format. Since not all browsers support VML, FrontPage provides the Downlevel Image File option on the Page Options dialog box to automatically save GIF versions of every drawing, AutoShape, and WordArt object you create to avoid the problems. If for some reason, the drawing, AutoShape, and WordArt tools are not available on menus and toolbar, you can enable the the VML Graphics option in the Page Options dialog box.

Set VML Options

1. Click the Tools menu, and then click Page Options.

2. Click the Authoring tab.

3. Select the VML Graphics (Office Drawing) check box.

4. Select the Downlevel Image File check box.

5. Click OK.

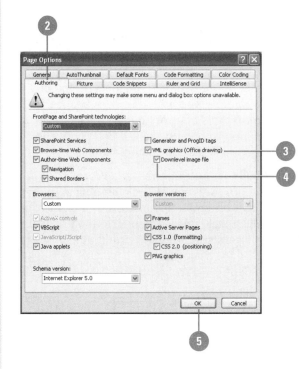

Creating a Drawing Canvas

If you intend to create a complex drawing composed of several objects, you can create a drawing area, known as a canvas, in which you can place your drawings. The canvas sets aside a separate area of the page for drawing, which you can resize just like any other object. There is a distinct advantage to using a drawing canvas. If a browser doesn't support VML, FrontPage can create one GIF file for the drawing canvas instead of individual GIF files for each object, which reduces file management and download time.

Create a Drawing Canvas

1. Click the View menu, click Page, and then open the Web page you want to use.

2. Click where you want to insert the drawing canvas.

3. Click the Insert menu, point to Picture, and then click New Drawing.

4. To resize the canvas, drag a black cropping handle.

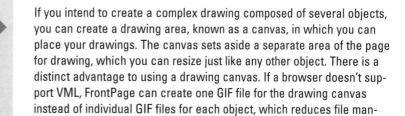

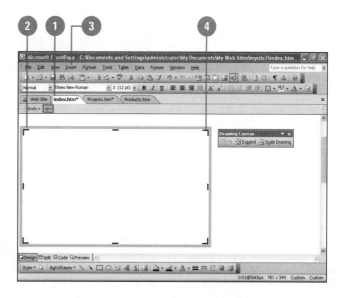

For Your Information

Drawing Objects

Drawing objects can be classified into three categories: lines, AutoShapes, and freeforms. **Lines** connect two points, **AutoShapes** are preset objects, such as stars, circles, or block arrows, and if you want to construct a new shape, you can draw a **freeform** shape.

Once you have created a drawing object, you can manipulate it in many ways, such as rotating it, coloring it, or changing its style. FrontPage also provides formatting commands that afford you precise control over your drawing object's appearance.

Drawing Lines and Arrows

The most basic drawing objects you can create on your pages are lines and arrows. FrontPage includes several tools for this purpose. The Line tool creates line segments. The Drawing toolbar's Line Style and Dash Style tools determine the type of line used in any drawing object—solid, dashed, or a combination of solid and dashed lines. The Arrow tool lets you create arrows that emphasize key features of your page. You can edit the style of the arrow using the Arrow Style tool.

Draw a Straight Line

1 Click the View menu, click Page, and then open the Web page you want to use.

2 Click the Line button on the Drawing toolbar.

3 Drag the pointer to draw a line on your page.

4 Release the mouse button when the line is the length you want. The endpoints of the line are where you started and finished dragging.

Did You Know?

You can constrain a line drawing. You can use keys on the keyboard to adjust lines as you draw them. To constrain the angle of the line to 15-degree increments, press and hold Shift as you drag the pointer. To draw the line from the center out, instead of from one endpoint to another, press and hold Ctrl as you drag the pointer.

You can display the Drawing toolbar. If the Drawing toolbar is not visible, click the View menu, point to Toolbars, and then click Drawing.

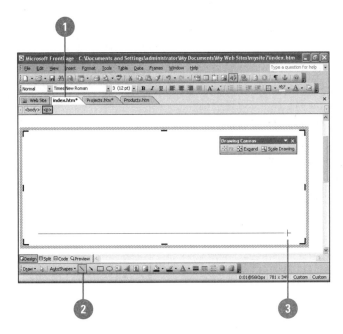

Edit a Line

1. Click the View menu, click Page, and then open the Web page you want to use.

2. Click the line that you want to edit.

3. Click the Line Style button on the Drawing toolbar, and then select a line thickness.

4. Click the Dash Style button on the Drawing toolbar, and then select a dash style.

5. Click the Line Color button list arrow on the Drawing toolbar, and then select a line color.

6. Drag the sizing handle at either end to a new location to change the size or angle of the line.

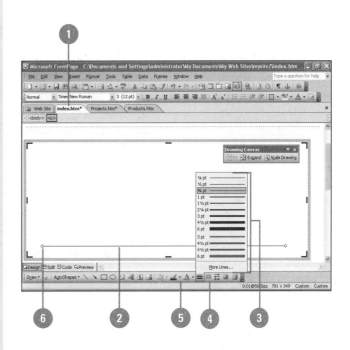

Draw a Curved Line

1. Click the View menu, click Page, and then open the Web page you want to use.

2. Click AutoShapes on the Drawing toolbar, and then point to Lines.

3. Click the Curve, FreeForm, or Scribble symbol.

4. To draw a curve, click a point on the screen, and then move the pointer. To draw a freeform, click a point, move the pointer, and then click to draw a straight line or drag to draw freely. To draw a scribble, drag the pointer.

5. Click the Line Color button list arrow on the Drawing toolbar to select a line color.

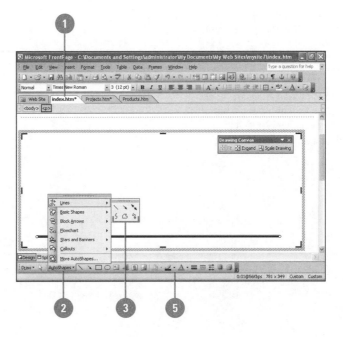

Drawing and Modifying Objects **179**

Drawing AutoShapes

You can choose from many different AutoShapes on the Drawing toolbar, ranging from hearts to lightening bolts. The two most common AutoShapes, the oval and the rectangle, are available directly on the Drawing toolbar. The rest of the AutoShapes are organized into categories that you can view and select from the AutoShapes menu. Once you have placed an AutoShape on a page, you can resize it using its sizing handles (small white circles that appear along the edge of an object). Many AutoShapes have an adjustment handle, a small yellow diamond located near a sizing handle, which you can drag to alter the shape of the AutoShape.

Draw an Oval or Rectangle

1. Click the View menu, click Page, and then open the Web page you want to use.

2. Click the Oval button or the Rectangle button on the Drawing toolbar.

3. Drag the pointer across the page where you want to place the oval or rectangle.

4. Release the mouse button when the object is the shape you want.

Did You Know?

You can draw a circle or square. Click the Oval button or the Rectangle button on the Drawing toolbar, and then press and hold Shift as you drag the shape.

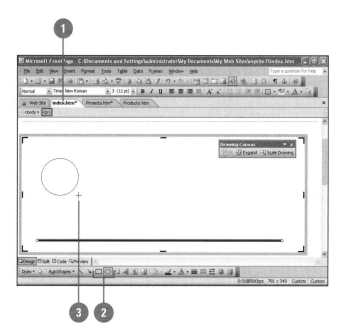

Draw an AutoShape

1. Click the View menu, click Page, and then open the Web page you want to use.

2. Click AutoShapes on the Drawing toolbar, and then point to the AutoShape category you want to use.

3. Click the symbol you want.

4. Drag the cursor across the page until the drawing object is the shape and size that you want.

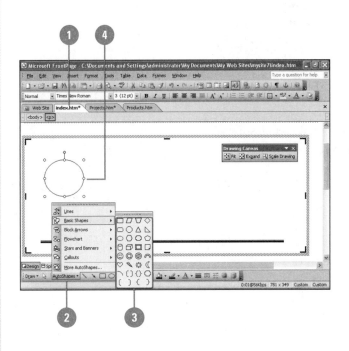

Resize or Adjust an AutoShape

1. Click the View menu, click Page, and then open the Web page you want to use.

2. Click the AutoShape you want to adjust.

3. Drag a white circle handle to resize the AutoShape or the yellow diamond handle to adjust the form of the AutoShape.

Did You Know?

You can replace one AutoShape with another and retain its settings. Click the AutoShape you want to replace, click Draw on the Drawing toolbar, point to Change AutoShape, and then select the new AutoShape.

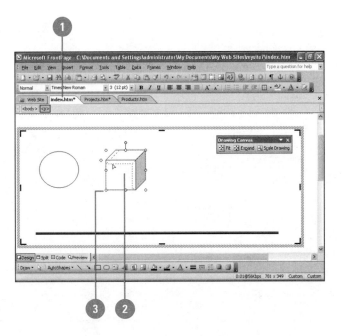

Inserting AutoShapes from the Clip Gallery

In addition to drawing AutoShapes, you can insert AutoShapes, such as computers and furniture, from the Clip Art task pane. These AutoShapes are called clips just like clip art. The Clip Art task pane gives you a miniature of each clip. You can click the clip you want to insert onto your page or click the clip list arrow to select other options, such as previewing the clip or searching for similar clips.

Insert an AutoShape from the Clip Gallery

1. Click the View menu, click Page, and then open the Web page you want to use.

2. Click the AutoShapes button on the Drawing toolbar, and then click More AutoShapes.

3. If necessary, use the scroll arrows to display more AutoShapes.

4. Click the shape you want to insert on your page.

5. Drag a handle to resize the shape on your page.

6. When you're done, click the Close button on the task pane.

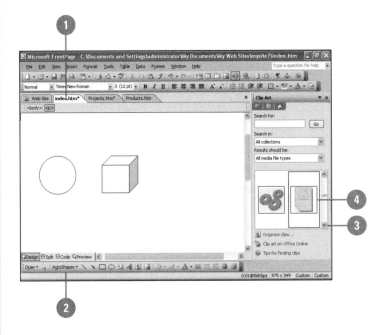

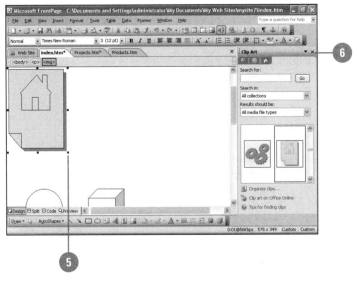

Moving an Object

After you create a drawing object, you can move it. You can quickly move objects using the mouse, or if you want precise control over the object's new position, use the Nudge command to move drawing objects in tiny increments up, down, left, or right. If you are not working in the Drawing canvas, you can also use the arrow keys to nudge objects.

Move an Object

1 Drag the object to a new location on the page.

Make sure you aren't dragging a sizing handle or adjustment handle. If you are working with a freeform and you are in Edit Points mode, drag the interior of the object, not the border, or you will end up resizing or reshaping the object, not moving it.

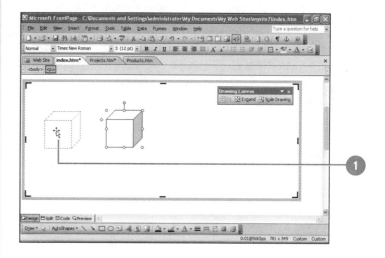

Nudge an Object

1 Click the object you want to nudge.

2 Click the Draw button on the Drawing toolbar.

3 Point to Nudge, and then click Up, Down, Left, or Right.

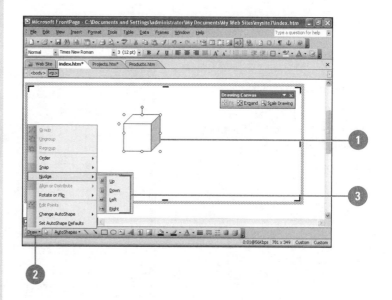

Choosing Object Colors

When you create a closed drawing object, you can select a fill color and a line color. When you create a drawing object, FrontPage uses the default color scheme to determine the line style and fill color. You can change the line and fill color settings using the same color tools you use to change a text color. An easy way to apply the current fill color to any object is to select the object, and then click the Fill Color button.

Change an Object's Fill Color

1. Click the drawing object whose fill color you want to change.

2. Click the Fill Color button list arrow on the Drawing toolbar.

3. Select the fill color you want.

4. Click Fill Effects if you want to change the fill effect too.

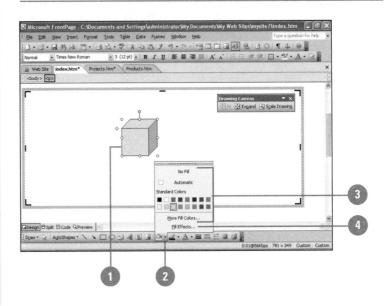

Remove a Fill

1. Click the drawing object whose fill you want to change.

2. Click the Fill Color button list arrow on the Drawing toolbar.

3. Click No Fill.

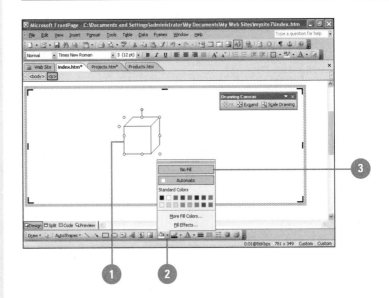

Change Colors and Lines in the Format Dialog Box

1. Click the drawing object you want to modify.

2. Click the Format menu, and then click AutoShape.

3. Click the Colors And Lines tab.

4. Set Fill, Line, and Arrows options.

5. Click OK.

Did You Know?

You can set the color and line style for an object as the default. Right-click the object, and then click Set AutoShape Defaults. Any new objects you create will use the same styles.

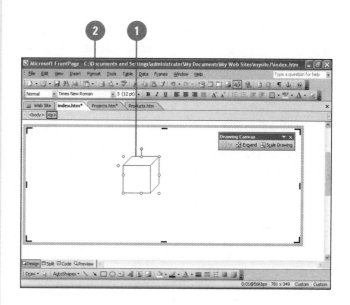

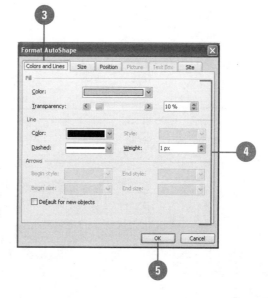

Applying Fill Effects

Applying a fill effect to a drawing object can add emphasis or create a point of interest in your page. FrontPage offers fill effects such as gradients, patterns, textures, and even clip art pictures. Spend a few minutes in the Fill Effects dialog box to create the right look for your drawing object.

Apply a Picture Fill

1 Select the object you want to fill, click the Fill Color button list arrow on the Drawing toolbar, and then click Fill Effects.

2 Click the Picture tab.

3 Click Select Picture.

4 Locate the picture you want, and then double-click it.

5 Click OK.

Apply a Gradient Fill

1 Select the object you want to fill, click the Fill Color button list arrow on the Drawing toolbar, and then click Fill Effects.

2 Click the Gradient tab.

3 Click the color or color combination you want.

4 Click the shading style option you want.

5 Click the variant you want.

6 Click OK.

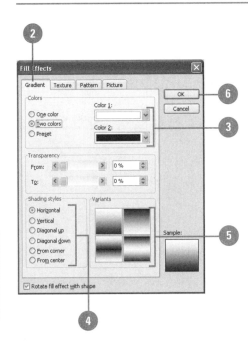

Apply a Pattern Fill

1 Select the object you want to fill, click the Fill Color button list arrow on the Drawing toolbar, and then click Fill Effects.

2 Click the Pattern tab.

3 Click the Foreground list arrow to select the color you want in the foreground.

4 Click the Background list arrow to select the color you want in the background.

5 Click the pattern you want.

6 Click OK.

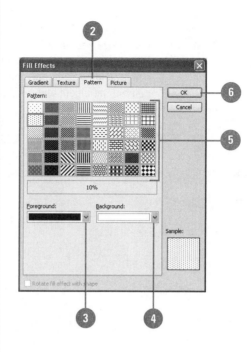

Did You Know?

You can change the fill to match the background. Select the object, click the Format menu, click AutoShape, click the Colors And Lines tab, click the Fill Color button list arrow, click Background, and then click OK.

You can apply fill effects to other objects. Apply fill effects to objects such as lines and WordArt to enhance your page.

Creating Shadows

You can give objects on your pages the illusion of depth by adding shadows. FrontPage provides several preset shadowing options, or you can create your own by specifying the location and color of the shadow. If the shadow is falling on another object in your page, you can create a semitransparent shadow that blends the color of the shadow with the color of the object underneath it.

Use a Preset Shadow

1. Click the drawing object to which you want to add a preset shadow.

2. Click the Shadow Style button on the Drawing toolbar.

3. Click a shadow style.

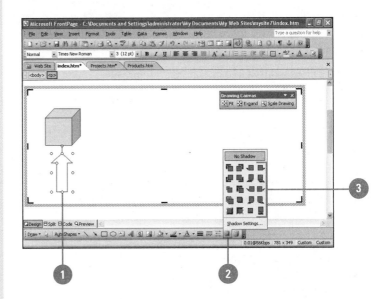

Change the Location of a Shadow

1. Click the drawing object with the shadow.

2. Click the Shadow Style button on the Drawing toolbar, and then click Shadow Settings.

3. Click the tool that creates the effect you want. The Nudge buttons move the shadow location slightly up, down, right, or left.

4. Click the Close button on the Shadow Settings toolbar.

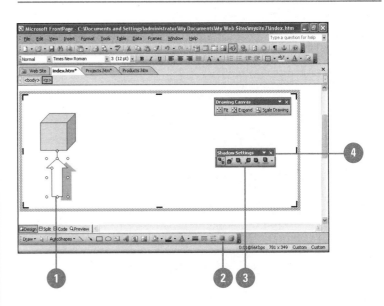

Change the Color of a Shadow

1 Click the drawing object with the shadow.

2 Click the Shadow Style button on the Drawing toolbar, and then click Shadow Settings.

3 Click the Shadow Color button list arrow on the Shadow Settings toolbar, and then select a new color.

4 Click the Close button on the Shadow Settings toolbar.

Did You Know?

You can remove a shadow. Click the drawing object with the shadow, click the Shadow button on the Drawing toolbar, and then click No Shadow.

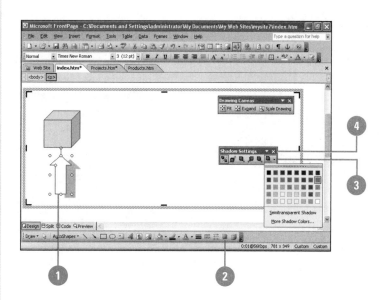

Adding 3-D Effects

You can add the illusion of depth to your Web pages by using the 3-D tool. Although not all objects can be turned into 3-D objects, most of the AutoShapes can. You can create a 3-D effect using one of the 20 preset 3-D styles supported by FrontPage, or you can use the 3-D tools to customize your own 3-D style. The settings you can control with the customization tools include the spin of the object, or the angle at which the 3-D object is tilted and rotated, the depth of the object, and the direction of light falling upon the object.

Apply a Preset 3-D Style

1 Click the drawing object you want to change.

2 Click the 3-D Style button on the Drawing toolbar.

3 Click a 3-D style.

> ### Did You Know?
>
> **You can add a different surface to your 3-D object.** Apply interesting surfaces, such as wire frame, matte, plastic, or metal, to your 3-D object by clicking the Surface button on the 3-D Settings toolbar.

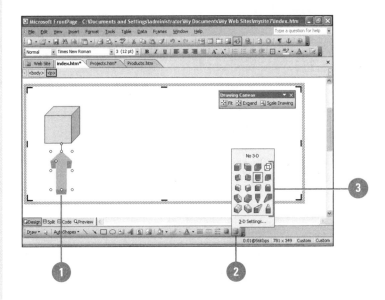

Tilt a 3-D Object

1 Click the 3-D object you want to change.

2 Click the 3-D Style button on the Drawing toolbar, and then click 3-D Settings.

3 Click the tilt setting you want.

4 Click the Close button on the 3-D Settings toolbar.

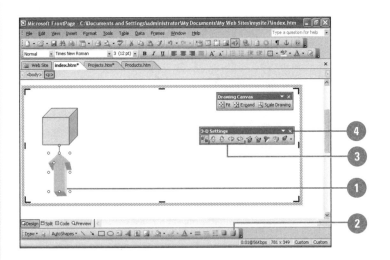

Set Lighting

1. Click the 3-D object, click the 3-D Style button on the Drawing toolbar, and then click 3-D Settings.

2. Click the Lighting button on the 3-D Settings toolbar.

3. Click the spotlight that creates the effect you want.

4. Click the Close button on the 3-D Settings toolbar.

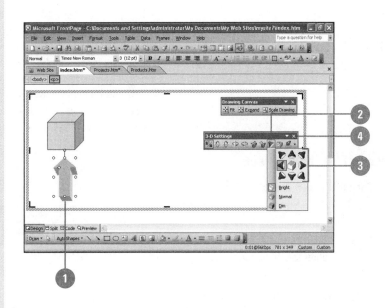

Set 3-D Depth

1. Click the 3-D object, click the 3-D Style button on the Drawing toolbar, and then click 3-D Settings.

2. Click the Depth button on the 3-D Settings toolbar.

3. Click the size of the depth in points, or enter the exact number of points you want in the Custom box.

4. Click the Close button on the 3-D Settings toolbar.

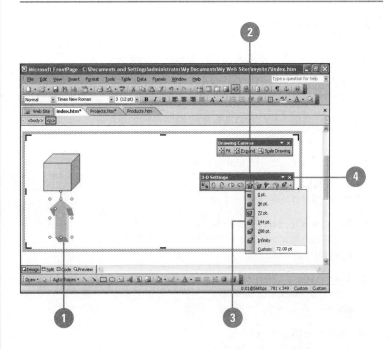

Did You Know?

You can change the direction of a 3-D object. Click the Direction button on the 3-D Settings toolbar. You can also use this button to add perspective to your objects or align them along a parallel.

Aligning or Distributing Objects

When you work with two or more similar objects, you need to ensure that they look good on the page. Objects often look best when you align them in relation to each other. For example, you can align three objects so that the tops of all three objects line up along an invisible line. Other times, you may want to distribute objects evenly across an area. FrontPage includes commands to distribute your items horizontally and vertically, and you can specify whether you want to distribute objects in their currently occupied space or across the entire page.

Align or Distribute Objects

1. Click the View menu, click Page, and then open the Web page you want to use.

2. Press and hold Shift while you click the objects that you want to align.

3. Click Draw on the Drawing toolbar, and then point to Align Or Distribute.

4. Click the alignment or distribution option you want.

   ◆ **Align Left.** Lines up the left edges of the selected objects.

   ◆ **Align Center.** Lines up the centers of the selected objects.

   ◆ **Align Right.** Lines up the right edges of the selected objects.

   ◆ **Align Top.** Lines up the top edges of the selected objects.

   ◆ **Align Middle.** Lines up horizontally the middles of the selected objects.

   ◆ **Align Bottom.** Lines up the bottom edges of the selected objects.

   ◆ **Distribute Horizontally.** Evenly distribute the objects horizontally.

   ◆ **Distribute Vertically.** Evenly distribute the objects vertically.

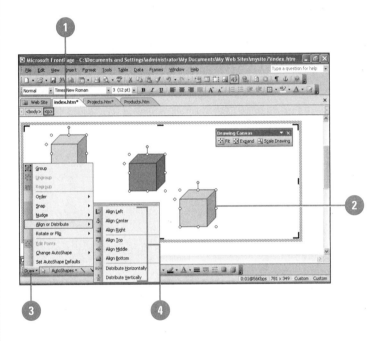

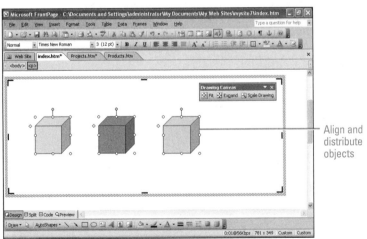

Align and distribute objects

Changing Object Stacking Order

The placement order determines the object stacking order. The first graphic that you place is on the bottom, and the last object that you place is on top. You can change the order of this stack of objects by using Bring to Front, Send to Back, Bring Forward, and Send Backward commands on the Draw menu on the Drawing toolbar.

Change Object Stacking Order

1. Click the View menu, click Page, and then open the Web page you want to use.

2. Select the object or objects you want to arrange.

3. Click the Draw button on the Drawing toolbar, point to Order, and then click the option you want.

   ◆ Click Bring To Front or Bring Forward to move a drawing to the top of the stack or up one location in the stack.

   ◆ Click Send To Back or Send Backward to move a drawing to the bottom of the stack or back one location in the stack.

Did You Know?

You can use a grid to help align objects. When you drag an object, you can instruct FrontPage to snap the object you're dragging to another object or to an invisible grid on the page. Click Draw on the Drawing toolbar, point to Snap, and then click To Grid or To Shape.

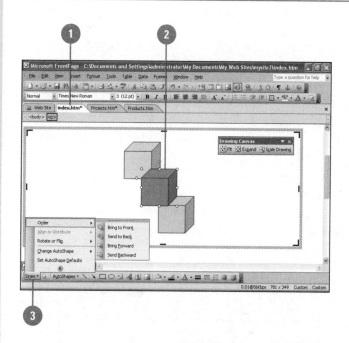

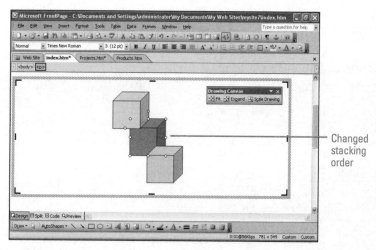

Changed stacking order

Rotating and Flipping an Object

Once you create an object, you can change its orientation on the page by rotating or flipping it. Rotating turns an object 90 degrees to the right or left; flipping turns an object 180 degrees horizontally or vertically. If you need a more exact rotation, which you cannot achieve in 90 or 180 degree increments, you can drag the green rotate lever at the top of an object to rotate it to any position. You can also rotate and flip any type of picture—including bitmaps—in a Web page. This is useful when you want to change the orientation of an object or image, such as changing the direction of an arrow.

Rotate an Object to any Angle

1. Click the object you want to rotate.

2. Position the pointer (which changes to the Free Rotate pointer) over the green rotate lever at the top of the object, and then drag to rotate the object.

3. Click outside the object to set the rotation.

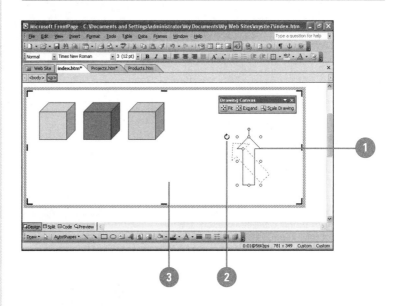

Rotate or Flip a Object Using Preset Increments

1. Click the object you want to rotate or flip.

2. Click the Draw button on the Drawing toolbar.

3. Point to Rotate or Flip, and then click a rotate or flip option.

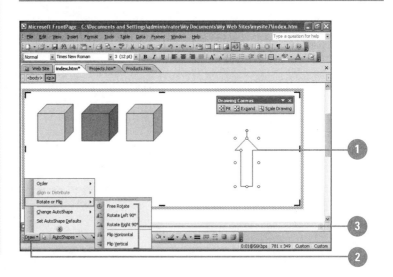

Rotate a Object Around a Fixed Point

1. Click the object you want to rotate.

2. Click the Draw button on the Drawing toolbar, point to Rotate or Flip, and then click Free Rotate.

3. Click the rotate handle opposite the point you want to rotate, and then press and hold Ctrl as you rotate the object.

4. Click outside the object to set the rotation.

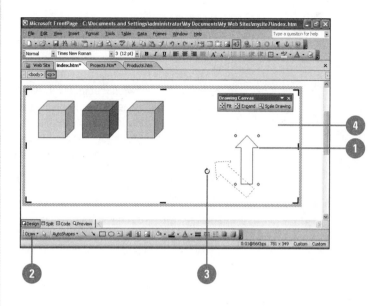

Rotate a Object Precisely

1. Right-click the object you want to rotate, and then click Format AutoShape.

2. Click the Size tab.

3. Enter the angle of rotation, or click the up or down arrows.

4. Click OK.

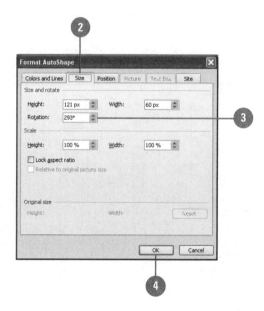

Grouping and Ungrouping Objects

Objects can be grouped together, ungrouped, and regrouped in FrontPage to make editing and moving information easier. Rather than moving several objects one at a time, you can group the objects and move them all together. Grouped objects appear as one object, but each object in the group maintains its individual attributes. You can change an individual object within a group without ungrouping. This is useful when you need to make only a small change to a group, such as changing the color of a single shape in the group. You can also format specific AutoShapes, drawings, or pictures within a group without ungrouping. Simply select the object within the group, change the object or edit text within the object, and then deselect the object. However, if you need to move an object in a group, you need to first ungroup the objects, make the change, and then group the objects together again. After you ungroup a set of objects, FrontPage remembers each object in the group and in one step regroups those objects when you use the Regroup command. Before you regroup a set of objects, make sure that at least one of the grouped objects is selected.

Group Objects Together

1 Select the objects you want to group together.

2 Click the Draw button on the Drawing toolbar, and then click Group.

Did You Know?

You can use the Tab key to select objects in order. Move between the drawing objects on your page (even those hidden behind other objects) by pressing the Tab key.

You can use the shortcut menu to select the Order and Grouping commands. Right-click the objects you want to group or reorder, point to Grouping Or Order, and then make your selections.

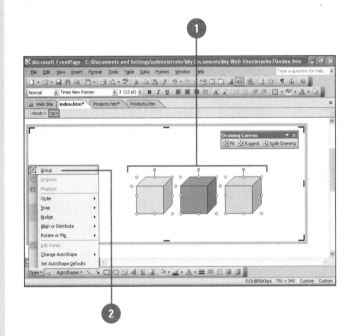

Ungroup a Drawing

1 Select the grouped object you want to ungroup.

2 Click the Draw button on the Drawing toolbar, and then click Ungroup.

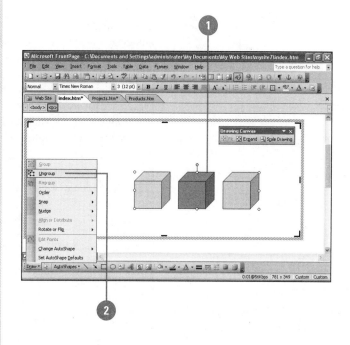

Regroup a Drawing

1 Select one of the objects in the group of objects you want to regroup.

2 Click the Draw button on the Drawing toolbar, and then click Regroup.

Did You Know?

You can troubleshoot the arrangement of objects. If you have trouble selecting an object because another object is in the way, try moving the first object out of the way temporarily.

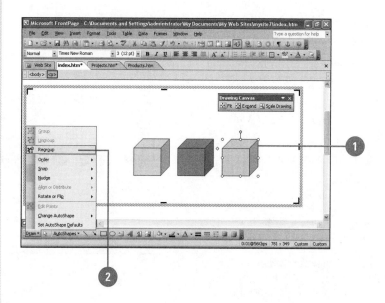

Adding WordArt

To add life to your Web site, you can add a WordArt object to your Web page. **WordArt** is an Office component that allows you to add visual enhancements to your text that go beyond changing a font or font size. You can select a WordArt style that stretches your text horizontally, vertically, or diagonally. You can also change the character spacing and reshape the text. Like many enhancements you can add to a document, WordArt is an object that you can move, resize, and even rotate. WordArt is a great way to enhance a newsletter or resume, jazz up an invitation or flyer, or produce a creative report cover or eye-catching envelope.

Create WordArt

1 Click the View menu, click Page, and then open the Web page you want to use.

2 Right-click any toolbar, and then click Drawing to display the Drawing toolbar.

3 Click the Insert WordArt button on the Drawing toolbar.

4 Double-click the style of text you want to insert.

5 Type the text you want in the Edit WordArt Text dialog box.

6 Click the Font list arrow, and then select the font you want.

7 Click the Size list arrow, and then select the font size you want.

8 If desired, click the Bold button, the Italic button, or both.

9 Click OK.

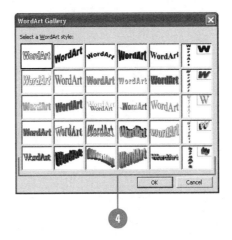

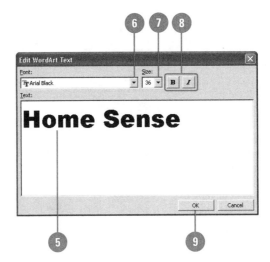

Did You Know?

You can display the WordArt toolbar. When you click a WordArt object, its selection handles and the WordArt toolbar reappear. If the toolbar doesn't appear, click the View menu, point to Toolbars, and then click WordArt.

10 With the WordArt object selected, drag any handle to reshape the object until the text is the size you want.

11 Use the WordArt toolbar buttons to format or edit the WordArt.

12 Drag the WordArt object to the location you want.

13 Click outside the WordArt text to deselect the object and close the toolbar.

7

Did You Know?

You can change the WordArt fill color to match the background. Click the WordArt object, click the Format WordArt button, click the Colors And Lines tab, click the Fill Color button list arrow, click Fill Effects, click the Patterns tab, click the Background list arrow, choose a background color, and then click OK.

You can add a fill effect to WordArt. To fill a WordArt object with a pattern or special effect, click the Fill Color button list arrow on the Drawing toolbar, click Fill Effects, and then click the fill effect you want.

Using WordArt Toolbar Buttons

Icon	Button Name	Purpose
	Insert WordArt	Create new WordArt
Edit Text...	Edit Text	Edit the existing text in a WordArt object
	WordArt Gallery	Choose a new style for existing WordArt
	Format WordArt	Change the attributes of existing WordArt
	WordArt Shape	Modify the shape of an existing WordArt object
	Text Wrapping	Wrap text around an existing object
Aa	WordArt Same Letter Heights	Make uppercase and lowercase letters the same height
Ab b	WordArt Vertical	Change horizontal letters into a vertical formation
	WordArt Alignment	Modify the alignment of an existing object
AV	WordArt Character Spacing	Change the spacing between characters

Using Rulers and Grid ▶

You can use rulers and a visible layout grid in Design view. Turning on the visible grid makes it easier to create, modify, and align objects of all types. Within the Page Options dialog box, you can select from a variety of options, such as ruler and grid measurement units and the display grid spacing and line color. To align several objects to a grid, you first turn Snap To Grid on. Then you drag the objects to align them to the grid.

Show or Hide Rulers and Grid

1. Click the View menu, and then point to Ruler And Grid.

2. Click Show Ruler or Show Grid.

3. To have objects snap to grid, click the View menu, point to Ruler And Grid, and then click Snap To Grid.

4. To hide or turn the options off, choose the commands again.

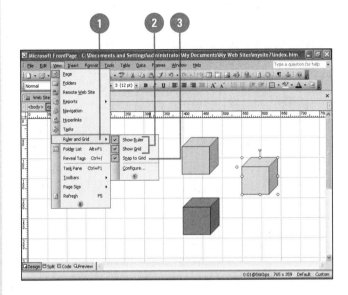

Set Rulers and Grid Options

1. Click the View menu, point to Ruler And Grid, and then click Configure.

2. Click the Ruler And Grid Units list arrow, and then select a measurement.

3. Select the spacing, line style, and line color for the display grid.

4. Specify the spacing you want for the snapping grid.

5. Click OK.

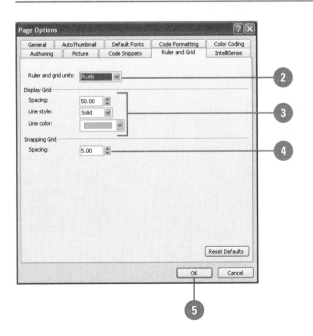

Laying Out and Formatting Web Pages with Tables

8

Introduction

Tables are a useful tool for laying out and formatting Web pages in Microsoft Office FrontPage 2003. Tables consists of horizontal rows and vertical columns. The intersection of a row and column is called a cell, which contains the information you want to present. A table in FrontPage has two main uses: page layout and data formatting.

A layout table creates a grid on your page, which you can use to position various elements—text and graphics—on the page to create an overall look. Due to limitations in HTML for arranging information, page layout is one of the most important aspects of using a table in FrontPage.

In addition to page layout, tables also make it easy to manage and present your data. These conventional tables that format your data in a tabular way, are like the ones you might create in some of the other Office programs, such as Microsoft Excel, PowerPoint or Word.

The main difference between layout tables and conventional tables is the additional page layout options to arrange and modify cell properties. If you create one type of table, yet determine later you need the other, you can switch between the two types.

Once you have your table designed, you can modify it by changing the cell formatting, and the way cells are viewed on your page. You can also add, modify and delete various cells, rows, and columns in your table. Adding a rounded corner or a shadow effect to your cells, could provide that extra touch. You might even have a table where you need to split a cell into two cells, or merge other cells into one cell.

Some of the final touches such as formatting your overall table, adding color, and including some graphical images to the table can really make your data stand out.

Creating a Layout Table

A layout table helps you organize data and design the overall look of a Web page. A layout table creates a grid on the page, which you can use to map out the location for each element you want to display on the page. You can create your own layout table grid or you can use one of table layout templates that comes with FrontPage. The templates provides a quick and easy way to create a table grid. Once you create a layout table, you can create additional cells and insert your Web content.

Create a Layout Table

1. Click the View menu, click Page, and then open the Web page you want to use.

2. Click the Table menu, and then click Layout Tables And Cells.

   TIMESAVER *Click the New button on the Standard toolbar to create a new page and open the Layout Tables And Cells task pane.*

3. Use one of the following methods to create a layout table.

   ◆ Click the Insert Layout Table link to create a one cell layout table.

   ◆ Click the Draw Layout Table button, and then drag to create a table.

   ◆ Click any of the templates in the Choose Layout area.

4. When you're done, click the Close button on the task pane.

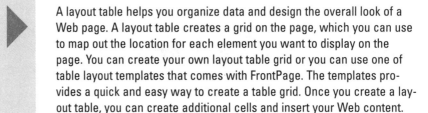

Insert Layout Table link

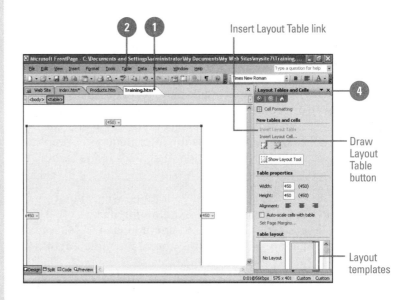

Draw Layout Table button

Layout templates

Did You Know?

You can switch between table types quickly. Click the Show Layout Tool button on the Layout Tables And Cells task pane or the Tables toolbar.

You can remove a table layout from a page. Click the No Layout template on the Layout Tables And Cells task pane.

Change Layout Table Properties

1. Click the View menu, click Page, and then open the Web page with the layout table you want to change.

2. Click the Table menu, and then click Layout Tables And Cells.

3. Use the table properties area to change the layout table.

   ◆ **Width.** Changes table width.

   ◆ **Height.** Changes table height.

   ◆ **Alignment buttons.** Changes table alignment on the page to the left, center, or right.

   ◆ **Auto-Scale Cells With Table.** Select to keep the width of the table equal to the sum of its cell width.

4. To set page margins, click Set Page Margins on the task pane, enter the margins you want, and then click OK.

5. When you're done, click the Close button on the task pane.

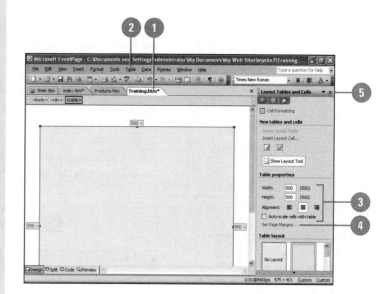

Did You Know?

You can display the Layout Tables And Cells task pane when you create a new page. Select the Show When Creating A New Page check box at the bottom of the Layout Tables And Cells task pane.

Creating Layout Cells

FrontPage makes a distinction between conventional cells and layout cells. Conventional cells contain no special properties, while layout cells do. These special properties, for example, allow you to have individual borders, rounded corners, shadows, and resize or reposition layout cells without affecting other layout cells. When you add a layout cell in a layout table, FrontPage adds and sizes rows and columns to create the cell in the location where you want it. The rows and columns serve only to position the cell. When you add more layout cells, the rows and columns change. After you create a layout cell, you can move and resize it to create the layout you want. Before you can move or resize a layout cell, you need to first select it (point to the edge, and then click the blue edge).

Create a Layout Cell

1. Click the View menu, click Page, and then open the Web page with the layout table you want to use.

2. Click the Table menu, and then click Layout Tables And Cells.

3. Click the Draw Layout Cell button on the task pane.

4. Drag a layout cell in the layout table.

5. When you're done, click the Close button on the task pane.

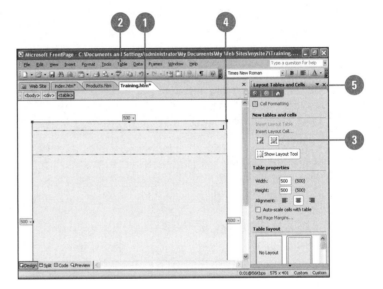

Move or Resize a Layout Cell

1. Click the View menu, click Page, and then open the Web page with the layout cells you want to change.

2. Point to the edge of the layout cell to display a blue edge.

3. Click the blue edge to select the layout cell.

4. To move the layout cell, drag the tab at the top of the cell with the cell size or the blue edge.

5. To resize the layout cell, drag a handle to the desired size.

Drag to move layout cell.

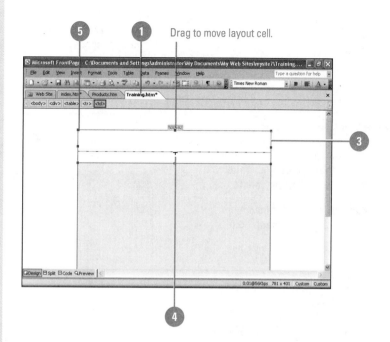

8

Modifying Layout Tables

Before you can modify a layout table, you need to first select it and you must not be in drawing mode. You can click the Draw Layout Cell button to change modes. To select a layout table, point to the table edge, and then click the green edge. When you select a layout table, list arrows appear at the edges, indicating the size of the row or column. You can click the list arrows to change row and column properties.

Modify a Layout Table

① Click the View menu, click Page, and then open the Web page with the layout table you want to use.

② Point to the edge of the layout table to display a green edge.

③ Click the green edge to select the layout table.

④ Click the list arrow for the row or column you want to modify, and then click Change Column Height or Change Width Height to open a dialog box. You can select some options directly from the submenu without opening the dialog box (if so, skip Steps 5 and 6).

⑤ Select the row or columns options you want. The column options include:

◆ **Column Width.** The column width.

◆ **Clear Contradicting Width.** Select to correct two or more cells in the same column with different heights.

◆ **Make Column Autostretch.** Select to let the browser determine the width of the column.

◆ **Use Column Spacer Image.** Select to control the width of the column by adding a transparent picture to the last row.

⑥ Click OK.

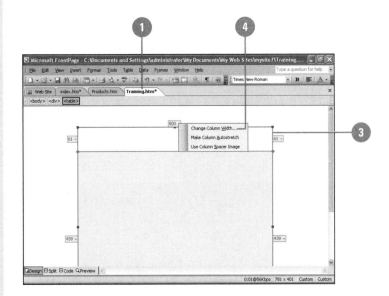

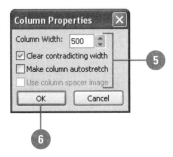

206

Modifying Cell Formatting

FrontPage give you several options to modify cell formatting to create the page layout you want. You can change the width, height, padding, alignment, and background color for a layout cell. Padding specifies the space between the cell border and the cell contents. You can also change the cell border thickness and color as well as the margins. These options are available on the Cell Formatting task pane.

Modify Cell Formatting

1. Click the View menu, click Page, and then open the Web page with the layout table you want to use.

2. Click the Table menu, and then click Cell Formatting.

3. Select the cell you want to format.

4. Select the layout cell properties on the task pane you want.

   ◆ **Width.** The cell width (in pixels).

   ◆ **Height.** The cell height (in pixels).

   ◆ **Padding.** The space (in pixels) between the cell border and the cell contents.

   ◆ **VAlign.** Cell content alignment in a browser.

   ◆ **BgColor.** The background color.

5. Specify the border thickness in pixels, color, and where to apply the border sides.

6. Specify the left, top, right, and bottom margins you want.

7. When you're done, click the Close button on the task pane.

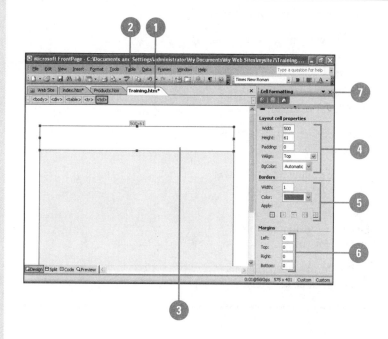

Modifying Cell Headers and Footers

Tables often have a header with a title for the table. You can show a header or footer for a layout table and format it to suit your needs and style. You can change the height, padding, alignment, background color, border width, and border color for the header or footer. These options are available in the Cell Header And Footer area on the Cell Formatting task pane.

Modify Cell Headers and Footers

1. Click the View menu, click Page, and then open the Web page with the layout table you want to use.

2. Click the Table menu, and then click Cell Formatting.

3. Click Cell Header And Footer on the task pane.

4. Select the Show Header check box and the Show Footer check box.

5. Select the header and footer options you want.

   ◆ **Height.** The header or footer height (in pixels).

   ◆ **Padding.** The space between the header or footer and its contents (in pixels).

   ◆ **VAlign.** Header or footer alignment in a browser.

   ◆ **BgColor.** The header or footer background color.

   ◆ **Border Width.** The border thickness between the cell header or footer and normal cells (in pixels).

   ◆ **Border Color.** The color between the cell header or footer and normal cells.

6. When you're done, click the Close button on the task pane.

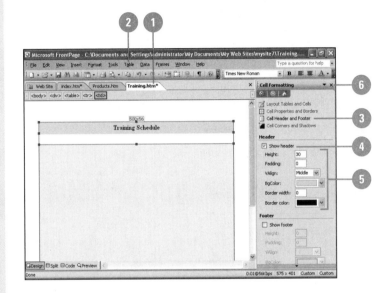

Modifying Cell Corners and Shadows

Adding rounded corners and shadows to the cells in your table can create a distinctive look. You can change the width, height, and color for cell corners and the width, softness, and color for cell shadows. Softness determines the sharpness of the shadow fade (0 to 100, where 0 is solid and 100 is the lightest shading). These options are available in the Cell Corners And Shadows area on the Cell Formatting task pane.

Modify Cell Corners and Shadows

1. Click the View menu, click Page, and then open the Web page with the layout table you want to use.

2. Click the Table menu, and then click Cell Formatting.

3. Click Cell Corners And Shadows on the task pane.

4. Select the cell you want to format.

5. Click the Use Default Image option.

6. Specify the width, height, color, and border color you want for cell corners, and then click the corners buttons to apply the options.

7. Specify the width, softness, and color you want for cell shadows, and then click the shadow buttons to apply the options.

8. When you're done, click the Close button on the task pane.

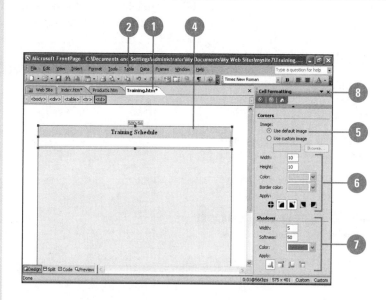

Creating Conventional Tables

Though you might want to reference and analyze information, the best way to initially display large amounts of data is through the use of tables. Tables are defined by their various components; the cell, the row, and the column. The number of rows determines the height of the table, and the number of columns the width. The combination of the two determines the total number of cells that can hold information. You can also create a table by drawing it, using the Draw Table feature on the Tables toolbar. You can create the table by drawing each individual cell. This is useful when you want to create a custom table.

Create a Conventional Table

① Click the View menu, click Page, and then open the Web page you want to use.

② Click where you want to create a table.

③ Click the Table menu, point to Insert, and then click Table.

④ Define the attributes of the table, some options include:

◆ **Rows.** The number of rows you want in your table.

◆ **Columns.** The number of columns you want in your table.

◆ **Alignment.** The position you want to assign the table text.

◆ **Specify Width.** The width of the table in pixels or percentages.

◆ **Cell Padding.** The space, in pixels, between the data and the inside of the table cell.

◆ **Cell Spacing.** The space (in pixels) between the cells.

◆ **Border Size.** The thickness level (in pixels) you want to assign to the table's border box.

⑤ Click OK.

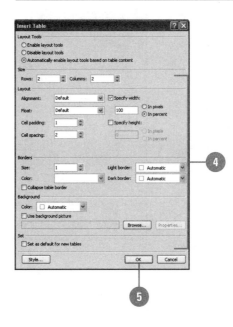

Draw a Table

1. Click the View menu, click Page, and then open the Web page where you want the table to appear.

2. Click the Table menu, and then click Draw Table.

3. Position the pointer on the page you want to represent the upper left corner of the cell, and then drag the cell to make the desired dimension. When you have the desired shape, release the mouse button and the cell snaps into position.

4. To divide the original cell into smaller cells, click the Draw Table button on the Tables toolbar, and then draw a line.

5. To remove a line, click the Eraser button on the Tables toolbar, and then move the cursor to your table. To erase a vertical or horizontal line, hold down the left mouse button and sweep the eraser icon across the line. As you cross the line, it briefly doubles, indicating that you are prepared to erase it. Release the mouse button and the line disappears.

6. When you're done, click the Draw Table button on the Tables toolbar to deselect it.

Did You Know?

You can resize a row or column quickly. Position the pointer (which changes to the double-headed arrow) on the row or column border you want to resize, and then drag the border to the size you want.

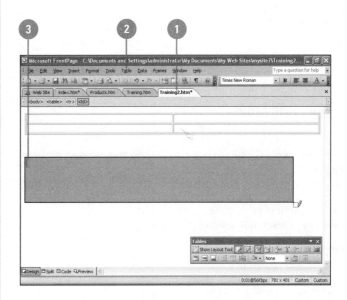

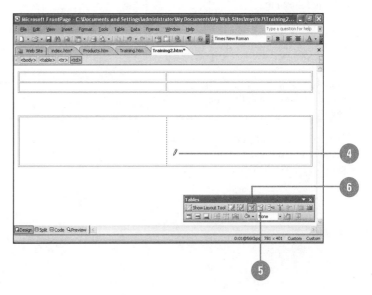

Entering Text in a Table

Once you create your table, you enter text into cells just as you would in a paragraph, except pressing the Tab key moves you from cell to cell. The first row in the table is good for column headings, whereas the left-most column is good for row labels. To enter text in cells, you need to know how to move around the table and select the rows and columns.

Enter Text and Move Around a Table

 1 Click the View menu, click Page, and then open the Web page you want to use.

2 Position the insertion point in the table where you want to enter text.

The insertion point shows where text you type will appear in a table.

3 Type your text, and then perform one of the following:

◆ Press Enter to start a new paragraph within that cell.

◆ Press Tab to move the insertion point to the next cell to the right (or to the first cell in the next row).

◆ Press the arrow keys or click in a cell to move the insertion point to a new location.

Press Tab to move to the first cell in the next row.

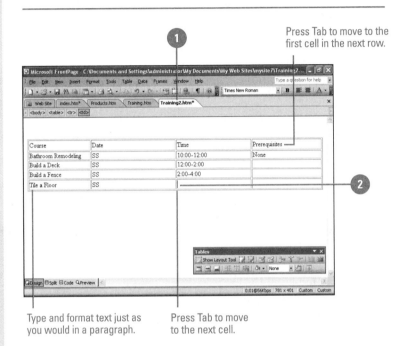

Type and format text just as you would in a paragraph.

Press Tab to move to the next cell.

Select Table Elements

Refer to this table for methods of selecting table elements, including:

- ◆ The entire table
- ◆ One or more rows and columns
- ◆ One or more cells

Before you can select text in a table, the Draw Table button on the Tables toolbar needs to be deselected.

Did You Know?

You can see the selection difference between layout and conventional tables. When you select a conventional table in Design view, it appears with a solid black background. When you select a layout table, it appears with a green border.

Selecting Table Elements

To Select	Do This
The entire table	Click in a cell, click the Table menu, point to Select, and then click Table.
One or more rows	Position the pointer along the left edge of the row you want to select (a black arrow appears), and then drag to select the rows you want, or click the Table menu, point to Select, and then click Row.
One or more columns	Position the pointer along the top edge of the column you want to select (a black arrow appears), and then drag to select the columns you want, or click the Table menu, point to Select, and then click Column.
A single cell	Drag a cell or click the cell with the black arrow, or click the Table menu, point to Select, and then click Cell.
More than one cell	Drag with the black arrow to select a group of cells.

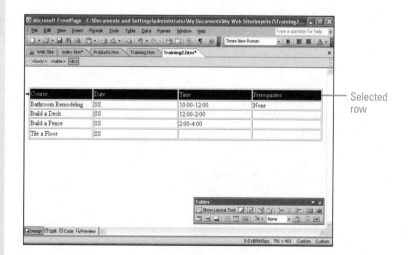

Selected row

Converting Text to a Table

If you have existing text separated by paragraphs, tabs, or commas, you can convert the text to a table. When text is separated by paragraphs, tabs, or commas, it's known as delimited text, which is commonly used to delineate data for tables, spreadsheets, and databases. During the conversion process, you can select the character used to separate the text on your page to create a table.

Convert Delimited Text to a Table

1 Click the View menu, click Page, and then open the Web page you want to use.

2 Select the delimited text you want to convert to a table.

3 Click the Table menu, point to Convert, and then click Text To Table.

4 Click the option to designate the character used to separate the text (commas, paragraphs, etc.).

5 Click OK.

Did You Know?

You can create a one-celled table. Click the None option in the Convert Text To Table dialog box.

HTML doesn't support tabs as a character separator. HTML doesn't directly support tabs as a character to separate text, so we recommend avoiding them, if possible, despite their presence on the Convert Text to Table dialog box.

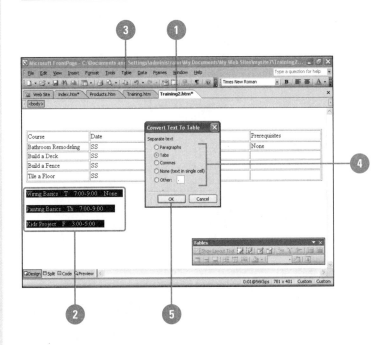

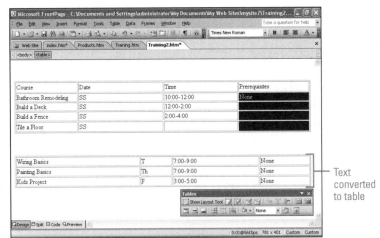

Text converted to table

Filling a Table with Information

A table needs information, and while you will normally enter most of that data manually when creating a new table, text can also be easily copied into a row or column of cells. The Fill Down and Fill Right commands allow you to propagate repeating content to table cells below or right of the currently selected cell.

Fill Cells with Information

1 Click the View menu, click Page, and then open the Web page you want to use.

2 Select the cell with the text to be copied along with the adjacent cells in a row or a column by dragging the cursor either to the right (row) or down (column).

3 Click the Table menu, point to Fill, and then click Right or Down. All selected cells, in the row, or column now contain the text from the original cell.

> **TIMESAVER** *Click the Fill Down button or Fill Right button on the Tables toolbar to perform the fill commands.*

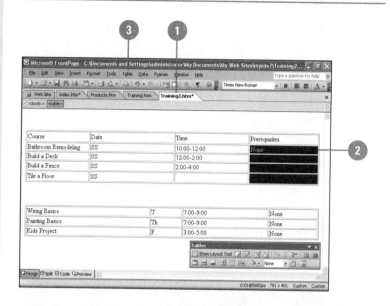

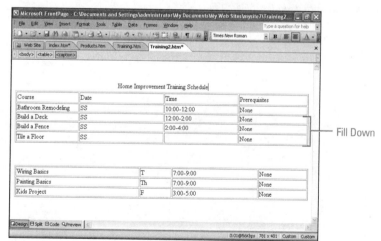

Fill Down

Creating Table Captions

A caption is an important way to provide information about the data in a table. When you insert a table caption, it appears at the top of the table, but you can move it to the bottom. When you enter caption text, the rows and columns in the table grow to accommodate the cell contents.

Add a Caption to a Table

1. Click the View menu, click Page, and then open the Web page you want to use.

2. Position the insertion point anywhere inside the table.

3. Click the Table menu, point to Insert, and then click Caption.

   The text insertion point appears at the top of the table (top is the default selection).

4. Type the caption for the table at the insertion point.

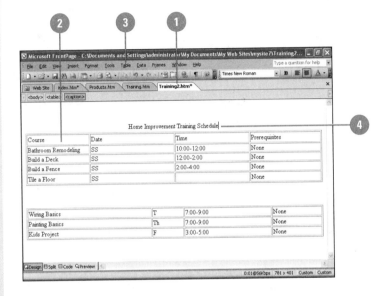

> ### Did You Know?
>
> **You can change caption alignment on the Formatting toolbar.** Select the caption, and then click Align Right, Align Left, or Center on the Formatting toolbar.

Change the Position of a Caption

1. Click the View menu, click Page, and then open the Web page you want to use.

2. Right-click the caption, and then click Caption Properties.

3. Click the Top Of Table option or the Bottom Of Table option.

4. Click OK.

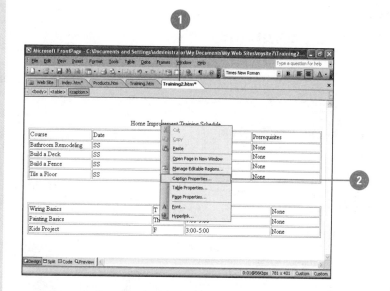

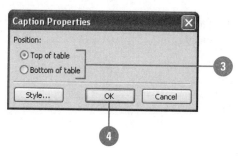

Adding Cells, Rows, or Columns to Tables

As you begin to work on a table, you might need to modify its structure by adding more rows, columns, or cells to accommodate new text, graphics, or other tables. The table realigns as needed to accommodate the new structure. When you insert rows, columns, or cells, the existing rows shift down, the existing columns shift right, and you choose what direction the existing cells shift. Similarly, when you delete unneeded rows, columns, or cells from a table, the table realigns itself.

Add a Cell, Row, or Column to a Table

1. Click the View menu, click Page, and then open the Web page you want to use.

2. Click to position the insertion point to the right of the cell where you want to add another cell.

3. To add a single cell, click the Table menu, point to Insert, and then click Cell. A new cell is added at the right end of the row containing the insertion point.

4. To add a row or column, click the Table menu, point to Insert, and then click Rows Or Columns.

   TIMESAVER *Click the Insert Rows button or the Insert Columns button on the Tables toolbar to perform the commands.*

5. Enter the number of columns or rows you want to add to the table, and the related options.

6. Click OK.

   The new columns or rows are added to the table underneath or to the right of the insertion point.

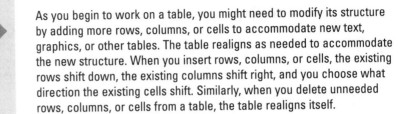
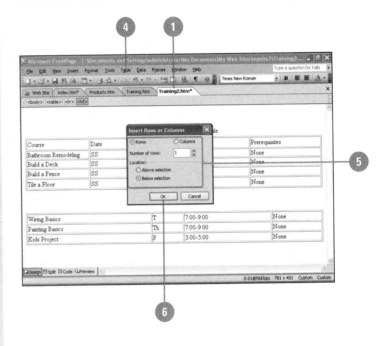

Resizing Rows and Columns

FrontPage provides three commands—Distribute Rows Evenly, Distribute Columns Evenly, and AutoFit To Contents—you can use to create evenly spaced rows and columns in a table. However, due to limitations in HTML regarding table dimensions, browsers often override table alignment settings, so its important to test pages with tables in several browsers. If you need to adjust a single row or column, you can use the mouse pointer to drag the border to a new location.

Resize Table Rows and Columns

1. Click the View menu, click Page, and then open the Web page you want to use.

2. Select the rows and columns you want to resize.

3. To distribute rows or columns evenly, click the Table menu, and then click Distribute Rows Evenly or Distribute Columns Evenly.

4. To minimize the size of rows and columns to fit the cell contents, click the Table menu, and then click AutoFit To Contents.

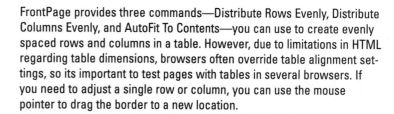
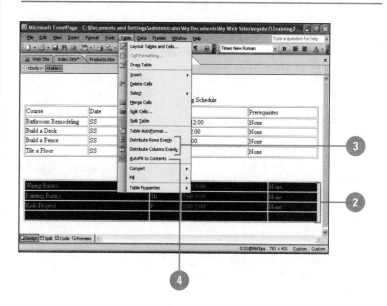

Resize Table Rows and Columns Using the Mouse

1. Click the View menu, click Page, and then open the Web page you want to use.

2. Position the pointer over the border between rows or columns you want to resize (cursor changes to a double-headed arrow), and then drag the border to resize it.

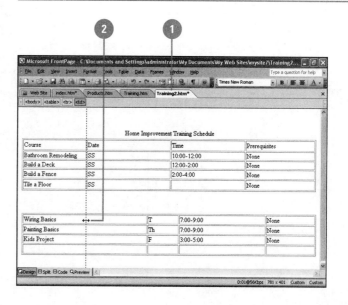

Splitting and Merging Cells

Cells can also be split or combined (also known as merged). Often there is more to modifying a table than adding or deleting rows or columns; you need to make cells just the right size to accommodate the text you are entering in the table. For example, a title in the first row of a table might be longer than the first cell in that row. To spread the title across the top of the table, you can merge (combine) the cells to form one long cell. Sometimes to indicate a division in a topic, you need to split (or divide) a cell into two.

Split a Cell into Two Cells

1. Click the View menu, click Page, and then open the Web page you want to use.

2. Right-click the cell you want to divide, and then click Split Cells.

   TIMESAVER *Click the Split Cells button on the Tables toolbar to perform the command.*

3. Click the Split Into Columns option or the Split Into Rows option.

4. Type the number of columns or rows into which you want the cells split.

5. Click OK.

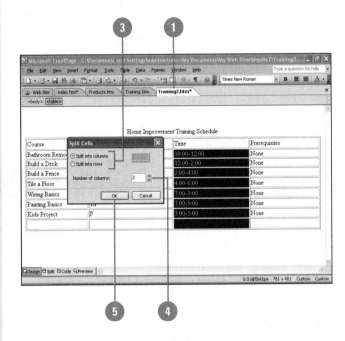

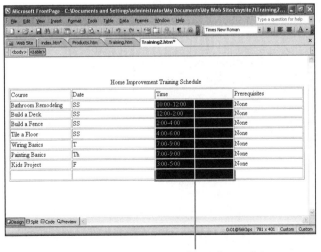

The column split in two.

Merge Cells Together

1. Click the View menu, click Page, and then open the Web page you want to use.

2. Click a column, row, or group of adjacent cells, and then drag to select them. You can begin with two cells or select an entire group of adjacent cells.

3. Click the Tables menu, and then click Merge Cells.

   TIMESAVER *Click the Merge Cells button on the Tables toolbar to perform the command.*

   The cells merge into a single, larger cell.

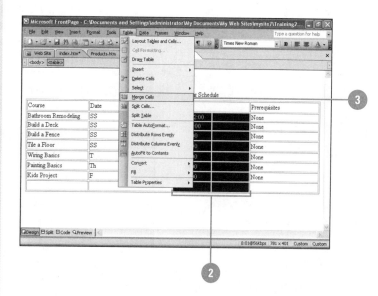

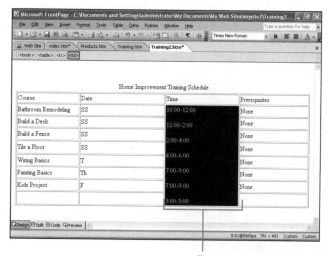

The two columns merge into one.

Deleting Table Elements

If you no longer need a table element, you can remove it. Tables, cells, rows, columns, and captions can all be easily deleted in Page view. You can use the commands on the Table menu or the Backspace and Delete keys. The Backspace key deletes the selected table, cell, column, or row and its contents, while the Delete key deletes only the contents of the selected table, cell, column, or row.

Delete a Table Element

1. Click the View menu, click Page, and then open the Web page you want to use.

2. Select the table, cell, row, column, or caption you want to delete.

3. Click the Table menu, point to Select, and then:

   ◆ To delete a table, click Table.

   ◆ To delete a cell, click Cell.

   ◆ To delete a row, click Row.

   ◆ To delete a column, click Column.

4. Click the Table menu, and then click Delete Cells.

   TIMESAVER *Click the Delete Cells button on the Tables toolbar to perform the command.*

Did You Know?

You can delete a table caption. Select the caption, and then press Delete.

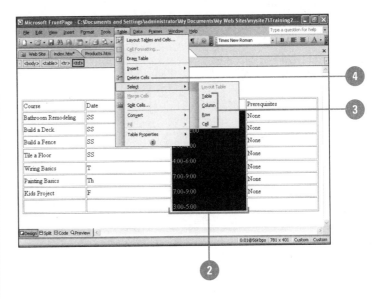

Aligning Cell Contents

You can align the cell content in a table to any border. FrontPage makes it easy with the alignment buttons on the Formatting and Tables toolbars. The Formatting toolbar contains the Align Left, Center, and Alight Right buttons and the Tables toolbar contains the Align Top, Center Vertically, and Align Bottom buttons.

Align Cell Contents

1. Click the View menu, click Page, and then open the Web page you want to use.

2. Select the rows or columns in which you want to align cell contents.

3. Use the alignment buttons on the Formatting toolbar.

   ◆ **Align Left**. Aligns to the left edge of the cell.

   ◆ **Center.** Aligns to the horizontal center of the cell.

   ◆ **Align Right**. Aligns to the right edge of the cell.

4. If necessary, right-click any toolbar, and then click Tables to display the Tables toolbar.

5. Use the alignment buttons on the Tables toolbar.

   ◆ **Align Top.** Aligns to the top of the cell.

   ◆ **Center Vertically.** Aligns to the vertical center of the cell.

   ◆ **Align Bottom.** Aligns to the bottom of the cell.

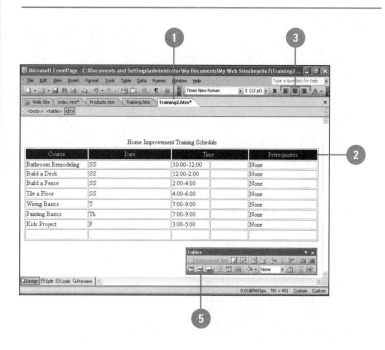

Changing Table Properties

Once you create a table and enter information, you can modify a variety of elements in the table, including alignment, cell spacing, cell padding (the space around the cell contents), height and width, border size, and color. You can change all of these properties in the Table Properties dialog box.

Change Table Properties

1. Click the View menu, click Page, and then open the Web page you want to use.

2. Right-click the table, and then click Table Properties.

3. You can set the table's layout modifying the following parameters or accepting the default settings.

   ◆ **Alignment.** Set the position for the table on the page (left, right, center).

   ◆ **Float.** Indicate whether you want text surrounding the table to flow around the left or right side of the table. If you do not want text to flow around the table at all, select Default.

   ◆ **Cell Padding.** Change the space between a cell border and its content by entering a number in the box.

   ◆ **Cell Spacing.** Change the space between the table cells by entering a number in the box.

   ◆ **Specify Width.** Set the width of the columns in pixels or percentage of the available screen space.

   ◆ **Specify Height.** Set the height of the columns in pixels or percentage of the available screen space.

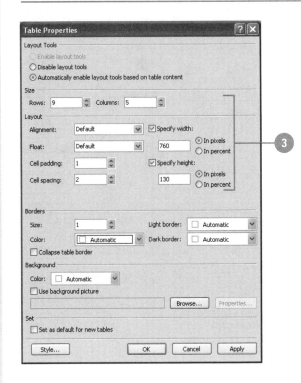

4 You can set the table's borders modifying the following parameters or accepting the default settings.

◆ **Size.** Enter the width of your table border in pixels. If you don't want a border, enter 0 (zero).

◆ **Color.** Select one color for the table border from the dialog box's list color menu.

◆ **Light Border and Dark Border.** Set a two-color border for a three-dimensional effect, and then select colors from the lists.

5 To select a color for the table background, in the Background area, click the Color list arrow, and then select a color from the Color palette.

6 Click OK.

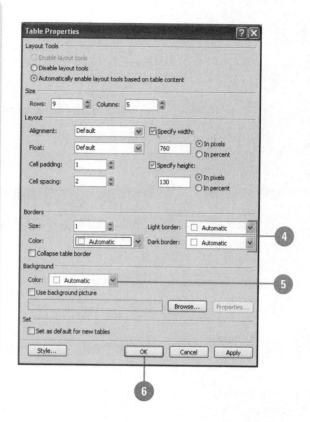

8

Changing Cell Properties

You can use the Cell Properties dialog box to resize rows or columns of cells and change the span between cells in a table. You can also change the cell alignment, size, and border or background color. If the text or images in a cell are larger than the set values, the table or its elements will be upsized to contain the content. The cell span feature is designed to create various widths or heights within cells on the same table.

Resize Cells, Rows, or Columns

1. Click the View menu, click Page, and then open the Web page you want to use.

2. Click to place the insertion point within a row or column you want to resize.

3. Click the Table menu, point to Select, and then click Row, Column, or Cell.

4. Right-click the selected element, and then click Cell Properties.

5. To set the width, click the Specify Width check box to select it, and then enter a value in pixels or in percent.

6. To set the height, click the Specify Height check box to select it, and then enter a value in pixels or in percent.

7. Click OK.

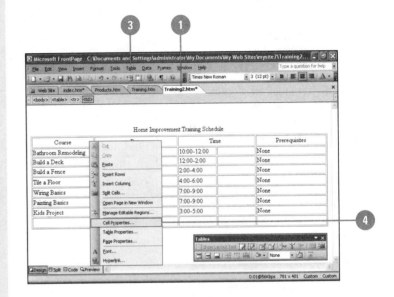

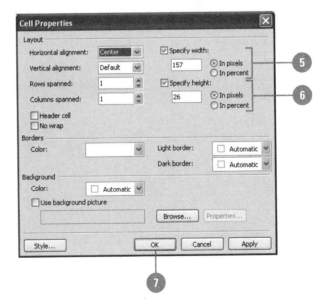

Change Cell Span

1. Click the View menu, click Page, and then open the Web page you want to use.

2. Right-click the selected cell, and then click Cell Properties.

3. Enter the number of rows and columns you want in the Rows Spanned and Columns Spanned boxes.

4. Click OK.

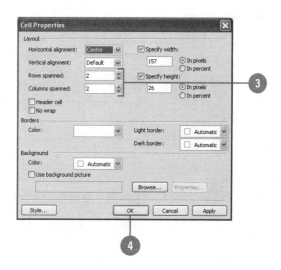

Change Cell Layout

1. Click the View menu, click Page, and then open the Web page you want to use.

2. Select the cell you want to change, right-click the cell, and then click Cell Properties.

3. Set the cell alignment options you want.

   ◆ **Horizontal Alignment.** Click the Horizontal Alignment list arrow, and then select an alignment.

   ◆ **Vertical Alignment.** Click the Vertical Alignment list arrow, and then select an alignment.

4. You can set the cell's layout using the following parameters:

   ◆ To set cells as header cells, select the Header Cell check box.

   ◆ To wrap your text within a cell, clear the No Wrap check box.

5. Click OK.

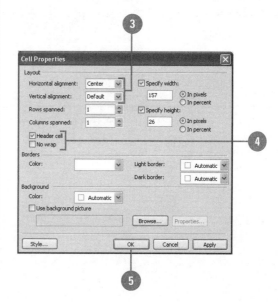

Formatting a Table

A uniform background color isn't always the best solution. For example, if you have a large table with a lot of columns, it might be easier for the reader to follow particular rows of information if your table uses alternating background colors for each row. Or perhaps you just want to have a different color in the first row or column (or both) to pull out the key terms that organize the data. Either way, you can use a color template to format your table, regardless of the number of cells it contains, or their arrangement.

Format a Table Quickly

1. Click the View menu, click Page, and then open the Web page you want to use.

2. Click the table to select it.

3. Click the View menu, point to Toolbars, and then click Tables.

4. Click the Table AutoFormat Combo button list arrow on the Tables toolbar.

5. Click the table format style you want.

Did You Know?

You can view the Tables toolbar.
Right-click any toolbar, and then click Tables.

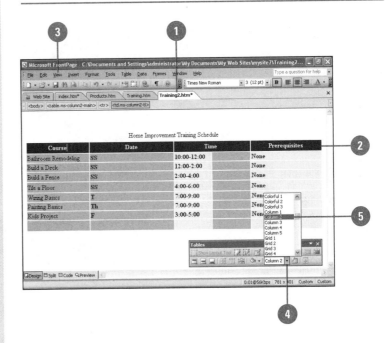

Format a Table Using AutoFormat

1. Click the View menu, click Page, and then open the Web page you want to use.

2. Click the table to select it.

3. Click the View menu, point to Toolbars, and then click Tables.

4. Click the Table AutoFormat button on the Tables toolbar.

5. Click a table style.

6. Click the format check boxes to select or clear additional formatting options.

7. Click OK.

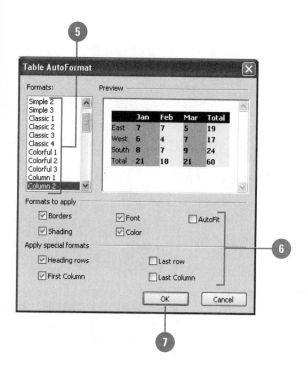

Adding Color to a Table

Tables are transparent by default, showing the background color or pattern of the Web page as the background of the table. If this is not the best design choice, consider adding a different color as the background. You can change the color table elements quickly using the Fill Color button on the Tables toolbar. If you want to change several color options at once, you can use the Table Properties dialog box. You can also add color to cells and borders. A cell border can contain one or two colors (the second color adds depth, or a 3-D type), and each individual cell within a table can have its own one or two-colored border.

Add Color to Table Elements Quickly

1. Click the View menu, click Page, and then open the Web page you want to use.

2. Select the table, column, row, or cell you want to add color.

3. Click the Fill Color button list arrow on the Tables toolbar.

4. Select a color on the menu.

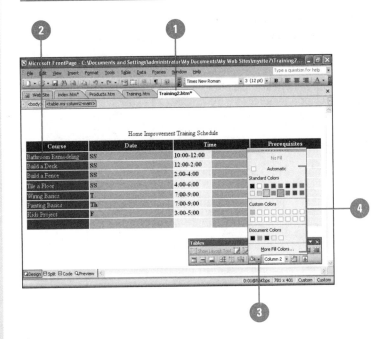

> ### Did You Know?
>
> **You can add color to a table using Table Properties.** Right-click the table, click Table Properties, click the background color, select a color, and then click OK.

Change Cell Border or Background Color

1. Click the View menu, click Page, and then open the Web page you want to use.

2. Right-click the table cell, and then click Cell Properties.

3. You can set the cell's border using the following parameters in the Borders area:

   ◆ To select a single-color border, click the Color list arrow, and then select a color.

   ◆ To select a two color border, select a color from the Light Border list arrow and one from the Dark Border list arrow.

4. You can set the cell's background using the following parameters in the Background area:

   ◆ Click the Color list arrow, and then select a color.

5. Click OK.

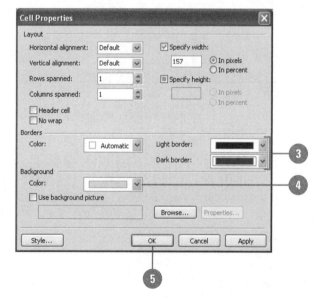

Adding Images to Tables

Because tables are supported by many browsers, they can be used to help lay out a page's text and graphics. Tables provide an ideal way to present images in a unified manner, which browsers can consistently display in the same way. You can insert pictures into a single cell or an entire table using the Cell Properties and Table Properties dialog boxes.

Add an Image to a Table or Cell

1. Click the View menu, click Page, and then open the Web page you want to use.

2. Right-click the table or cell, and then click Table Properties to add a table image or Cell Properties to add a cell image.

3. Select the Use Background Picture check box.

4. Click Browse.

5. Locate and select the picture you want to use, and then click Open.

6. Click OK.

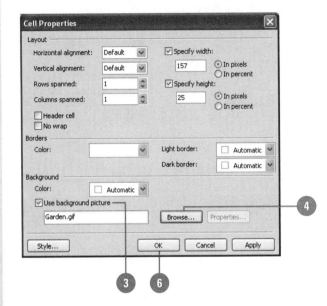

Creating Frames and Borders

Introduction

A Microsoft Office FrontPage 2003 Web site contains frames pages. A frames page is a type of HTML page that breaks up the browser display into different areas, known as **frames**. Each frame can display a different page. Pages are shown in frames by creating a hyperlink to the page and indicating the frame as a portion of the link. Frames are useful to Web masters because the user interface is stable and the frames contain built-in navigation. Frames pages are used for many different types of Web sites and pages, such as catalogs or sites containing a collection of articles.

Frames pages don't actually contain content; they are holders that indicate which content pages to display within the boundaries the frames page defines. It is much like a picture frame without a picture. For example, you can click a hyperlink within a frame, and have the linked page open in a different frame, called a target frame because it is the target of the link. Frames can also be split (vertically or horizontally), resized, or deleted by dragging frame borders. Frame borders can be seen or hidden by the user. You, as the webmaster, can determine the size of the margins inside each frame, the amount of space between frames, and whether a frame can be resized within a browser or if scroll bars should be included.

If you continually use the same frame page to create Web pages for your site, you can save time by creating a template. You can modify an existing frames page template to create a customized one, or you can create one from scratch. FrontPage comes with a variety of frames page templates—Banner and contents, Contents, Header, Footer, and Footnotes—from which you can create a customized template.

Enabling Frames

Before you can work with frames, you need to enable the Frames features in FrontPage on the Authoring tab in the Page Options dialog box. It's a good idea, therefore, to see whether your browser supports frames before continuing your work in a frames page template.

Enable Frames in FrontPage

1. Click the Tools menu, and then click Page Options.

2. Click the Authoring tab.

3. Select the Frames check box.

4. Click OK.

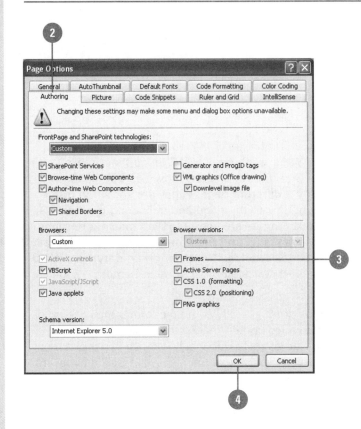

Viewing a Frames Page

Frame borders   Frames menu

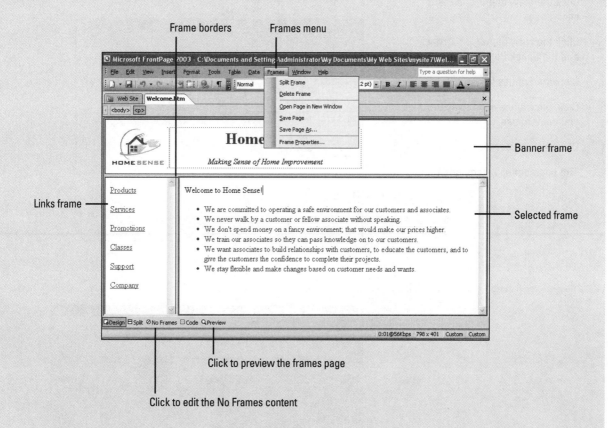

Links frame

Banner frame

Selected frame

Click to preview the frames page

Click to edit the No Frames content

Creating a Frames Page Using a Template

When you first work with borders you should use a frames page template, because templates are pre-configured so that you can easily move between frames. The Page Templates dialog box comes with a set of built-in templates—Banner and contents, Contents, Header, Footer, and Footnotes—from which you can create a frames page. With a template, you decide what occupies the initial page (the page that is visible in each frame when you first visit a frames page), which can either be a new page or one you've previously created.

Create Frames Pages

① Click the View menu, and then click Page.

② Click the New button list arrow, and then click Page.

③ Click the Frames Pages tab.

④ Click the frames page template you want to use.

⑤ Click OK.

The page opens in template form.

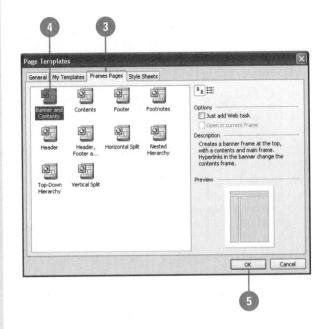

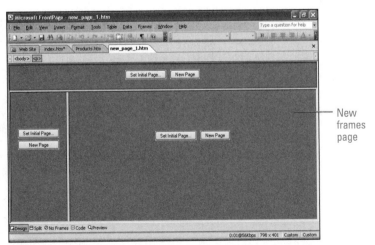

New frames page

Inserting an Inline Frame

Inline frames resemble normal frames pages except an inline frame and its contents are embedded in an existing Web page. So you don't have to create a separate frames page to introduce embedded content. An **inline frame** can also create a frame within a frame. And anything you can do with a regular page can be done with an inline frame. Just as with any other frame, inline frames are customizable. Using the Inline Frame command on the Insert menu, you can add multiple inline frames to your Web page quickly.

Add an Inline Frame in a Web Page

1. Click the View menu, and then click Page.

2. Click the Insert menu, and then click Inline Frame.

   An inline frame appears on your page.

3. Click Set Initial Page.

4. Browse and locate the page you want to embed in the selected frame, and then click the page to be imported. The URL for the page appears in the Address box.

5. Click OK.

   The selected page is now imported into the frame.

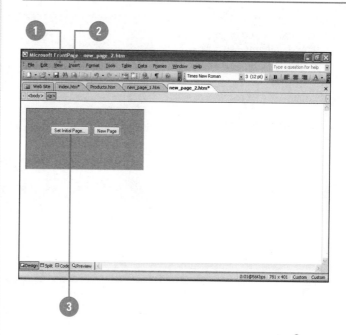

Did You Know?

You can place an inline frame in an inline frame. If you are working from a template or have inserted several inline frames, you can place new inline frames within existing frames by placing the insertion point in the desired frame, and then click Inline Frame. The inline frame appears in the designated spot.

9

Adding Content to Frames

After you create a frames page using a template or insert an inline frame, you can add content to the frames. Each frame offers two option buttons: Set Initial Page or New Page. Using Set Initial Page, you can insert an existing page. Using New Page, you can create the contents of the frame from scratch.

Insert an Existing Page in a Frame

1 Click the View menu, click Page, and then open the frames page you want to add content.

2 Click a frame to select it.

3 Click Set Initial Page.

4 Select a file or Web page to insert in a frame.

5 Click OK.

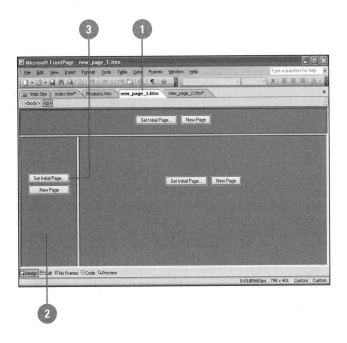

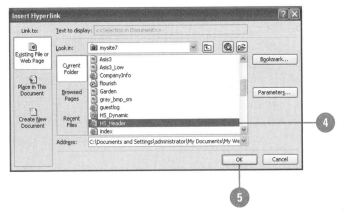

Insert a New Page in a Frame

1. Click the View menu, click Page, and then open the frames page you want to add content.

2. Click a frame to select it.

3. Click New Page.

4. Enter and format content on the page like any other Web page.

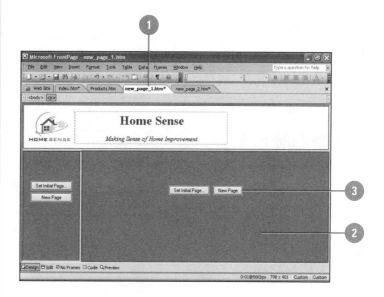

Resize a Frame

1. Click the View menu, click Page, and then open the frames page you want to modify.

2. Position the pointer over the frame border you want to resize.

3. Drag the frame border to a new location.

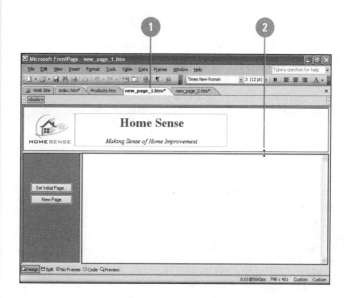

9

Changing Frame Properties

You can edit the properties of a normal or inline frame at any time. The Frame Properties dialog box allows you to change all aspects of working with a frame in one place. You can specify or change the frame name, the initial page, long description, title, frame size, margins, and other browser related options. These options allow you to customize the overall appearance of your frames page.

Change Frame Properties

1. Click the View menu, click Page, and then open the frames page you want to change.

2. Right-click the frame, and then click Frame Properties.

3. Change the frame properties you want.

   ◆ **Name.** The name that hyperlinks specify to load their contents in the frame.

   ◆ **Initial Page.** The page that is first displayed in a frame when a visitor browses the site.

   ◆ **Long Description.** The URL that contains more information about the current frame.

   ◆ **Title.** The description of the frame.

   ◆ **Frame Size.** The width and height of the frame in pixels, percentages, or units that create proportional spacing.

   ◆ **Margins.** The margins of the frame in pixels.

   ◆ **Resizeable In Browser.** Select to allow visitors to resize frames in a browser.

   ◆ **Show Scrollbars.** When the scrollbars appear on screen. Set to Never Appear, Always Appear, or Appear If Needed.

4. Click OK.

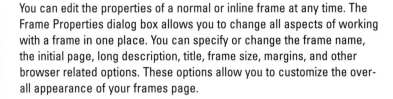

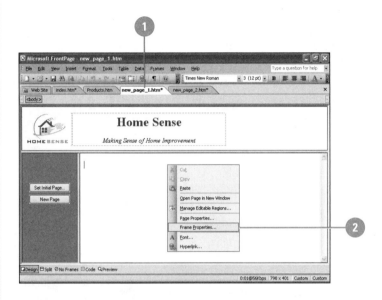

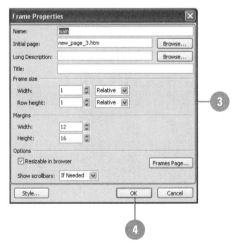

Change Inline Frame Properties

1. Click the View menu, click Page, and then open the frames page you want to change.

2. Right-click the frame, and then click Inline Frame Properties.

3. Change the inline frame properties you want.

   ◆ **Name.** The name that hyperlinks specify to load their contents in the frame.

   ◆ **Initial Page.** The page that is first displayed in a frame when a visitor browses the site.

   ◆ **Title.** The description of the frame.

   ◆ **Frame Size.** The width and height of the frame in pixels or percentages.

   ◆ **Margins.** The margins of the frame in pixels.

   ◆ **Alignment.** The position for the inline frame on the page (left, right, or center).

   ◆ **Scrollbars.** When the scrollbars appear on screen. Set to Never Appear, Always Appear, or Appear If Needed.

   ◆ **Alternate Text.** The text that you want the browser to display if the browser doesn't support frames.

   ◆ **Show Border.** If you want a border drawn around the inline frame.

4. Click OK.

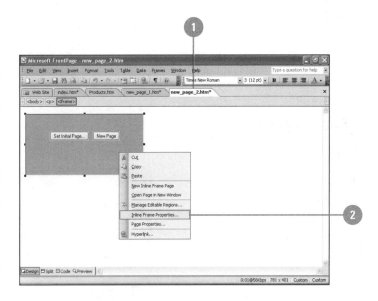

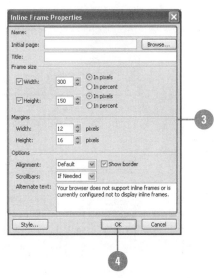

9

Saving Frames Pages

After you've prepared your frames page, you need to save it. Saving pages in a frames page involves a few more steps than simply a normal Web page. You need to save each page in a frame as well as the entire frames page itself. When you save a frames page, or the **frameset**, you're also saving instructions for the placement and sizing of individual frames on the page.

Save a Page in a Frame

1. Click the View menu, click Page, and then open the frames page you want to save.

2. Click the frame displaying the page you want to save.

3. Click the Frames menu, and then click Save Page As.

4. Enter (or click) the file name for the page displayed in the thumbnail's selected frame.

5. To edit the page title, click Change Title, type a title for the page, and then click OK.

6. Select the type of Web page you want saved.

7. Specify a location where you want the page saved.

8. Click Save.

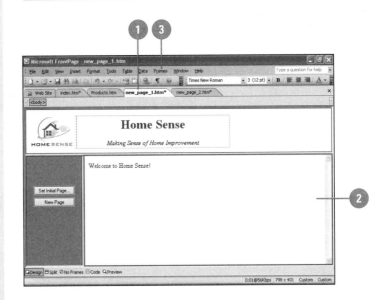

Did You Know?

The title is different from the file name. The title you see in the browser's title bar is the title of the frames page, not the title of the page displayed in that frame.

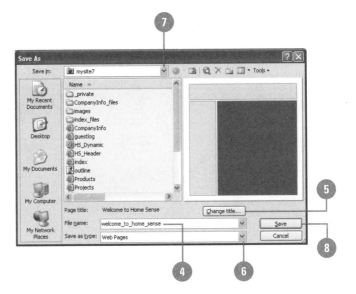

Save a Frameset

1 Click the View menu, click Page, and then open the frames page you want to save.

2 Click the File menu, and then click Save As.

The Save As dialog box opens, complete with a thumbnail showing the layout of the page with the affected elements highlighted with a dark blue box.

3 Type a file name for the highlighted frames page.

4 To edit the page title, click Change Title, type a title for the page, and then click OK.

5 Specify a location where you want to save the Frameset.

6 Click Save.

If any pages in a frame have not been saved, the Save As dialog box opens, asking you to save the page.

7 If necessary, click Save for each additional page in a frame.

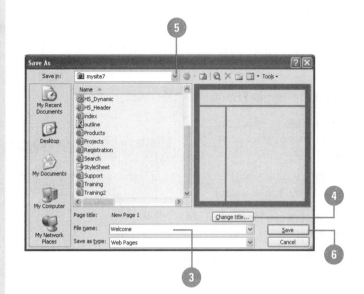

Did You Know?

You can reselect the frames page. Press and hold Shift while you click any frame border.

9

Targeting a Frame

Sometimes you want a link in one frame to display content in another frame. This type of link is called a target frame. When you link a target page to a frame, you need to know the name of the frame you want to target, and the name of the Web page file you want to link to the frame.

Create or Edit the Target Frame

1. Click the View menu, click Page, and then open the frames page you want to use.

2. Select the normal (create) or hyperlinked (edit) text or graphic.

3. Click the Insert Hyperlink button on the Standard toolbar.

4. Enter or verify the file name for the targeted frame.

5. Click the Target Frame button.

6. Select the option you want.

   ◆ In the Current Frames Page area (a map of your frames page), click the frame you want to designate as the target frame.

   ◆ In the Common Targets box, click the target frame you want to designate as the target.

7. Click OK.

8. Click OK.

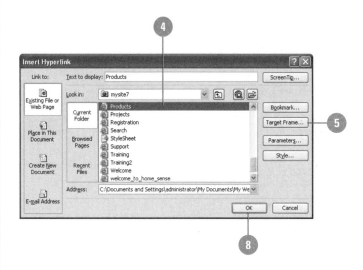

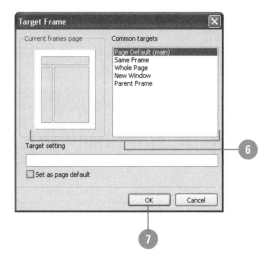

Editing Frames Pages

Editing the content of a frame is another key in developing a solid site. When working in Page view, select the frame you want to edit by clicking it. The frame might be too small for you to work in easily. If this is the case, you'll want to open it in a larger window. Frame margins set the distance between the frame content and the border.

Open a Frame in a Window for Editing

1. Click the View menu, click Page, and then open the frames page you want to change.

2. Right-click anywhere in the frame. A dark blue border appears around the frame you're editing and a shortcut menu opens.

3. Click Open Page In New Window.

   The frame is now large enough to work in easily.

4. Click the File menu, and then click Close to return the page to its original size.

Did You Know?

You can show or hide scrollbars. Right-click in the frame, click Frame Properties, click the Show Scrollbars list arrow, click If Needed, Never, or Always, and then click OK.

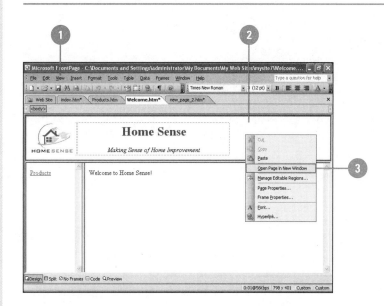

Deleting a Frame

When you no longer need a frame, you can delete it from a frames page. When the frame is deleted, the Web page in the frame is deleted, but the page is still available in your Web site folders. After you delete a frame, the remaining frames on the Web page expand to fill the space left by the frame you deleted. If the frames page contains only one frame, you cannot delete that frame.

Delete a Frame

1. Click the View menu, click Page, and then open the frames page you want to change.

2. Click the frame you want remove to select it.

3. Click the Frames menu, and then click Delete Frame.

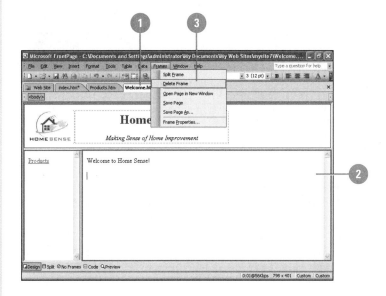

Splitting Frames

There are two ways to split a frame: by dragging its border, or by using the Split Frame command on the Frames menu. When you split a frame, FrontPage creates a new frame and the content in the original frame remains intact.

Split a Frame Quickly

1. Click the View menu, click Page, and then open the frames page you want to change.

2. Click the frame you want to split to select it.

3. Hold down Ctrl while you drag the frame border.

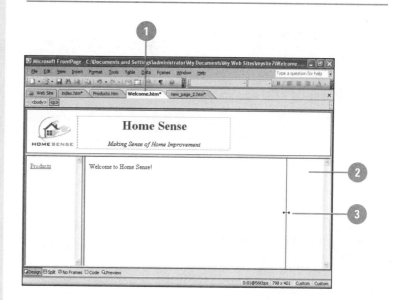

Split Frames in Columns or Rows

1. Click the View menu, click Page, and then open the frames page you want to change.

2. Click the frame you want to split to select it.

3. Click the Frames menu, and then click Split Frame.

4. Click the Split Into Columns option to split the frame vertically, or click the Split Into Rows option to divide the frame horizontally.

5. Click OK.

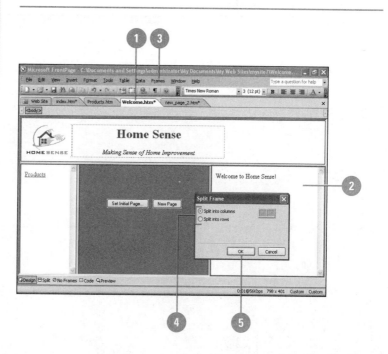

Show or Hide Border Frames

You can display or hide borders around frames. When you display a border, you can also set the spacing between borders to achieve the look you want. If you hide borders, you can still see them when you work on the page in Design view. The hidden frame borders appear as a thin gray line.

Display or Hide Borders Around Frames

1. Click the View menu, click Page, and then open the frames page you want to change.

2. Right-click anywhere on the frames page, and then click Frame Properties.

3. Click Frames Page.

4. If necessary, click the Frames tab.

5. Select or clear the Show Borders check box to display or hide border frames.

6. If you select the Show Borders check box, enter the amount of space, in pixels, you want between borders.

7. Click OK.

8. Click OK.

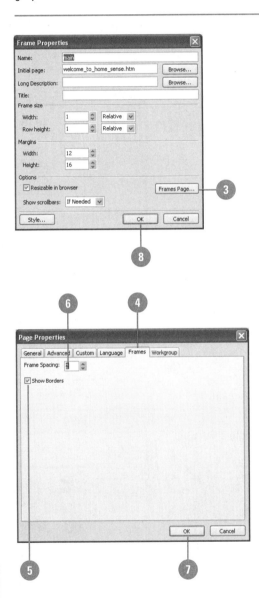

Inserting a Shared Border in a Frame

Frames pages can also contain shared borders—areas at the top, bottom, left, or right of a page—that are common to multiple pages in a Web site. Shared borders are used to include the same content on more than one page. Shared borders give your work a consistent appearance and often contain link bars to navigate to other frequently accessed pages within the site, or even to important pages external to the site. Another advantage of shared borders is that you only need to edit content in one place to update all the pages that use the border. If, for example, some vital piece of information needs to be changed, you can change it on one page and the information is updated everywhere it appears within a shared border.

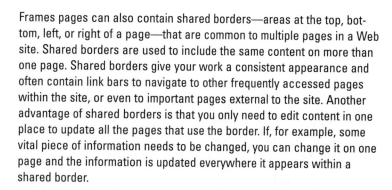

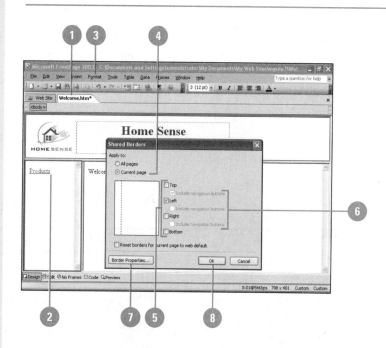

Insert a Shared Border in a Frame

1. Click the View menu, click Page, and then open the frames page you want to change.

2. Click the frame in which you want to add a shared border to select it.

3. Click the Format menu, and then click Shared Borders.

4. Click the Current Page option.

5. Select one or more of the check boxes for each border you want to use.

6. If you want, select the Include Navigation Buttons check box for the borders you want to use.

7. To change the shared border background color, click Border Properties, make your changes, and then click OK.

8. Click OK.

See Also

See "Adding Shared Borders" on page 62 for more information on working with shared borders.

Customizing a Frames Page Template

If you continually use the same frames page to create Web pages for your site, you can save time by creating a template. You can modify an existing frames page template to create a customized one, or you can create one from scratch. FrontPage comes with a variety of frames page templates—Banner and contents, Contents, Header, Footer, and Footnotes—from which you can create a customized template.

Customize an Existing Frames Page Template

1. Click the View menu, and then click Page.

2. Open a frames page template.

3. Right-click in any frame, and then click Frame Properties.

4. Make any modifications to the size of the frame, margins, name and so forth that you desire, and then click OK.

5. Click the File menu, and then click Save As.

6. Click the Save As Type list arrow, and then click FrontPage Template.

7. Type the file name for your custom template.

8. Click Save.

9. Type the name you want to use as a title for the template. This is the title that will appear in the list of templates on the Frames Pages tab in the New dialog box.

10. Type the text describing what the template does. This text is displayed in the Description area on the Frames Pages tab.

11. Click OK.

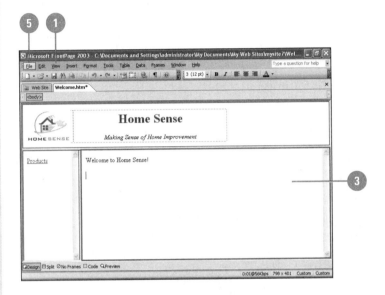

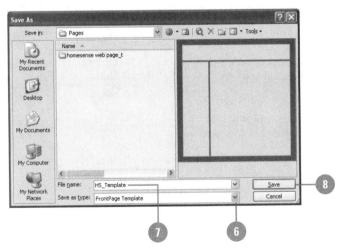

Adding Functionality to Web Pages

Introduction

So far, you examined many of the key features available for webmasters in Microsoft Office FrontPage 2003. Using FrontPage, you can easily add Web functionality to give your Web site a professional look with minimal effort and no programming expertise. You will be working with what FrontPage calls Web Components—Hit Counters, Page Banners, and other key components. Using FrontPage, you can place these components directly on your Web page through the Insert menu.

You can insert a scheduled image—a graphic element that may or may not be on screen at any given time. You can also add a timestamp to your site to let your visitors know when the last time the site was revised. Keeping your site current will bring back visitors; also, by adding a discussion group, you are sure to increase activity on your Web site as visitors come back for more information.

If you have data in a Microsoft Office Excel spreadsheet, chart, or PivotTable, you can insert it into a Web page. When you insert Excel data into a Web page, visitors to your site can view and interact with the data online without having to install the Office Excel program on their computer. The Excel Web component includes a toolbar with sorting and data analysis tools. FrontPage allows you to include information from MSN and MSNBC on your Web site. You can insert maps, Web searches, and stock quotes from MSN and headline news from MSNBC.

Other navigational tools such as, a search form so that you can search your site, a navigation bar to guide your visitors through your site, and a Table of Contents to let your visitors go to a specific page or topic are all tools that are essential for a successful Web site. When you publish your Web site with some Web Components, such as hit counters, the site needs to include FrontPage Server Extensions; see Chapter 12, "Publishing and Managing a Web Site," for more details.

What You'll Do

Insert Hit Counters

Work with Page Banners

Include a Page

Insert Scheduled Images

Use Site Parameters and Substitution

Insert Timestamps

Insert Microsoft Excel Data

Insert MSN Content or MSNBC News

Insert a Search Form

Insert Navigation Bars

Insert a Table of Contents

Create Discussion Groups

Create a Project Web Site

Inserting Hit Counters

A hit counter tabulates and displays the number of times a page has been visited. From the earliest days of the World Wide Web, Web site designers have attempted to keep track of the number of visitors who walked through their virtual doors. Today, hit counters remain popular. They give established Web sites credibility, and if you hope to attract advertisers, some record of Web site traffic is a minimal requirement. FrontPage offers a variety of counters that you can import directly to your Web site. You can also create your own, unique hit counter in GIF format. After you've added a hit counter to your page, it can be set to any number, or reset at any time back to zero to restart the count.

Insert a Hit Counter

1. Click the View menu, click Page, and then open the Web page you want to use.

2. Position the insertion point where you want the hit counter to appear.

3. Click the Web Component button on the Standard toolbar.

4. Click Hit Counter.

5. Click Finish.

6. Click the hit counter style option you want.

7. Select the Fixed Number Of Digits check box, and then enter the number of digits you want.

8. Click OK.

   The words Hit Counter appear in brackets on the Web page as a placeholder. When you are linked to a server equipped with FrontPage Server Extensions or Microsoft SharePoint Team Services, you can click the Preview or Preview In Browser commands to test your hit counter.

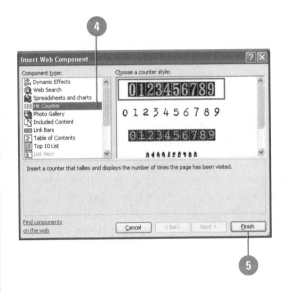

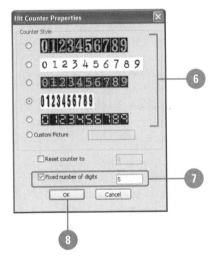

Reset a Hit Counter

1. Click the View menu, click Page, and then open the Web page with the hit counter.

2. Double-click the hit counter.

3. Select the Reset Counter To check box, and then enter a counter number.

4. Click OK.

   The words Hit Counter appear in brackets on the Web page as a placeholder. When you are linked to a server equipped with FrontPage Server Extensions or Microsoft SharePoint Team Services, you can click the Preview or Preview In Browser commands to test your hit counter.

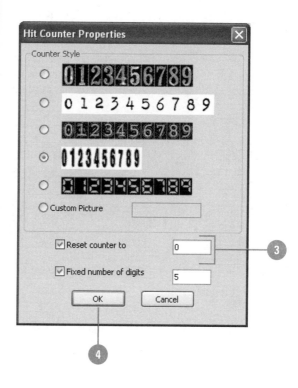

Did You Know?

You need to turn on support for features that require FrontPage Server Extensions. If not turned on by default, click the Tools menu, click Page Options, click Authoring tab, select the Browse-time Web Components check box, and then click OK.

You can create your own hit counter. Click the Custom Picture option in the Hit Counter Properties dialog box, and then enter the location and name of the file in GIF format you want to substitute for your own hit counter. Your GIF file hit counter must include all numbers from zero through nine.

10

Working with Page Banners

Page banners are blocks of text, such as headlines, column and section headers, and the Web site name. Page banners maintain the styles and graphics of a theme if you are using one. If you are not using themes, you can enter the text and then format it yourself by selecting the font, style, and size. A good way to add banners to more than one page is to position the banner inside a shared border or frame.

Insert a Page Banner

1 Click the View menu, click Page, and then open the Web page you want to use.

2 Click where you want to place the page banner.

3 Click the Insert menu, and then click Page Banner.

4 Click the Picture option or the Text option, and then enter the text for the banner.

5 Click OK.

◆ If you selected the Text option, the text you entered for the banner appears as a placeholder on the page.

◆ If you selected the Picture option, the stylized, graphically-enriched version of your banner appears on the page.

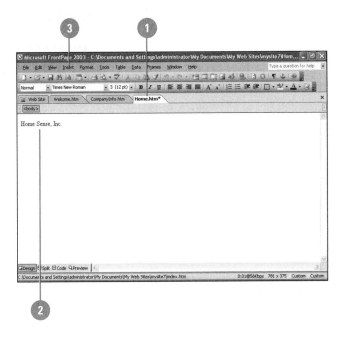

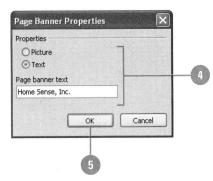

Edit and Format a Page Banner

1. Click the View menu, click Page, and then open the Web page with the page banner.

2. Right-click the banner you want to edit, and then click Font.

    The Font dialog box opens, displaying the Font tab.

3. If necessary, select the font settings you want.

4. Click the Character Spacing tab.

5. To change character spacing, click the Spacing list arrow, select a spacing option (either Normal, Expanded, or Condensed), and then enter the amount of spacing you want in the By box.

6. To change character position, click the Position list arrow, and then select a positioning option (either Baseline, Sub, Super, Top, Text-Top, Middle, Bottom, or Text-Bottom).

7. Click OK.

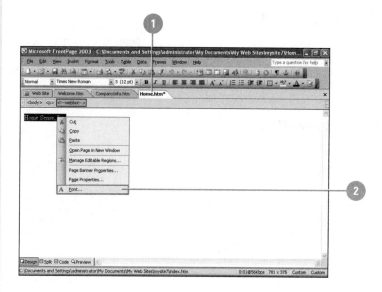

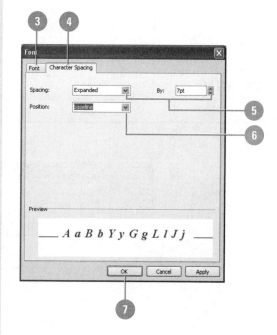

10

Including a Page

You can use Frontpage's Include Page component to merge the contents of one Web page into another. If you have parts of a page, such as boilerplate text and graphics like a header or footer, you use on a regular basis in different pages, you can use the Include Page component to make sure the material is the same in all instances. When you want to change the material, you only need to change it in one place.

Insert an Include Page

1. Click the View menu, click Page, and then open the Web page you want to use.

2. Click where you want to place the include page.

3. Click the Web Component button on the Standard toolbar.

4. Click Included Content.

5. Click Page.

6. Click Finish.

7. Click Browse, locate and select the file with the page you want to include, and then click OK.

8. Click OK.

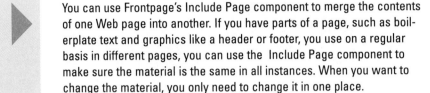

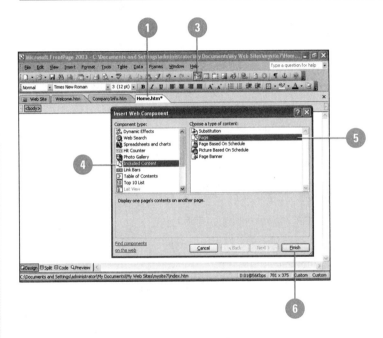

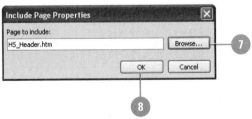

Inserting Scheduled Images

A **scheduled image** is a graphic element that may or may not be on screen at any given time. These images are scheduled to appear at fixed intervals or at a single preset time (such as when you have prepared a new page and you want the Web site to update to that page at a specific time). FrontPage uses the Web server's clock to time the appearances of graphics.

Insert a Scheduled Image

1. Click the View menu, click Page, and then open the Web page you want to use.

2. Click where you want to display the graphic.

3. Click the Web Component button on the Standard toolbar.

4. Click Included Content.

5. Click Page Based On Schedule to import a Web page or click Picture Based On Schedule to import a picture.

6. Click Finish.

7. Type the Relative URL (the Net address of a page relative to the address of the current page), or click Browse, locate and select a photo, and then click OK.

8. Enter the Starting and Ending times in the appropriate boxes.

9. Click OK.

   The picture you selected now appears in the pre-selected position. The picture will now appear and re-appear based on the schedule you selected.

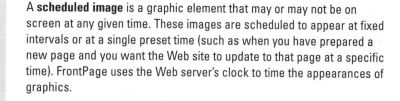

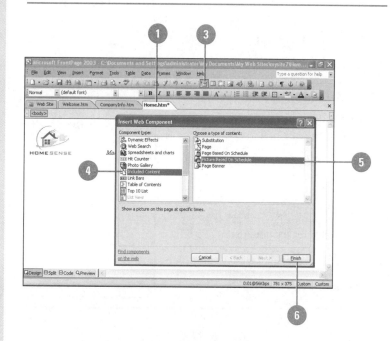

Using Site Parameters and Substitution

Site parameters are commonly used references in several places in a Web site that periodically change. For example, if you use a list of names, such as company employees, on your Web site that change from time to time, you can create site parameters for each name. When a name changes, you only need to change it in one place. After you create a site parameter, you can use the Substitution component to insert the parameter in a page.

Create a Site Parameter

1. Click the View menu, click Page, and then open the Web page you want to use.

2. Click the Tools menu, and then click Site Settings.

3. Click the Parameters tab.

4. Click Add.

5. Type a parameter name.

6. Type a value for the parameter.

7. Click OK.

8. Click OK.

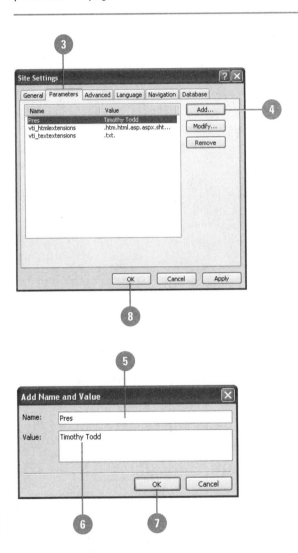

Insert a Substitution

1. Click the View menu, click Page, and then open the Web page you want to use.

2. Click where you want to insert a substitution.

3. Click the Web Component button on the Standard toolbar.

4. Click Included Content.

5. Click Substitution.

6. Click Finish.

7. Click the Substitution With list arrow, and then click a site parameter.

8. Click OK.

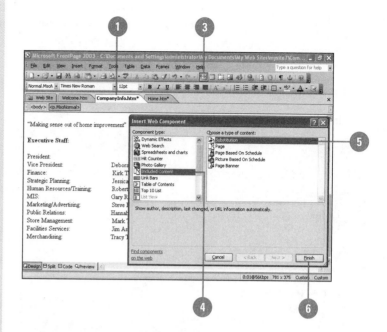

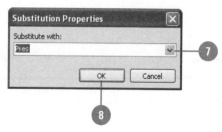

10

Inserting Timestamps

A **Timestamp** is a FrontPage component that displays the date, time, or both, when the page was either created or last revised. Timestamps are easy ways for visitors to tell if the Web site's been updated since their last visit.

Insert a Timestamp

1. Click the View menu, click Page, and then open the Web page you want to use.

2. Click where you want to place the timestamp.

3. Click the Insert menu, and then click Date And Time.

4. Click one of the display option buttons.

   ◆ **Date This Page Was Last Edited.** Displays the date the page was last saved with FrontPage.

   ◆ **Date This Page Was Last Automatically Updated.** Displays the date the page was last changed (manually in FrontPage or automatically by someone else in the Web site).

5. Click the Date Format list arrow, and then select a format.

6. If necessary, click the Time Format list arrow, and then select a format.

7. Click OK.

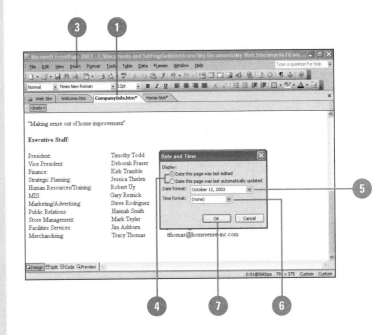

Did You Know?

You should avoid data format that use numbers for months. The expression 6/11/2004 means June 11 in some parts of the world and November 6 in others.

Inserting Microsoft Excel Data

If you have data in a Microsoft Office Excel spreadsheet, chart, or PivotTable, you can insert it into a Web page. When you insert Excel data into a Web page, visitors to your site can view and interact with the data online without having to install the Office Excel program on their computer. The Excel Web component includes a toolbar with sorting and data analysis tools.

Insert Microsoft Office Excel Data

1. In Excel, copy the data you want to use in FrontPage.

2. In FrontPage, click the View menu, click Page, and then open the Web page you want to use.

3. Click where you want to place the Excel spreadsheet, chart, or PivotTable.

   The following steps vary depending on the item you select.

4. Click the Web Component button on the Standard toolbar.

5. Click Spreadsheets And Charts.

6. Click Office spreadsheet, Office Chart, or Office PivotTable.

7. Click Finish.

8. Click the Data Source tab, click the Data Typed Into A Data Sheet option, and then click Data Sheet.

9. Click the first cell to Paste.

10. Click the Paste button on the Commands And Options dialog box.

11. Click the Type tab, and then select a chart type.

12. Click the Close button on the Commands And Options dialog box.

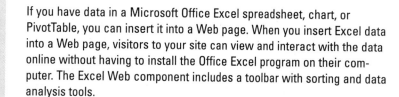

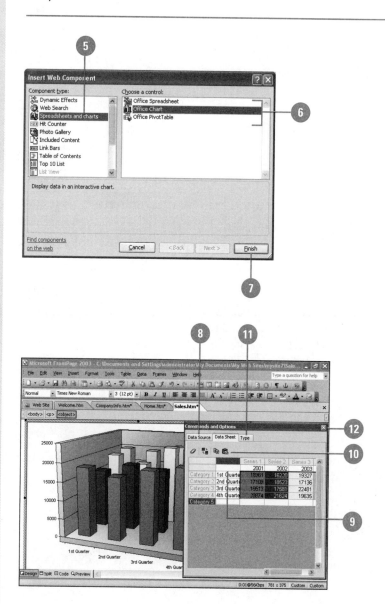

Inserting MSN Content or MSNBC News

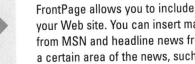

FrontPage allows you to include information from MSN and MSNBC on your Web site. You can insert maps, Web searches, and stock quotes from MSN and headline news from MSNBC. If you only want to provide a certain area of the news, such as business, living and travel, headlines, sports, technology, or weather, you can pick and choose the ones you want to use. By providing your visitors with this information, you can give them another reason to stay at your site.

Insert Maps or News

① Click the View menu, click Page, and then open the Web page you want to use.

② Click where you want to place a map or the news.

③ Click the Web Component button on the Standard toolbar.

④ Click an MSN or MSNBC component type.

⑤ Click the component you want to use.

⑥ Click Finish.

⑦ If a wizard opens, requesting additional information, enter the information, step through the wizard, and then click Finish.

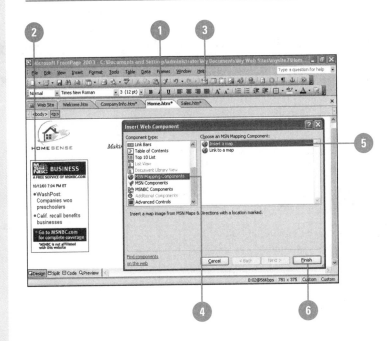

Inserting a Search Form

When visitors come to a Web site, they typically look for a search form to help them find information. FrontPage includes a Web component that makes it easy to create a search form and index the content on your site, so visitors can enter keywords and phrases to conduct searches.

Insert a Search Form

1. Click the View menu, click Page, and then open the Web page you want to use.

2. Click where you want to place the search form.

3. Click the Web Component button on the Standard toolbar.

4. Click Web Search.

5. Click Current Web.

6. Click Finish.

7. Type a text label for the search form.

8. Type the width in character for the search label.

9. Type labels for the button, click to start the search and to clear the search box.

10. Click the Search Results tab.

11. To rank the results, select the Display Score check box.

12. To display score data, select the Display File Date and the Display File Size check boxes.

13. Select the date and time formats you want.

14. Click OK.

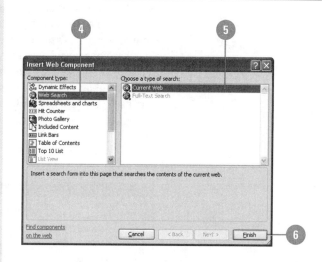

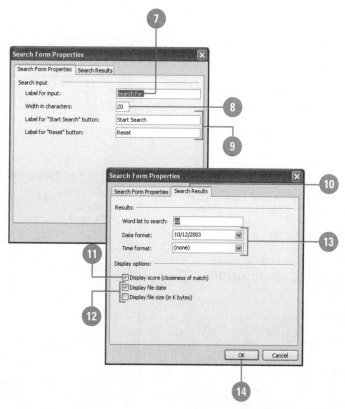

Inserting Navigation Bars

The larger the Web site, the more important it is that visitors be able to navigate easily through your Web site. One of the most effective tools in that area is the Navigation Bar, a FrontPage component that can be positioned in the shared border area of your Web pages. A Navigation Bar is actually a collection of hyperlinks used to guide visitors through a Web site. The hyperlinks usually lead to primary pages, such as a contact page or the site's home page. Link bars can be placed on every page of your Web site, so visitors can always navigate easily without getting lost in a maze of pages. These bars can also have buttons and text hyperlinks. You can create buttons, much as you can create hit counters, or you can set up your Web's navigation system and have FrontPage automatically generate the link bars for you.

Create a Link Bar

1. Click the View menu, click Page, and then open the Web page you want to use.

2. Click where you want to place the link bar.

3. Click the Insert menu, and then click Navigation.

4. Click Bar With Custom Links.

5. Click Next.

6. Select the link bar style you want to use, and then click Next.

7. Select the orientation for the link bar.

8. Click Finish.

9. Enter a name for your new link bar, and then click OK.

10. Click Add Link.

11. Browse to locate the page you want to add, select it, and then click OK.

12. Click OK.

   The page appears with + Add Link as a placeholder, which you can click to add a link.

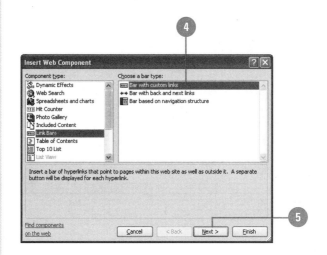

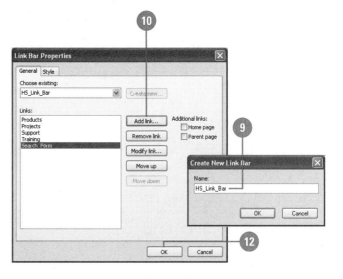

Change Link Bar Properties

1. Click the View menu, click Page, and then open the Web page you want to use.

2. Right-click the link bar, and then click Link Bar Properties.

   The Link Bar Properties dialog box opens, displaying the General tab.

3. Select the options you want.

   ◆ To add a link, click Add Link, select the new link, and then click OK.

   ◆ To remove a link, select the link you want to delete, and then click Remove Link.

   ◆ To change a link, click Modify Link, make your changes, and then click OK.

4. Click the Style tab, and then change the settings you want for the link bar.

5. Click OK.

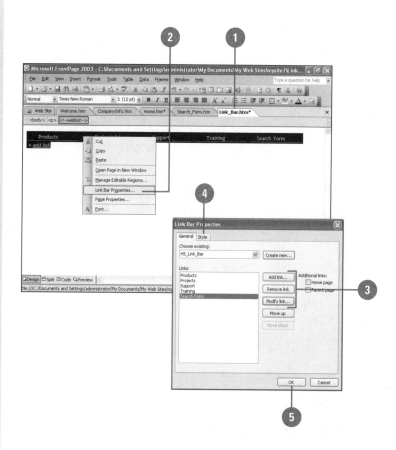

For Your Information

Understanding the Types of Link Bars

Custom Link Bar. Import any Web pages from your Web site or external sites. This type of link bar can be set up on a custom basis, and you're free to add or remove pages at any point.

Link Bar With Back And Next Links. Uses your navigation system to track the last page that a visitor has read as well as the next page in the Web site.

Link Bar Based On Your Site's Navigation Structure. Uses the Navigation view structure to determine which hyperlinks to include on its bar and what to call them.

Inserting a Table of Contents

A Table of Contents (TOC) not only lets visitors know what's on your Web site, but tells users where to find it. You can base your Table of Contents on either the categories assigned to your pages or the navigational structure of your Web site. A TOC based on the navigational structure might also include pages containing hyperlinks that are not included in the navigational structure, so a visitor can click any feature listed in the TOC and be transported directly to that location. The TOC can be edited and formatted. FrontPage even offers the option of automatically resetting the TOC whenever an editorial change is made.

Create a Table of Contents

1. Click the View menu, click Page, and then open the Web page you want to use.

2. Click where you want to produce a Table of Contents.

3. Click the Web Component button on the Standard toolbar.

4. Click Table Of Contents.

5. Click For This Web Site.

6. Click Finish.

7. Enter the relative URL of the page that serves as the TOC starting point (use Browse if necessary).

8. Select the size of the styled text you want to use in your header.

9. Select the check boxes you want.

   ◆ **Show Each Page Only Once.** TOC only lists each page once.

   ◆ **Show Pages With No Incoming Hyperlinks.** Includes pages not linked to other pages.

   ◆ **Recompute Table Of Contents When Any Other Page Is Edited.** Updates the TOC when any page is edited.

10. Click OK.

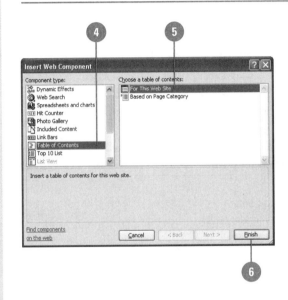

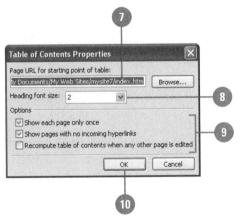

Create a TOC from Categories

1. Click the Folders button on the Views bar, right-click a page you want to assign to a category, and then click Properties.

2. Click the Workgroup tab.

3. Click the category you want to assign to this page (select the check box).

4. Click OK.

5. Repeat the first four steps for each page that you want to assign to a category.

6. In Page view, position the insertion point where you want your TOC located.

7. Click the Insert menu, and then click Web Component.

8. Click Table Of Contents, and then click Based On Page Category.

9. Click Finish.

10. Select the categories whose pages you want to include in your Table of Contents. These selected categories will appear in the Selected Categories box.

11. Click the Sort Files By list arrow, and then select an option:

    ◆ Document Title sorts the list alphabetically

    ◆ Date Last Modified sorts the list, in ascending order, by date

12. To display the Date The File Was Last Modified or Comments Added To The File, check the appropriate option.

13. Click OK.

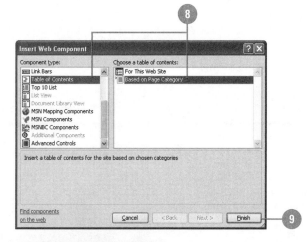

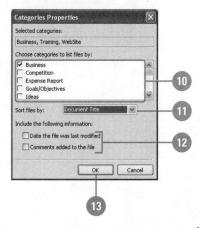

10

Creating Discussion Groups ▶

As webmaster, it's your assignment to provide a forum for those visitors who want to discuss subjects related to your Web site. You will want to add hyperlinks that take readers to related materials on certain subjects; provide a search engine so visitors can locate the subjects they have interest in; and some form of a message board so that visitors can post their thoughts. You can set up the possibility of creating a discussion group based on your Web site. Be aware that some of this material might not be supported by all browsers.

Create a Discussion Group

① Click the New button list arrow on the Standard toolbar, and then click Web Site.

② Click the Discussion Web Site Wizard icon.

③ To add this template to your Web Site, select the Add To Current Web Site check box.

④ Click OK.

⑤ Read the opening comments, and then click Next.

⑥ Select the check boxes with the main features you want in your discussion, and then click Next.

⑦ Enter a name that will appear on the Web site for the discussion forum, name the folder that will contain the discussion, and then click Next.

⑧ Click the input fields option you want that the user must complete to post to the forum (for most non-commercial Web sites, the Subject, Comments option works best), and then click Next.

⑨ Click the Yes or No option to determine whether this will be an open forum to all users, or a closed forum where users must input a password to participate, and then click Next.

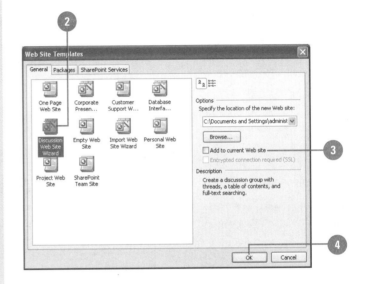

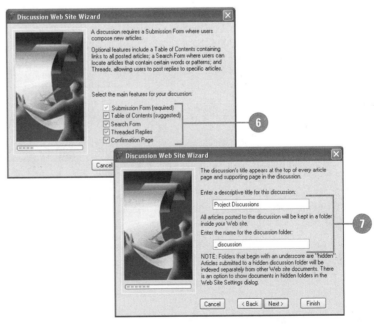

10 Click the option to determine whether posts should be sorted from most current to oldest, or oldest to most current from top to bottom on the page, and then click Next

11 Click the option to determine whether you want the Table of Contents for the discussion forum to be the home page of the Web (this would only be appropriate if the discussion was the central focus of the Web site), and then click Next.

12 Click the option to determine whether you want the Search Form to report for matching document.

13 If available and you want to use a theme, select a theme, otherwise, click Next.

To select a theme to the discussion Web, click Choose Web Theme. Select the themes and properties that you want to use, and then click OK.

14 Click the option to determine whether or not to apply frames to the discussion Web, and then click Next.

15 When you're done, click Finish.

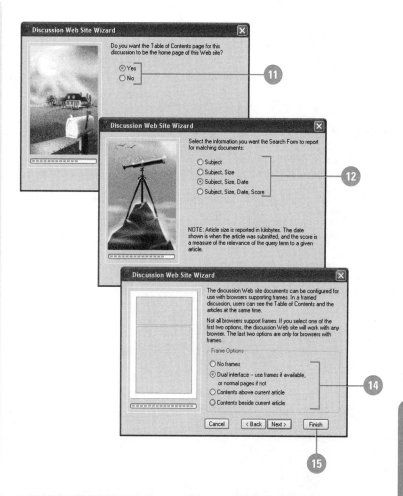

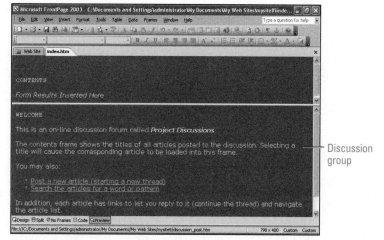

Discussion group

Creating a Project Web Site

You can create a project Web site that contains a list of members, a schedule, status, an archive, and discussions in one easy step. All you need to do is select the Project Web Site Wizard in the Web Site Templates dialog box and FrontPage does all the rest. You don't even need to answer any wizard questions.

Create a Project Web Site

1. Click the New button list arrow on the Standard toolbar, and then click Web Site.

2. Click the Project Web Site icon.

3. Click OK.

4. Double-click the index.htm file to open the project Web site home page to view the site.

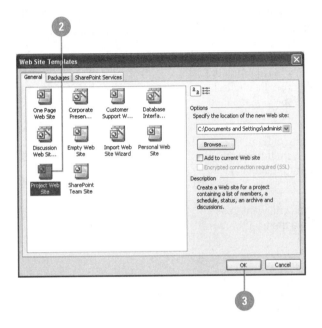

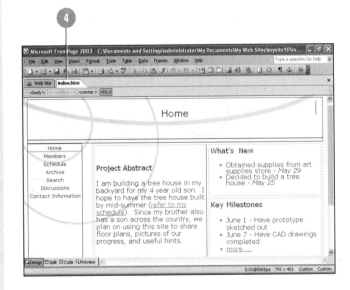

Gathering User Input Using Forms

Introduction

In this chapter, you're going to create Web page forms, using Microsoft Office FrontPage 2003. Forms that appear on Web pages are similar to paper forms. Web page forms share the same purpose (gathering information about your visitors) and use many of the same devices (check boxes, information fields, etc.) as paper forms. The most popular types of forms include:

◆ Request

◆ Registration

◆ Feedback

◆ Contact information

◆ Survey

◆ Guest book

◆ Order (shipping and billing information)

◆ Log On (prompts visitors to enter name and password)

◆ Search (enables visitors to search your site)

After some initial design and thought for your form page, you can get started by adding it to your Web site, and then you can design and display all the various information that you want to gather using text boxes, check boxes, option buttons, labels, list menus, and push buttons. You can also further customize your form by adding pictures, and setting certain rules for entering the data in certain fields.

Your server will require either FrontPage Server Extensions or SharePoint Team Services for the FrontPage forms to function on your Web site. Your Web administrator or ISP can let you know whether this software is included on your server.

Understanding Form Fields

One of the keys to creating a form is the creation of fields. There are many different types of fields, including text boxes, text areas, option buttons, list menus, and push buttons. In addition to these fields, there are also Advanced Buttons, which you can customize through font and color selection, and Group Boxes, which you can use to segregate clusters of related controls into one group. Password fields are basically one-line text boxes used to add passwords to your site so that you can restrict access (to charge for membership, for example). When a site visitor enters their password, it appears on screen as a collection of asterisks to secure confidentiality.

After you've decided what types of fields to add to the form, you can define what you want them to do and how you want them to look. You can even set properties for each field, such as the length of a text field, or the available options on a list menu. You can insert form fields using the Form submenu on the Insert menu. If an item on the Form submenu is grayed out, the command is not available. You need a Web server equipped with FrontPage Server Extensions or SharePoint Team Services to active the commands. After you create a form, you have to determine how to collect and display the visitor data.

Form Field Element Types

Field Element Type	Description
Text Box	Enter short, one line text, such as a name
Text Area	Enter multiple line text, such as a comment
File Upload	Upload a file provided by the visitor
Check Box	Select between two values, such as yes/no
Option Button	Select one value from a list of values
Group Box	A titled border that surrounds a group of related elements
Drop-Down Box	Select an item from a list of several choices
Push Button	A button that executes an action
Advanced Button	A button that executes an action, yet also displays HTML content on the front
Picture Form Field	A picture
Label	An invisible element that surrounds a form field and its title
Hidden	An invisible element that the browser uses to execute an action

Validating Forms

To make sure that the visitor fills out the forms correctly, you will have to set data entry rules, a process also known as **Validation**. You can further guide the user by setting the format in which the data is accepted. If you're asking for a telephone number, for example, set up your text box so that it only accepts numbers and hyphens. You can also pre-set the number of character spaces so the visitor doesn't inadvertently leave out or add a number. A Validate button is provided in field related dialog boxes, where you can set validation rules.

After you've collected the information, you need to access it. FrontPage offers form han-dlers, server programs that are executed when a form is submitted to your site. Using these form handlers you can produce a database of visitor information and even offer users access to special features. You can have the results saved (or e-mailed) as either a text or HTML file.

You can also add a confirmation page (the form the visitor has just filled out is displayed and the visitor is given the opportunity to either edit or confirm it); create keyboard shortcuts (displayed as an underlined letter in the field label); or allow visitors to navigate the form using the Tab key.

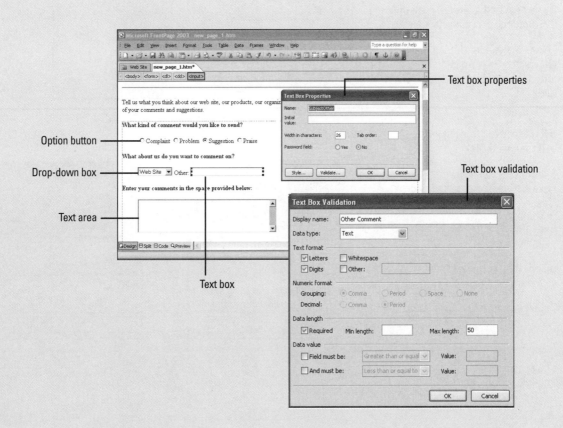

Option button

Drop-down box

Text area

Text box

Text box properties

Text box validation

11

Creating Forms

FrontPage offers numerous types of forms so that you can collect information from visitors to your site. You can start from scratch and create the form by adding information fields to a blank form, or you can use one of the wizard templates. When you first create a form, FrontPage inserts a rectangular box with a perforated line-dash perimeter. Inside this box, you can add everything from check boxes and text fields to list boxes and submit buttons.

Create a Form Using a Wizard or Template

1. Click the New button list arrow on the Standard toolbar, and then click Page.

2. Click the Form Page Wizard icon (a wizard) or the Feedback Form or Guest book icon (templates).

3. Click OK.

4. If you selected a wizard, read the instructions, and then click Next.

   This takes you to a dialog box that allows you to add questions to the form and maintains a list of them. Click Add for a list of potential new questions.

5. Select the type of input you want, and then click Next.

6. Select the items you want to collect from users, and then click Next.

7. Repeat the cycle, adding more questions.

8. Select the presentation options you want, and then click Next.

9. Select the output options you want, and then Next.

10. Click Finish.

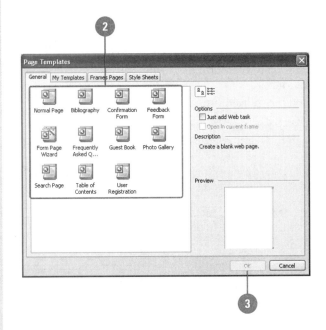

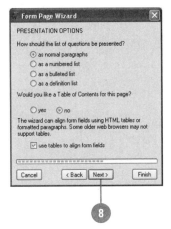

Create a Form

1. Click the View menu, click Page, and then open the Web page you want to use.

2. Click the Insert menu, point to Form, and then click Form.

   A rectangular box with a perforated line-dash perimeter appears, accompanied by two push buttons, labeled Submit and Reset.

3. To add space before or after the push buttons, so you can insert other form fields, click to position the insertion point before or after the buttons, and then press Enter, as necessary.

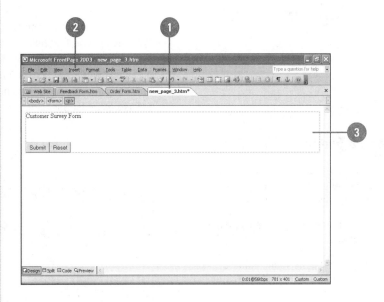

Delete a Form Field

1. Click the View menu, click Page, and then open the Web page you want to use.

2. Click the field you want to delete to select it.

3. Press Delete.

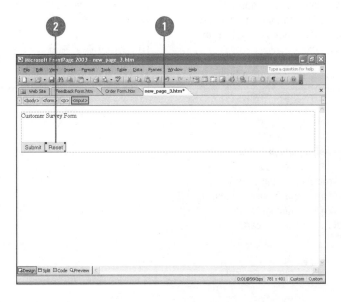

11

Inserting Text Boxes

You can insert two types of text boxes in a form, Text Box and Text Area. Text boxes ask for information and provide a field where a visitor can type an answer. Text boxes are used for collecting relatively small quantities of information, such as the visitor's online name. Text areas are small text windows best suited for brief text entries. This window scrolls vertically and horizontally to maximize its available space. They are ideal for use as guest books.

Insert a Text Box or Text Area

1 Click the View menu, click Page, and then open the Web page you want to use.

2 Click in the form where you want to place the text box or text area.

3 Click the Insert menu, point to Form, and then click Text Box or Text Area.

A text box or text area appears in the form with an insertion point next to it. You can click to place the insertion point before or after the text box.

4 Type the label next to the box.

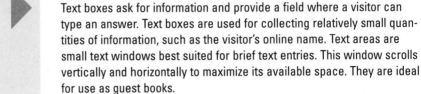
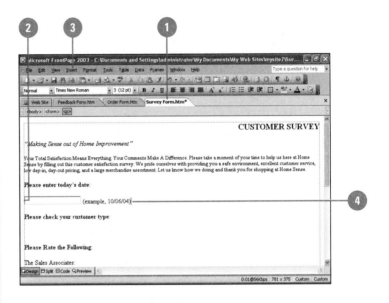

Change Text Properties

1. Click the View menu, click Page, and then open the Web page you want to use.

2. Double-click the text box or text area.

3. Enter a name that will identify the text box.

4. Enter the text to be displayed in the text box when a site visitor first opens the form. As you type, the characters will be counted in the Width In Characters box.

5. Specify the field specific options for text boxes or text areas.

   ◆ For text boxes, click the Yes option to create a password to your Web site so that you can restrict access. When a Web site visitor enters their password, it appears as asterisks for confidentiality.

   ◆ For text areas, type the number of lines in which you want the area.

6. Click OK.

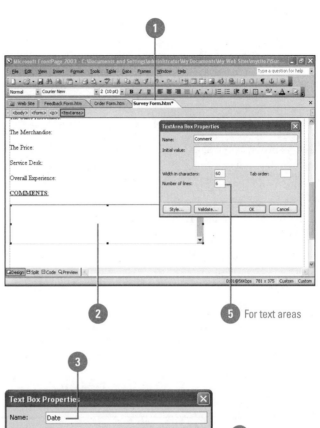

5 For text areas

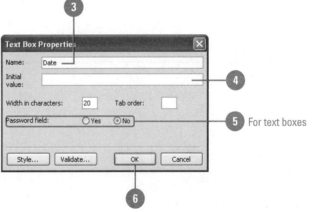

3

4

5 For text boxes

6

11

Setting Form Tab Order

When you fill out a form, many times it is easier for visitors to move from field to field using the Tab key instead of clicking the mouse each time. Many form elements have a Tab Order field. Tab order determines which fields in a form receive the focus (active where you can enter data) when the visitor presses the Tab key. A form field with lower tab values receives the focus before any fields with higher values.

Set Tab Order

1 Click the View menu, click Page, and then open the Web page you want to use.

2 Double-click the form field in which you want to change the tab order field value.

3 Type the tab order value you want (lower numbers appear before higher numbers).

4 Click OK.

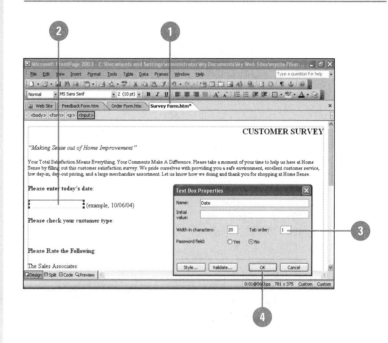

Inserting Drop-Down Boxes

The drop-down box allows visitors to choose one option from a scrollable list of choices. For example, you can create a list of all 50 states from which the visitor can choose one. The advantage of using a drop-down box is that the visitors are forced to select an option from the list, which prevents data input errors.

Insert a Drop-Down Box

1. Click the View menu, click Page, and then open the Web page you want to use.

2. Click in the form where you want to place the drop-down box.

3. Click the Insert menu, point to Form, and then click Drop-Down Box.

4. Double-click the drop-down box.

5. Type a name for the drop-down box.

6. Click Add.

7. Type the name of the list item you want to list.

8. To have the item selected initially, click the Selected option.

9. Click OK.

10. Perform Steps 6 through 9 for each item you want to include in the list.

11. Enter a height for the drop-down box.

12. Click the Yes or No option to allow multiple selections.

13. Click OK.

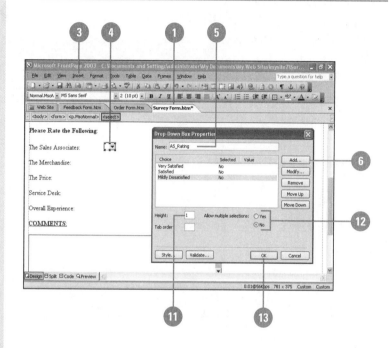

Inserting Check Boxes

Check boxes are provided to allow users multiple choices from a list or series of options. Check boxes are just what they sound like—a statement which you can either confirm, by checking the box, or decline by leaving the box blank.

Insert a Check Box

1. Click the View menu, click Page, and then open the Web page you want to use.

2. Click in the form where you want to place the check box.

3. Click the Insert menu, point to Form, and then click Check Box.

4. Type the check box label next to the box.

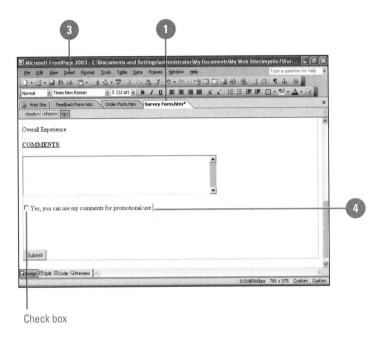

Check box

Change Check Box Properties

1. Click the View menu, click Page, and then open the Web page you want to use.

2. Double-click the check box you want to change.

3. Enter a name that identifies the check box in the form results.

   The name is not displayed on the form.

4. Enter a value to associate with the check box.

   This value is returned with the form results and is displayed on the default confirmation page.

5. Click the Checked option or the Not Checked option to set up the default state when a visitor opens the form.

6. Click OK.

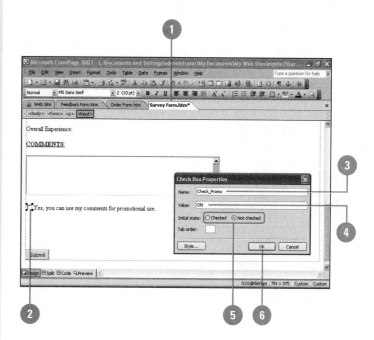

Adding Option Buttons

Option buttons (also known as Radio Buttons) are used when asking a visitor a question with more than one possible answer. Only one option button in a group can be selected at a time. FrontPage groups option button within a form with the same name. Typically assigning the same name to fields creates errors, but not with the option button. You need to assign option buttons in the same group with the same name to function properly.

Add an Option Button

1. Click the View menu, click Page, and then open the Web page you want to use.

2. Click in the form where you want to place the option button.

3. Click the Insert menu, point to Form, and then click Option Button.

4. Type the text that you want to appear with the option buttons.

5. Double-click an option button within the group.

6. Type a group name (the same one for each option button in the group).

7. Click OK.

8. Repeat steps 5 through 7 for each option button in the group.

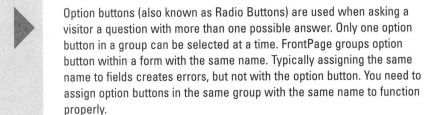

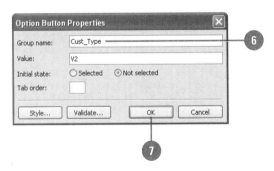

Activating a Label

After you type a label next to a check box or option button, you can specify whether Web site visitors select the check box or option button by clicking the box or button, or its label. If you want your visitors to click the label, you need to active the label.

Activate a Label

1. Click the View menu, click Page, and then open the Web page you want to use.

2. Select both the text and the check box or option button to which you want to activate the label.

3. Click the Insert menu, point to Form, and then click Label.

   The text label appears surrounded by a perforated border, which indicates the label is active.

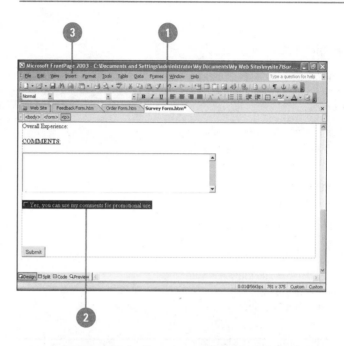

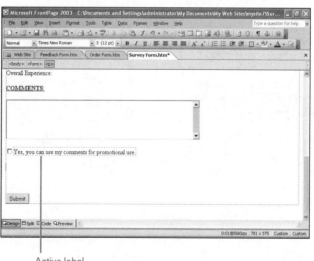

Active label

11

Inserting Buttons

Push buttons are functional components that are used when the visitor needs to do something. When you insert a form field, two buttons appear, Submit and Reset. The Submit button is a command that a visitor has to click to submit the form when completed, while the Reset button is a command that a visitor has to click to reset the form and start over. You can create a push button to perform an action.

Insert a Push Button

① Click the View menu, click Page, and then open the Web page you want to use.

② Position the insertion point in the form where you want to place the push button.

③ Click the Insert menu, point to Form, and then click Push Button.

A push button appears in the form.

④ Double-click the push button.

⑤ Enter a name that identifies the push button in the form results. The name is not displayed on the form.

⑥ Type the label that appears on the button.

⑦ Click the button type you want (Normal is the standard button, Submit is a button that submits the completed form, or Reset is a button that clears the form so the visitor can start over).

⑧ Click OK.

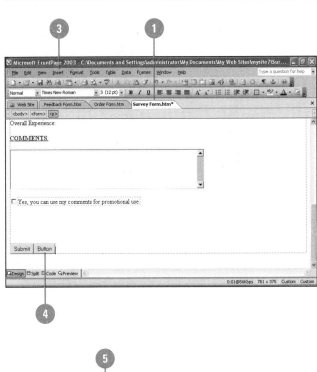

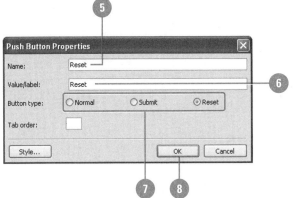

Insert an Advanced Button

1. Click the View menu, click Page, and then open the Web page you want to use.

2. Position the insertion point in the form where you want to place the push button.

3. Click the Insert menu, point to Form, and then click Advanced Button.

   An Advanced button appears in the form with selected default button text.

4. Type a name for the button.

5. Right-click the advanced button, and then click Advanced Button Properties.

6. Click the Button Type list arrow, and then select a button type.

7. Type a name to identify the button.

8. Click OK.

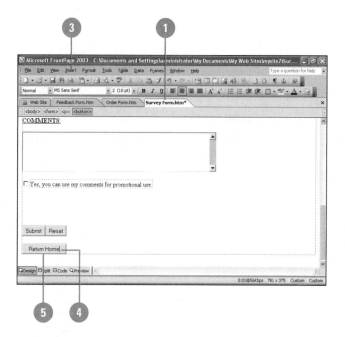

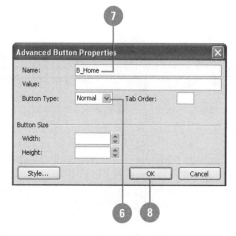

11

Inserting Pictures

You can insert a picture in a form, which you can use as a button. If you want, you can use a picture button, like a push button, to perform an operation. You can insert a picture in a form in a similar way you insert a picture in a Web page.

Insert a Picture in a Form

1. Click the View menu, click Page, and then open the Web page you want to use.

2. Position the insertion point in the form where you want to place the picture.

3. Click the Insert menu, point to Form, and then click Picture.

4. Locate and select the picture you want to use.

5. Click Insert.

Did You Know?

You can change the name that identifies the picture. Right-click the picture button, click Form Field Properties, enter a name in the Name box, and then click OK.

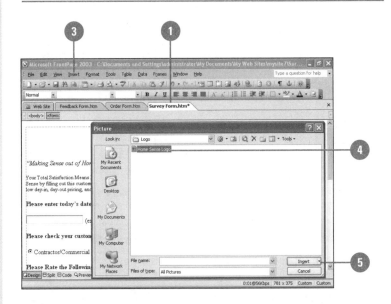

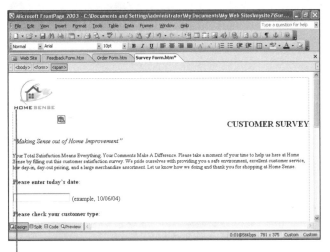

Inserted picture

Adding File Uploads

If you need to receive files from co-workers or visitors to your Web site, you can add a File Upload field to your form. When you add the File Upload field to a form, a text box and push button entitled Browse appear on the page. Visitors can use the text box to enter a path and file name or the Browse button to select a file to upload to your Web site. The file is transferred when you submit the form. If there is a problem, visitors can reset the form, and then try again.

Add a File Upload Field

1. Click the View menu, click Page, and then open the Web page you want to use.

2. Click in the form where you want to place the file upload field.

3. Click the Insert menu, point to Form, and then click File Upload.

4. Select the file upload destination folder for the current form.

5. Click OK.

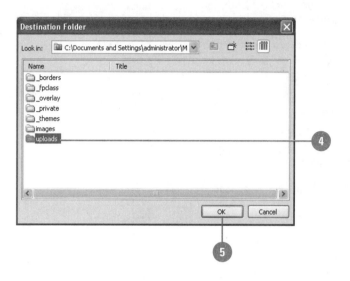

Change File Upload Properties

1. Click the View menu, click Page, and then open the Web page you want to use.

2. Double-click the file upload field.

3. Type an internal name for the field.

4. Specify the width of the field.

5. Click OK.

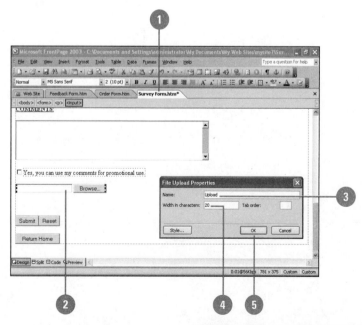

11

Formatting Form Fields

After you create a form field, such as a text box, text area, option button, list menu, or push button, you can format the text associated with the field in the same way you format any other text using formatting dialog boxes.

Format a Form Field

1. Click the View menu, click Page, and then open the Web page you want to use.

2. Double-click the form field you want to format.

3. Click Style.

4. Click Format.

5. Click a formatting command (Font, Paragraph, Border, Numbering, and Position).

6. Make the formatting selections you want, and then click OK.

7. Click OK.

8. Click OK.

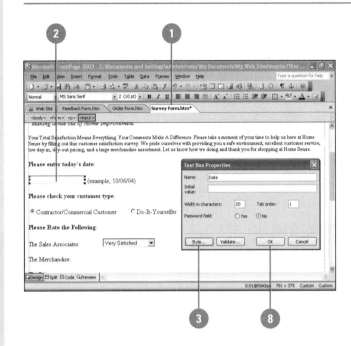

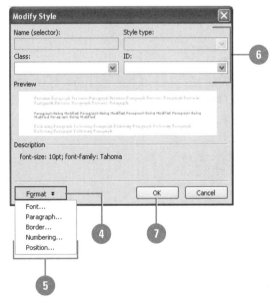

Setting Rules for Entering Data

For some form fields—text box, text area, option button, or list box—you can set rules that visitors to your Web site are required to follow to provide consistent results for gathering data. If you see a Validate button in a field's Property dialog box, you can set rules for entering data. Each Validation dialog box provides different options depending on the field.

Set a Rule for Entering Data

1. Click the View menu, click Page, and then open the Web page you want to use.

2. Double-click the form field (text box, text area, option button, or drop-down box) to which you want to set rules.

3. Click Validate.

4. Select the options you want to set rules for entering data.

   ◆ For a drop-down box or option button, select the Data Required check box.

   ◆ For text box or text area, click the Data Type list arrow, select the type of data you require in the text box, and then select other related options.

5. Click OK.

6. Click OK.

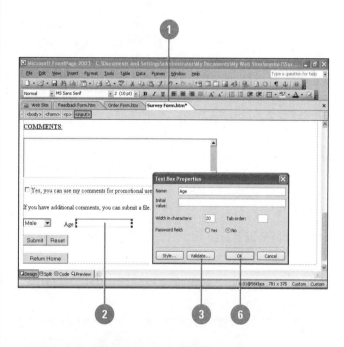

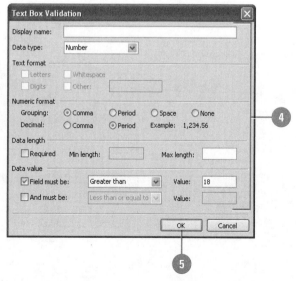

11

Connecting to a Database

When you have a lot of data about your site visitors, you'll want to save that information so that you can use the content. You can save the information in a form to a database by creating a database connection. A **database connection** is a connection that specifies the name, location, and type of database you want to access. You can create a new database, connect to an existing one, or connect to the sample Northwind database to try out the process. FrontPage comes with a wizard that creates one form for the visitor to submit information and another form for you to track the results. The Web site enables you to view, update, delete, or add records. To view the data once you set up the connection, your Web site must be hosted or published on a Web server configured with Active Server Pages (ASP), Active Data Objects (ADO), FrontPage 2002 Server Extensions or later or SharePoint Team Services, and Internet Information Server (IIS) version 4.0 (or later).

Create a Database Connection

1. Click the New button list arrow on the Standard toolbar, and then click Web Site.

2. Click Database Interface Wizard icon.

3. Click OK.

4. Click the option to create an ASP or ASP.NET page, and then click Next.

5. Click the option to create a new base, connect to an existing one, or connect to the sample Northwind database, and then click Next.

   For the purposes of this example, create a new database.

6. Type a name for your database connection, and then click Next.

7. Edit the list of columns and submission fields for the database using Add, Modify, Delete, Move Up or Move Down, and then click Next.

8. Click Next to continue.

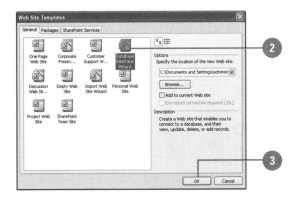

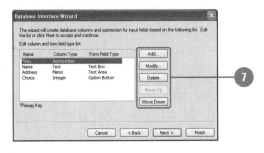

9. Select the table or view you want to use.

10. Specify a location for the database files (use the default location provided or click Browse to select a location), and then click Next.

11. Click Next to continue.

12. Select the check boxes for the database interface pages you want to use, and then click Next.

13. Type a user name, password, and password confirmation.

14. Click Finish.

Did You Know?

You can connect a database to part of a form. Instead of creating an entire set of forms, you can also set up a database connection to an area in a form. To set up a database connection, click the Insert menu, point to Database, and then click Results. The Database Results Wizard dialog box opens. Click the Use A New Database Connection option or the Use An Existing Connection option, and then follow the wizards instructions to create a new database or use an existing database.

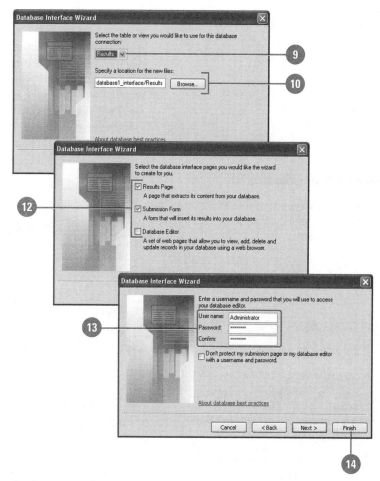

Database connection

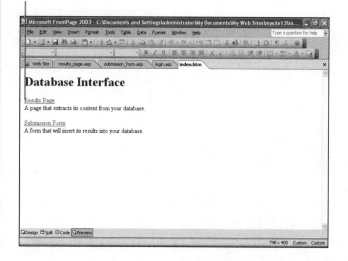

Saving Form Results

Once you create a form and collect information from visitors on the Web, you can save the form results to a database or file, or send the form results in an e-mail message. You can save the results to an ODBC-compliant database or a text or HTML file. When a site visitor fills out a form and submits it, FrontPage enters the data directly into a database or file, or sends an e-mail message. By default, form results are saved to a text file. The Save Results component (which saves the form results) requires FrontPage Extensions or SharePoint Team Services, both on the Web server you use to develop the site and the one visitors use.

Save Form Results to a File

1. Click the View menu, click Page, and then open the Web page you want to use.

2. Right-click the form, and then click Form Properties.

3. Click the Send To option.

4. Click Options.

5. Click the File Results tab.

6. Enter the location and name of a new file, or click Browse, locate and select the file to which you want to save the results, and then click Open.

7. Click the File Format list arrow, and then select a file format (such as HTML or Formatted Text).

8. Click OK.

9. Click OK.

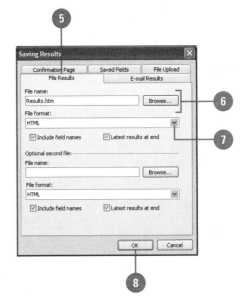

Save Form Results to a Database

1. Click the View menu, click Page, and then open the Web page you want to use.

2. Right-click the form you want to save the results from, and then click Form Properties.

3. Click the Send To Database option.

4. Click Options.

5. Click the Database Connection To Use list arrow, and then select an existing database connection.

6. Click the Table To Hold Form Results list arrow, and then select the table where you want to place the form results data from.

7. Click the Saved Fields tab.

   The fields in the form are listed. For each field, you must specify the database column in which you want to save the data.

8. Click the form field you want to modify.

9. Click Modify.

10. Click the Save To Database Column list arrow, select the column where you want to save the form field data, and then click OK.

11. Repeat steps 8 through 10 for each form field, and then click OK.

12. Click OK.

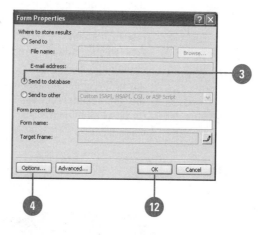

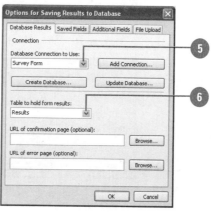

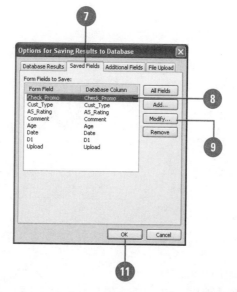

Sending Form Results as E-Mail

Once you create a form and collect information from visitors on the Web, you can send the form results in an e-mail message. As you send the results in an e-mail, you can also save the results to a file at the same time, so you have two records of the form results. To help automate part of the process, you can set e-mail settings and insert form field information in the e-mail message. The Save Results component (which saves the form results) requires FrontPage Extensions or SharePoint Team Services, both on the Web server you use to develop the site and the one visitors use.

Send Form Results as E-Mail

1. Click the View menu, click Page, and then open the Web page you want to use.

2. Right-click the form, and then click Form Properties.

3. Click the Send To option.

4. Type the e-mail address to which you are sending the form results.

5. If you want, specify a file to save the results in a file as well as being sent via e-mail.

6. Click Options.

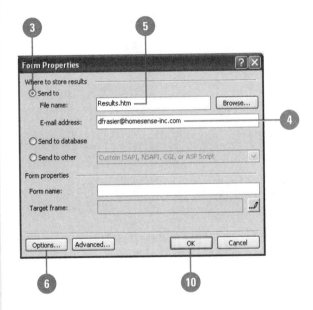

7 Click the E-Mail Results tab.

8 Perform one or more of the following steps:

◆ In the E-Mail Format box, select the text format you want from the list menu.

◆ In the Subject Line box, type the text that you want in the subject line of the e-mail (the default subject line in the e-mail is Form Results).

◆ If you want the subject line of the e-mail to contain the results of one field from the form, select the Form Field Name check box, and then type the name of the field in the Subject Line box.

◆ In the Reply-To Line box, a specific e-mail address can appear as the sender of the e-mail (the From or Reply To line in the e-mail). Enter the address.

◆ If the form contains a field that collects the site visitor's e-mail address, that address can be used as the sender's address. Select the Form Field Name check box, and then type the name of the form field in the Reply-To Line box.

9 Click OK.

10 Click OK to close the Form Properties dialog box.

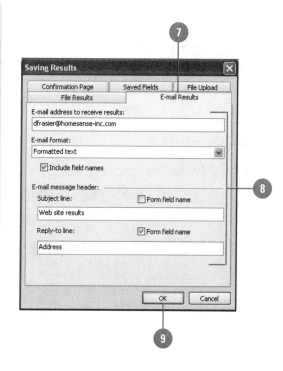

11

Creating a Confirmation Page

Use Form Confirmation Pages so that your site visitors can confirm that the information they've entered on a form is correct and, if changes need to be made, the visitors can reset the form and begin again. By default, FrontPage creates a generic confirmation page, but you can create your own confirmation page—from a template or custom page—to replace the default one.

Create a Confirmation Page Using a Template

1. Click the New button list arrow on the Standard toolbar, and then click Page.

2. Click the Confirmation Form icon.

3. Click OK.

4. Modify the text you want displayed after a visitor has submitted a form anywhere on the page, and then select the text.

5. To modify a field (bracketed text), double-click the field, type a field name, and then click OK.

6. To add more confirmation fields, click the Insert menu, click Web Component, click Advanced Controls, click Confirmation Field, and then click Finish.

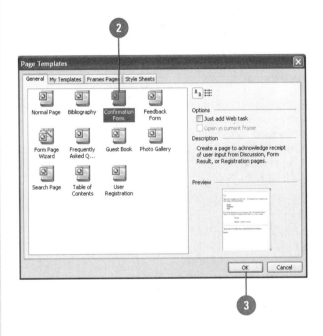

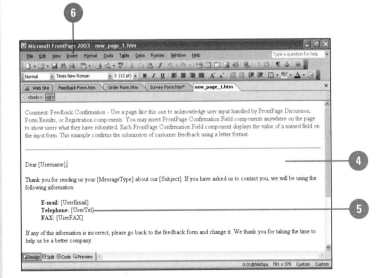

Create and Attach a Custom Confirmation Page

1. Click the File menu, click New, and then click Blank Page on the task pane.

2. Enter the text you want displayed after a visitor has submitted a form anywhere on the page, and then select the text.

3. Click the Insert menu, and then click Web Component.

4. Click Advanced Controls.

5. Click Confirmation Field.

6. Click Finish.

7. Enter the form field from which to display your information. This name must match the name you assigned the form field when you selected its properties.

8. Click OK.

   The name of the field is displayed in brackets on the form. When the confirmation form is displayed to a site visitor, the field displays the visitor's entry.

9. Repeat these steps for each field you want to display.

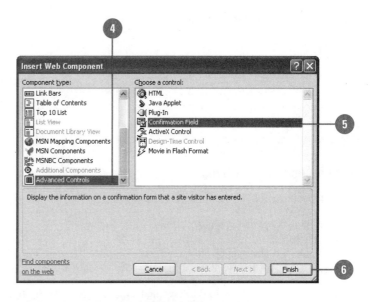

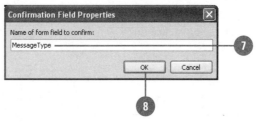

Form field name

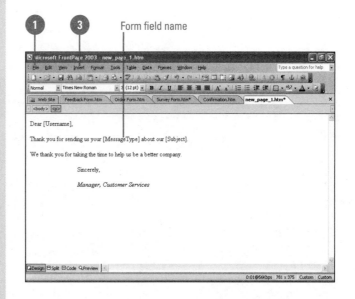

Creating a Custom Form Handler

You can also set up a form to save results using a custom form handler. A form handler is a program on a server that is executed when a site visitor submits a form. You can use your custom script (ISAPI, NSAPI, CGI, or ASP Script) as a form handler.

Create a Custom Form Handler

1. Click the Folders button on the Views bar.

2. Right-click the folder that contains the script, and then click Properties on the shortcut menu. A dialog box opens containing the name of your page followed by the word Properties.

3. Select the Allow Scripts To Be Run check box.

4. If you want other users to be able to view files in your directory, select the Allow Files To Be Browsed check box.

5. Click OK.

6. Click the View menu, and then click Page.

7. Right-click the form, and then click Form Properties.

8. Click the Send To Other option, click the list arrow, and then click Custom ISAPI, NSAPI, CGI, or ASP Script formats.

9. Click Options.

10. Click the Method list arrow, and then select one of the following formats for submitting data to the form handler:

    ◆ **Get.** Encodes the form's name-value pair and assigns the data to a server variable named Query_String.

    ◆ **Post.** Passes the name-value pair to the form handler as input.

    ◆ **Default.** Leaves the Encoding Type text box empty.

11. Click OK.

12. Click OK.

Publishing and Managing a Web Site

Introduction

Now that you know how to plan, build, and run a Microsoft Office FrontPage 2003 Web site, the only areas that remain are publishing and managing the Web site. Publishing a Web site is the process of copying all of the files that make up a Web to a predetermined destination, while managing a Web site is the process of administering the
day-to-day maintenance, which includes viewing reports and creating, assigning, and performing tasks.

You can publish copies of your Web site content files, and also copies of additional FrontPage files. However, it will require the server to display pages and perform Web functions. Using Remote Site view, you can publish an entire Web site or individual files.

FrontPage 2003 can publish to any Web server running any version of the FrontPage Server Extensions. However, Web part pages and any pages that use features on the Data menu in FrontPage 2003 require SharePoint Services 2.0 or later. These features will not work on any other type of Web server.

In addition to recording who's assigned to various tasks, FrontPage also keeps track of the review status for a file. If you are managing a large Web site and you want to keep the project on task, you need to continually monitor the review status of individual items. FrontPage provides several reports to help you keep track of the project workflow and task assignments.

You can apply XML (Extensible Markup Language) formatting. This format is ideal for producing extensive, highly-structured data from an application in a consistent manner. XML tags, however, employ a much tighter rule system with regard to XML syntax. If a single missing tag or mis-formatted attribute happens, XML makes the entire document unreadable.

Using Remote Site View

The Remote Site view allows you to compare the content of the current local Web site and a target remote Web site. Typically, the local Web site contains the development version of a site and the remote Web site on a Web server contains the "live" site on the Internet. Using Remote Site view, you can publish an entire Web site or individual files. If you display Remote Site view for a site you have not published, a blank window appears with the message *Click "Remote Web Site Properties..." to setup a remote site*. You can publish your files to a Web site with FrontPage Server Extensions or SharePoint Team Services, WebDAV (Distributed Authoring and Versioning), FTP (File Transfer Protocol), or Windows file system.

Specify the Remote Web Site Location

1. Open the Web site you want to publish, click the View menu, and then click Remote Web Site.

2. Click the Remote Web Site Properties button.

3. Click the Remote Web Site tab.

4. Click the option with the remote Web server type in which you want to publish your files.

    ◆ **FrontPage or SharePoint Services.** The site is running FrontPage Server Extensions or Windows SharePoint Services; use http://URL.

    ◆ **WebDAV.** The site supports WebDAV; use http://URL.

    ◆ **FTP.** The site supports FTP; use ftp://URL.

    ◆ **File System.** The site resides on a local or network drive; use C:\MyWeb or \\Server\MyWeb.

5. Type the remote Web site location or use Browse to select it.

6. Click OK.

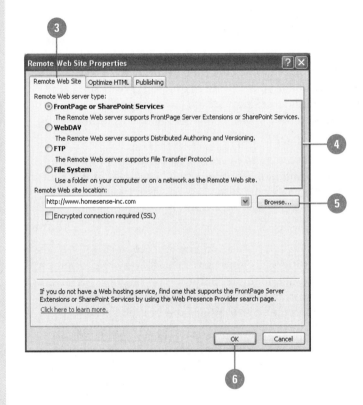

Change Publishing Properties

1. Open the Web site you want to publish, click the View menu, and then click Remote Web Site.

2. Click the Remote Web Site Properties button.

3. Click the Publishing tab.

4. Click the publish options you want.

   ◆ Changed Pages Only

   ◆ All Pages, Overwriting Pages Already On Destination

   ◆ Include Subsites. Select the check box to publish all Web sites contained within the main Web site.

5. Click the option you want to specify how FrontPage compares file in the two Web sites.

   ◆ Determine Changes By Comparing Source And Destination Sites

   ◆ Use Source File Timestamps To Determine Changes Since Last Publish

6. To keep a log of changes, select the Log Changes During Publish check box.

7. To display the log for the most recent publish operation, click View Log File.

8. Click OK.

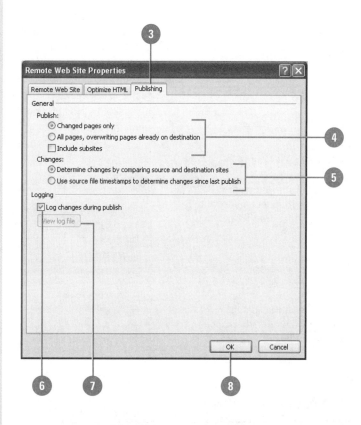

Entering the Publishing Destination

When you publish your site to a folder on your local file system, you enter a location using the syntax *C:\\sitefolder*, where C is the drive letter. When you publish your site to a folder on a network server, you enter a location using the **Universal Naming Conventions (UNC)**. UNC is a convention that produces a machine-independent way to locate a file. The UNC name employs the syntax \\server\share\path\foldername. When you publish your site to a folder on a Web server on the World Wide Web, you enter a Uniform Resource Locator (URL). A URL consists of three parts: the prefix http://, which indicates a Web address; a network identification, such as www for the World Wide Web; and a Web site name, or domain name, such as homesense-inc.com.

12

Optimizing HTML

Sometimes Web developers leave things in Web pages, such as comments, whitespace, and other HTML attributes, which have no value to visitors. FrontPage allows you to optimize your HTML code when you publish a Web site or Web page or when you are working on a page in Design view. Optimizing HTML code makes the code easier to read and faster to download on the Web. FrontPage is more aggressive optimizing individual pages in Design view. If the changes cause problems you can undo the change.

Optimize Published HTML Code

1. Open the Web site you want to optimize, click the View menu, and then click Remote Web Site.

2. Click the Remote Web Site Properties button.

3. Click the Optimize HTML tab.

4. Select the When Publishing, Optimize HTML By Removing The Following Elements check box.

5. Click the options you want. Some of the common ones include:

   ◆ **All HTML Comments.** Select to remove all comments; selects all the comments check boxes.

   ◆ **HTML Whitespace.** Select either check box to remove leading or all whitespace.

6. Click OK.

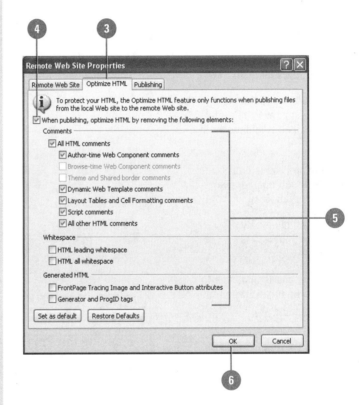

Optimize HTML Code in Design View

1. Open the Web page in which you want to optimize in Design view.

2. Click the Tools menu, and then click Optimize HTML.

3. Select the check boxes with the settings you want to optimize. Some of the common options include:

   - **All HTML Comments.** Select to remove all comments; selects all the comments check boxes.

   - **Merge Adjacent Tags.** Select to combine multiple tags into one.

   - **Empty Tags.** Select to remove tags with no content.

   - **Unused Styles.** Select to remove unused styles.

   - **Word HTML.** Select to remove extra HTML elements from Microsoft Word.

4. Click OK.

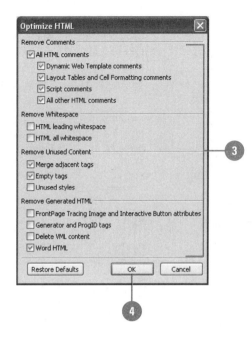

12

Publishing a Web Site

Publishing a Web site refers to the process of copying all of the files that make up a Web to a predetermined destination. In FrontPage, you typically publish your site for one of two reasons. The first reason is to launch the site on either a company intranet (a network limited to members of a specific group, usually a business) or on the World Wide Web. The second reason is to back up the site on either your computer or a network drive. Using the FrontPage Publish Web command you can publish all your Web files, only those that have been edited, or individual files. You can publish your Web files to a folder on your local or network drive, or on a Web server. When you publish a site, FrontPage maintains all the hyperlinks, as well as the original Web's theme.

Publish a Web Site

1. Open the Web site you want to publish.

2. Click the File menu, and then click Publish Site.

3. If necessary, click the Remote Web Site Properties button to connect to a Web server.

4. Display the folder with the local Web site.

5. Display the folder with the remote Web site.

6. Click the Local To Remote option.

7. Click Publish Web Site.

8. If a file conflict occurs, a dialog box appears, click Ignore And Continue, Overwrite Remote Files, or Cancel.

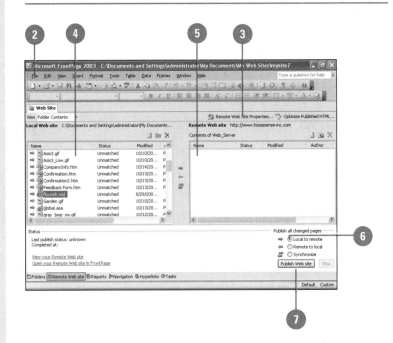

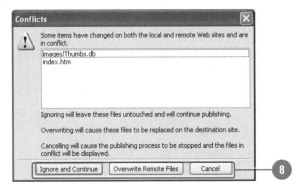

Using FrontPage Server Extensions or SharePoint Services

Before you can publish a Web site to a Web server that uses Web components, such as hit counters, you need to install FrontPage Server Extensions or Windows SharePoint Services on the Web server. See Chapter 10, "Adding Functionality to Web Pages," for more information on Web components. Some features in FrontPage, such as Web part pages and any pages that use features on the Data menu in FrontPage 2003 require SharePoint Services 2.0 or later. These features will not work on any other type of Web server.

FrontPage 2003 doesn't come with a new version of FrontPage Server Extensions. Instead, you can use FrontPage Server Extensions 2002, which are compatible and

available from Microsoft's MSDN (Microsoft Developers Network) Web site, or Windows SharePoint Services. If you plan to install Windows SharePoint Services, you don't need to install FrontPage Server Extensions.

Windows SharePoint Services is an engine that enables you to create Web sites to share information. SharePoint sites provide communities for team collaboration, enabling users to work together on documents, tasks, and projects. Windows SharePoint Services is part of Windows .NET Server 2003. To install Windows SharePoint Services, you need to install Windows .NET Server 2003 first; see Chapter 13, "Working Together on a SharePoint Team Site," for more details.

Microsoft's MSDN Web site

Click to download FrontPage Server Extensions

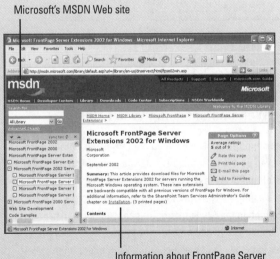

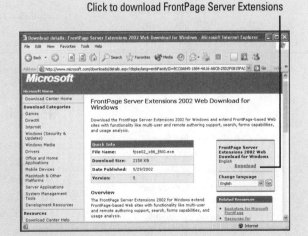

Information about FrontPage Server Extensions 2002

Publishing a Web Page

Publish a Web Page

① Open the Web site you want to publish.

② Click the File menu, and then click Publish Site.

③ Display the folder with the local Web site and select the Web page you want to publish.

④ Display the folder with the remote Web site.

⑤ Click the Local To Remote option.

⑥ Click the Right Arrow (-->) button between the two Web sites.

⑦ If a file conflict occurs, a dialog box appears, click Ignore And Continue, Overwrite Remote Files, or Cancel.

Did You Know?

You can publish an individual file in Folders view or Folders list. Right-click the file(s) you want to publish, and then click Publish Selected Files.

You can display certain files in the local Web site. In Remote Web Site view, click the View list arrow, and then click Folder Contents, Files To Publish, Files Not To Publish, or Files In Conflict.

In addition to publishing an entire Web site, you can also publish individual files and folders. Instead of waiting for FrontPage to compare all the files to find the one or two you changed, you can quickly select the files and publish them. When you are working on a large Web site, publishing individual files gives you the control you need and saves times.

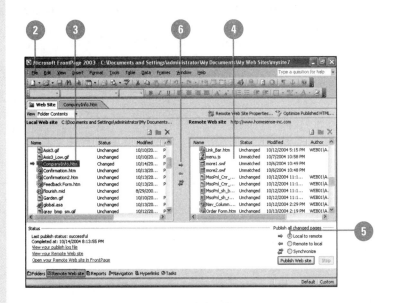

For Your Information

Publishing Web Content using Web Folders

FrontPage also supports publishing Web content using Web folders (provided the Web server is running FrontPage Server Extensions or Windows SharePoint Services). Web folders are http locations that you can access using My Network Places. You can use the Add Network Place icon in the My Network Places window to create a Web folder. You can use Windows Explorer to copy Web files from the Web site folder (typically in My Webs) to the Web folder on the Web server.

Updating a Web Site

Historically, a site that does not periodically update its material will not attract many repeat visitors. Housekeeping, therefore, is a crucial component of Web maintenance. You can opt to publish only those files that have been edited or altered in some way. FrontPage can compare the files in the working site on your local computer to the published files on the server, and determine if changes have been made on each file. If it detects a more recent version on your computer, that's what gets published. You can also choose which files you don't want to publish. For example, if a page is incomplete, not directly part of your Web site, or simply out-of-date, you can mark the file as Don't Publish. If you have multiple developers working on pages, the local and remote sites might become different. You can synchronize files from the remote site.

Update a Web Site

1. Open the Web site you want to update, and then modify the Web pages you want to update.

2. Click the File menu, and then click Publish. An arrow appears next to files that need to be updated.

3. Click the Remote Web Site Properties button, click the Publishing tab, click the Changed Pages Only option, and then click OK.

4. To mark a file as don't publish, right-click the Web page you don't want to publish, and then click Don't Publish. A small stop sign icon appears next to the file.

5. Click the publishing option you want to use.

   ◆ **Local To Remote.** Copies changed files from the local to the remote site.

   ◆ **Remote To Local.** Copies changed files from the remote to the local site.

   ◆ **Synchronize.** Copies all remote files to local.

6. Click Publish Web Site.

Changed file

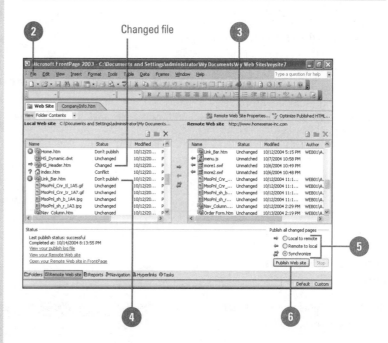

12

Checking Browser Compatibility

FrontPage can help to check the compatibility of your browser with FrontPage capabilities to make sure your Web site works properly. In the Page Options dialog box, you can select the Web server technologies and newest browser you want to support, and then FrontPage turns off the options beyond the capabilities of the specified browser. After you create your site, you can search for compatibility problems.

Match Browser Capabilities

1. Click the Tools menu, and then click Page Options.

2. Click the Authoring tab.

3. Click the FrontPage And SharePoint Technologies list arrow, and then select an option.

4. Click the Browsers list arrow, and then click a browser option.

5. If available, click the Browser Versions list arrow, and then click the newest version.

6. Click OK.

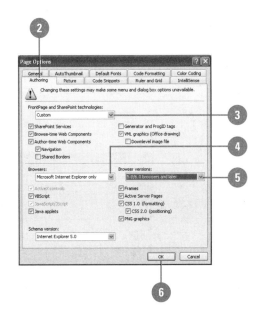

Search for Compatibility Problems

1. Click the Tools menu, and then click Browser Compatibility.

2. Click the option to specify which pages you want to search.

3. Click Check.

4. To open the Web page with the problem, double-click it.

5. To save the list of compatibility problems as a Web page, click Generate HTML Report.

6. Click Close.

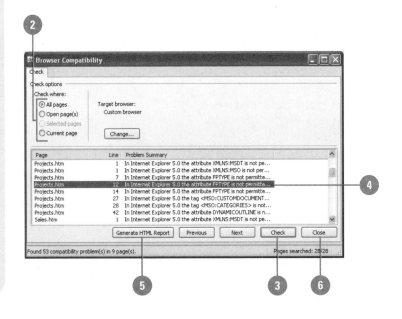

Generating Reports for a Web Site

Site reports can offer extensive information and records regarding your site's performance and its visitors. With FrontPage, you can generate reports on a wide variety of on-site activities.

- ◆ **View A Web Site Summary.** Provides general data regarding your site's content, from the number of files to a list of hyperlinks on your site.

- ◆ **View Problems.** Produces reports on maintenance problems, such as large pages (big files download slowly) or pages containing broken hyperlinks.

- ◆ **Manage Workflow.** Reports that help you manage your workflow (to make sure pages aren't too long or are inconsistent in size) by showing the status of your Web pages. Files in your site can be categorized, assigned to different authors, or checked in and out using source control.

- ◆ **Monitor Web Site Usage.** Reports that keep a record of items such as most popular pages and types of browsers used to visit your site.

Web Site Reports

Web site reports come in several different types:

- ◆ The **Site Summary** report displays an overview of your site's vital statistics, from number of files to number of hyperlinks.

- ◆ **File** reports the age of all files, who is assigned to them, when they were last edited, and when they first appeared on your site. It reports on: All Files, Recently Added Files, Recently Changed Files, and Older Files.

- ◆ **Shared Content** reports page usage for Dynamic Web Templates, Shared Borders, Style Sheet Links, and Themes.

- ◆ **Problem** reports on display-related problems on your site, such as component errors, files that are taking too long to download, or broken hyperlinks. It reports on: Unlinked Files, Slow Pages, Broken Hyperlinks, and Component Errors.

- ◆ **Workflow** reports on file status and assignments in your site, including review status, the person the file is assigned to, and so on. It reports on: Review Status, Assigned To, Categories, Publish Status, and Checkout Status.

- ◆ **Usage** reports on visits to your site, including page hits, browsers used by site visitors, etc. It reports on: Usage Summary, Monthly Summary, Weekly Summary, Daily Summary, Monthly Page Hits, Weekly Page Hits, Daily Page Hits, Visiting Users, Operating Systems, Browsers, Referring Domains, Referring URLs, and Search Strings.

12

Viewing Reports for a Web Site

FrontPage provides a collection of reports to help you manage your Web site. You can view any of the reports using Reports view. For usage reports you can even chart the statistical information in the report. While you're viewing a report, you can sort information by category, filter information by category values, and edit individual entries.

View Reports for a Web Site

① Click the View menu, and then click Reports.

② Point to a submenu to display a list of reports.

③ Click a report. The report opens.

④ To open other reports from within Reports view, click the list arrow at the left of the Reports View toolbar.

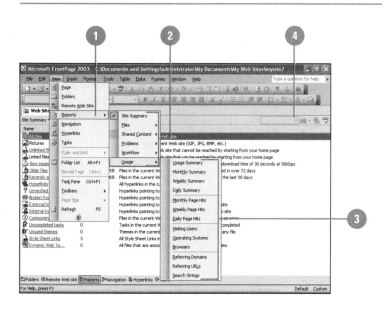

For Your Information

Charting Usage Data

FrontPage provides usage reports to help you manage your Web site, and to understand what areas of the site are most effective. To help you evaluate the report data, you can chart the statistical information. Click the View menu, click Reports, point to Usage, and then click a usage report. Click the Usage Chart button list arrow on the the Reports View toolbar, and then click a chart type. To change the interval for a usage report, click the Report Setting list arrow on the Reports View toolbar, and then click an interval. If usage data doesn't appear in Reports view, you need to turn on usage processing for FrontPage Extensions on the Web server.

Work with Reports

1. Click the View menu, click Reports, point to a submenu to display a list of reports, and then click a report.

2. To sort choices in a report by the information in a column (Name, Title, Assign To, etc.), click the column heading.

3. To filter a report by a specific column values, click the list arrow next to the column header, and then select a filter method.

   ◆ **All.** Removes a filter already in place.

   ◆ **Custom.** Opens the Custom AutoFilter dialog box, where you can apply a filter using two conditions.

4. To edit a field in a report, click the report line, click the field, and then edit the field or select an option from a list.

See Also

See "Customizing Reports View" on page 344 for information on changing the information gathered in Reports view.

Did You Know?

You can perform commands on the report files. Right-click a report entry, and then click a command, such as Open, Copy Report, Remove Filters, Publish Selected Files, Don't Publish, and Properties.

Working with Tasks

Files can be assigned to an individual or to an entire workgroup. Within a workgroup environment, product managers assign files to different workgroups. Product managers can then monitor the progress of the workgroups through the Assigned To and Review Status reports. Within the Tasks view, the product managers can oversee the individual workgroup monitors as well as each assigned task.

When assigning a file, you can add a review status that explains the type of work done on the file. If a file requires a legal review, for example, create the review status legal review, indicate the file's status, and then assign it to the person responsible for accomplishing this task. When the legal review is complete, that person can classify the task as approved.

It's also possible to view your site's files on an assignment basis by using the Assigned To report, which displays your Web files by assignment. The Assigned To report displays these files in a column format and provides the following information:

- ◆ **File name.** Name of the file

- ◆ **Title.** Title of the file

- ◆ **Assigned To.** User name or workgroup to which the task is assigned

- ◆ **Assigned Date.** Date the file was assigned

- ◆ **Assigned By.** Who assigned the file

- ◆ **Comments.** Comments that describe work that needs to be done on a file, or any other information you feel is necessary

- ◆ **Type.** Type of file (.gif, .css, .htm, etc.)

- ◆ **In Folder.** Folder in the Web site where the file is stored

Files can be sorted in any column heading displayed in the Assigned To report. You can also filter the values displayed in any of the report columns. The filtering choices for that column can be obtained by clicking the column heading.

Tasks can be assigned to individuals or a workgroup and feature a description of the work comprising the task. When dealing with files (whether they're pictures, text, or sound bites), you can associate a task and a file, and then assign it to yourself in the capacity of a co-worker.

In the Tasks view, you can monitor the many tasks on your site. Tasks view uses a column format and provides status information about each task under these column headings:

- ◆ **Status.** Indicates whether the task is completed or in progress

- ◆ **Task.** Name of the task

- ◆ **Assigned to.** User name or workgroup to which the task is assigned

- ◆ **Priority.** High, medium, or low

- ◆ **Associated with.** Name of the file, if any, that the task is associated with

- ◆ **Modified date.** Last time the file was modified

- ◆ **Description.** Description of work that needs to be done, or any other information

Creating Tasks

Developing a Web site requires a lot of tasks. Changes made to one page require updates on another. Keeping track of all these changes can be difficult to handle. To help you keep track of all the details, you need a task list. In FrontPage, you can create tasks to help you remember what needs to get done. If you have several people working on a Web site, you can create and assign tasks for them to accomplish.

Create and Assign a Task

1. Click the View menu, and then click Tasks.

2. Click the Edit menu, point to Tasks, and then click Add Tasks.

3. Type the name of the task.

4. Click the Assigned To list arrow, and then select a person or workgroup, or enter a person or workgroup's name.

5. Click a priority option (the default is Medium).

6. Type a description for the task. This field can be used to describe the work that needs to be completed on the task.

7. Click OK.

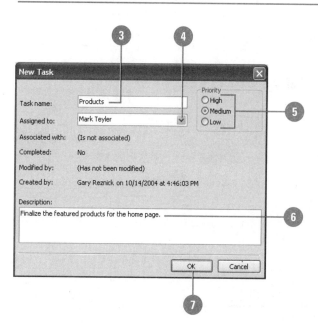

Did You Know?

You can edit a task. In Tasks view, right-click the task you want to edit, click Edit Task, make the changes you want, and then click OK.

12

Creating Tasks Associated with Files

When you create a task in Page view while you're editing a page, that task is automatically associated with the page file. The name of the file associated with the task is displayed in the Associated With field. When you begin a task associated with a different type of file, FrontPage opens the file in its associated editor (Word for .doc files, Notepad for .txt files, etc.). If the task is not associated with a file, the task is not performed. FrontPage can also create tasks automatically for some operations. When you check spelling or create a new page, you can set a task option to automatically create tasks for pages with misspellings or for page with needed work.

Create and Associate a Task with a File

1. Click the View menu, click Folder List, and then open the Web page you want to associate with a task.

2. Click the file you want to associate with a task.

3. Click the Edit menu, point to Tasks, and then click Add Tasks.

4. Type the name of the task.

5. Click the Assigned To list arrow, and then select a person, or enter a person's name.

6. Click a priority option (the default is Medium).

7. Type a description for the task. This field can be used to describe the work that needs to be completed on the task.

8. Click OK.

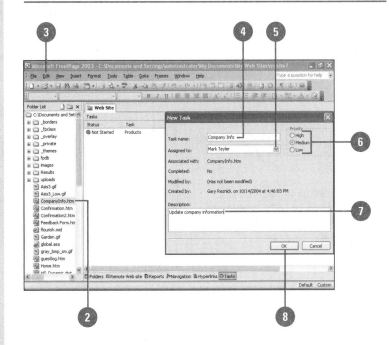

> ### Did You Know?
>
> **You can delete a task.** In Tasks view, right-click the task you want to remove, and then click Delete Task.

Create a Spelling Task

1. Click the View menu, click Page, and then open the Web page you want to check spelling.

2. Click the Tools menu, and then click Spelling.

3. When the Spelling dialog box appears, select the Add A Task For Each Page With Misspellings check box.

4. Click Start.

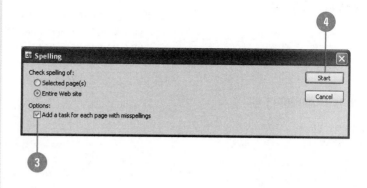

Create a New Page Task

1. Click the New button list arrow, and then click Page.

2. Click an icon with the new page you want to create.

3. Select the Just Add Web Task check box.

4. Click OK.

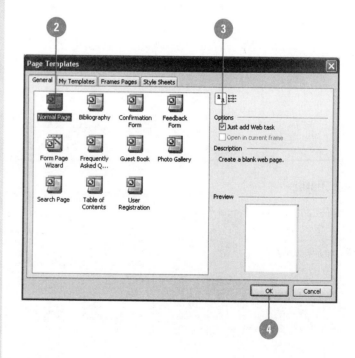

12

Viewing Tasks

Tasks view maintains a list of pending work items for the current Web site. by default, Tasks view displays only tasks not started or in progress. If you want to display completed tasks, you need to display task history. If you want to sort tasks, you can click the column headings in Tasks view to arrange tasks in ascending or descending order.

View Task Assignments

1. Click the View menu, and then click Tasks.

2. To sort choices in Tasks view by the information in a column (Name, Title, Assign To, etc.), click the column heading.

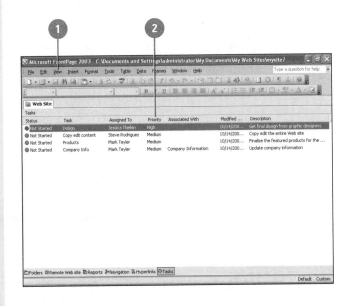

View Task History

1. Click the Edit menu, and then point to Tasks.

2. Click Show History.

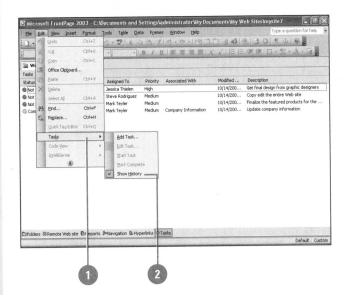

Performing Tasks

FrontPage makes it easy to locate and work on tasks. In Tasks view you can start a task's associated file, either a Web page or a file created in another program. This way you don't have to manually search for a Web page or file. After you complete a task, you can mark it complete. If a task is designated as Completed, you can change its description but not its name.

Perform a Task

① Click the View menu, and then click Tasks.

② Right-click the task you want to perform, and then click Start Task.

When you start a task associated with a page, FrontPage opens it in Page view, where you can make changes to complete the task.

Mark a Task Complete

① Click the View menu, and then click Tasks.

② Right-click the task you want to mark, and then click Mark Complete.

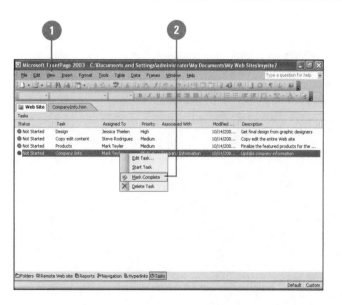

12

Controlling Workflow Status

In addition to recording who's assigned to various tasks, FrontPage also keeps track of the review status for a file. If you are managing a large Web site and you want to keep the project on task, you need to continually monitor the review status of individual items. To help you manage the process, you can use the Properties dialog box to create a master list of user names you can assign tasks and a master list of review status names. After you create the master lists, you can select the items from the Assign To and Review Status lists.

Set Workgroup Properties

1. Click the View menu, and then click Folder List.

2. Right-click the file you want to set workgroup properties, and then click Properties.

3. Click the Workgroup tab.

4. Select the general and usage options you want. Some of the common options include:

   - **Available Categories.** Lists the category name defined within the current Web site.

   - **Assigned To.** Specifies who's assigned to work on this file. Click Names to add or remove names from the master Assign To list.

   - **Review Status.** Records the results of the most recent review for the current file. Click Statuses to add or remove status types from the master Review Status list.

5. Click OK.

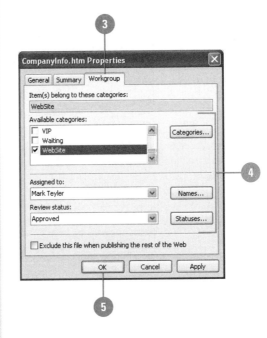

Viewing Workflow Task Assignments

If you are working in a workgroup, managing tasks assignment can be a big job. FrontPage provides several reports to help you keep track of the project workflow and task assignments. The Assign To report displays information provided during the creation of the task. You can sort the tasks by the assigned person or workgroup to pinpoint what needs to get done.

View Task Assignments

1. Click the View menu, point to Reports, point to Workflow, and then click Assigned To.

   Reports view appears, displaying task assignments.

2. To sort choices in a report by the information in a column (Name, Title, Assign To, etc.), click the column heading.

3. To filter a report by a specific column values, click the list arrow next to the column header, and then select a filter method.

   ◆ **All.** Removes a filter already in place.

   ◆ **Custom.** Opens the Custom AutoFilter dialog box, where you can apply a filter using two conditions.

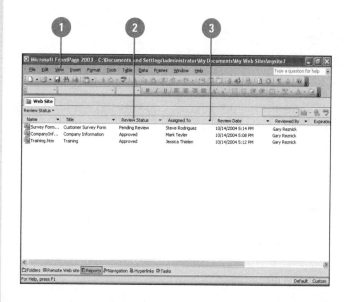

12

Checking Documents In and Out

If you are working in a workgroup, there is a chance that two people might start to work on the same file at the same time, which creates a conflict. Problems occur when one or the other saves the file overwriting changes the other one might be making. To avoid this problem, the Web site administrator can enable document check-in and check-out. This locks out other people from making changes and saves a copy for possible restoration. When a file is checked out to you, a green check mark appears in the Folder List. A gray padlock means the file is checked out to someone else.

Enable Document Check-In and Check-Out

1. Click the Tools menu, and then click Site Settings.

2. Click the General tab.

3. Select the Use Document Check-In And Check-Out check box.

4. Click the option you want to check out files from a remote or local site.

5. Select or clear the Prompt To Check Out File When Opening A Page check box.

6. Click OK, and then click Yes to confirm the change.

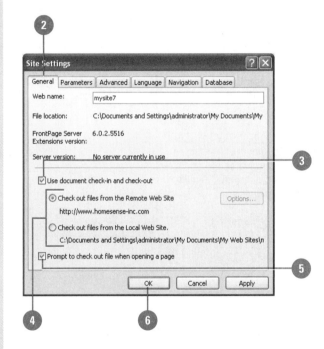

Set Document Check-In and Check-Out

1. Click the View menu, and then click Folder List, or display Folders view.

2. Right-click the file you want to check-in or check-out, and then click Check-In or Check-Out.

View the Check-Out Status Report

1. Open the Web site you want to view status, and then click the Reports button in Design view.

2. Click the Reports button list arrow, point to Workflow, and then click Checkout Status.

3. To sort choices in a report by the information in a column (Name, Title, Assign To, etc.), click the column heading.

4. To filter a report by a specific column values, click the list arrow next to the column header, and then select a filter method.

   ◆ **All.** Removes a filter already in place.

   ◆ **Custom.** Opens the Custom AutoFilter dialog box, where you can apply a filter using two conditions.

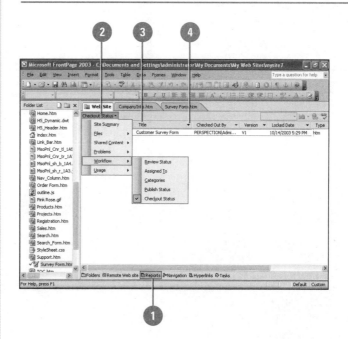

12

Applying XML Formatting

XML, or Extensible Markup Language, is an alternative to HTML. This format is ideal for producing extensive, highly-structured data from an application in a consistent manner. The difference between XML and HTML is subtle but profound: XML describes a Web document's content, while HTML tags describe how the document looks. HTML tags assign certain characteristics to the text they surround. XML is ideal for data-intensive Web environments and, unlike HTML, supports customized tags for specific data. XML tags, however, employ a much tighter rule system with regard to XML syntax. So much as a single missing tag or mis-formatted attributes makes the entire document unreadable.

Apply XML Formatting

1. Click the View menu, and then click Page.

2. Click the Code button at the bottom of the window.

3. Right-click anywhere on the page, and then click Apply XML Formatting Rules. FrontPage scans the XML code for missing or incomplete tags.

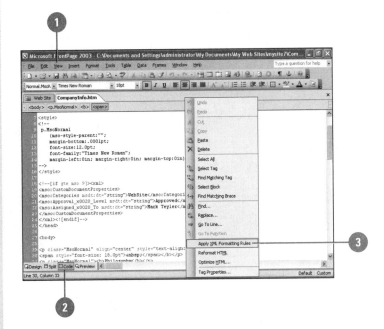

Working Together on a SharePoint Team Site

13

Introduction

Microsoft SharePoint technology, known as SharePoint Team Services, is a collection of products and services which provide the ability for people to engage in communication, document and file sharing, calendar events, sending alerts, tasks planning, and collaborative discussions in a single community solution. SharePoint enables companies to develop an intelligent application which connects their employees, teams, and information so that users can be part of a Knowledge Community. Before you can use SharePoint Team Services, SharePoint needs to be set up and configured on a Windows 2003 Server by your network administrator or Internet service provider.

   With Microsoft Office FrontPage 2003, you can create a new SharePoint site using a template. The SharePoint Web Site template creates a standard Team Site with a team events calendar, library for shared documents, task list, and contact list. You can also add SharePoint Web applications to create a related Web site using SharePoint package templates. The package templates allows you to create an issue tracking site with management tools, a news and reviews site with discussions and voting, and a Web log site with discussions, favorite links and a log search.

   SharePoint is integrated into Office 2003 and enables you to share data and documents using the Shared Workspace task pane directly from Office Word 2003, Office PowerPoint 2003, or Office Excel 2003. The Shared Workspace task pane allows you to see the list of team members collaborating on the current project, find out who is online, send an instant message, and review tasks and other resources. You can use the Shared Workspace task pane to create one or more document workspaces where you can collect, organize, modify, share, and discuss Office documents. The Shared Workspace task pane displays information related to the document workspaces stored on SharePoint Team Services.

What You'll Do

View SharePoint Team Services

Administer SharePoint Team Services

Create Sites Using SharePoint Templates

Create Sites Using SharePoint Packages

Store Documents in the Library

View Team Members

Set Up Alerts

Assign Project Tasks

Create an Event

Create Contacts

Hold Web Discussions

Work with Shared Workspace

Install Windows 2003 and SharePoint Server 2003

323

Viewing SharePoint Team Services

Microsoft SharePoint displays the contents of its home page so you can work efficiently with your site. The available pages are: The Home Page, Manage Content Page, Manage Users Page, Change Portal Site Navigation Page, Change Settings Page, and Site Settings Page. You can navigate within the site by clicking on each of the links within the home page. Certain Administrative Access rights are needed in order to view these pages.

Home Page view is the first page your users see when they access the URL for Microsoft SharePoint Server. If you are within a Windows 2003 Active Domain and have a Domain Account, you will not be prompted to type in your user credentials and password. If you do not have an account, you will be asked to type in your credentials to have the page display your SharePoint Site. Please contact your Systems Administrator if you do not have access to the SharePoint Server.

Documents and Lists Page view allows you to manage content to your SharePoint Site. You can create Portal sites, a Document Library, upload Graphic Images in an Image Library Site, Create Calendar Events, create an Address Book of Contents, setup Project Events, Create a Web Discussion site, and setup Surveys. Within your Document and Lists page you will be able to administer your content to provide users with content management capabilities.

Manage Users Page view allows you to add users to your SharePoint Site. If their e-mail address is located within their Domain Account on Windows 2003, SharePoint will e-mail the users you created, and then invite them to join in to the SharePoint Server. From the Manage Users page you can add, delete, and change the permissions of a user for your site.

Home Page

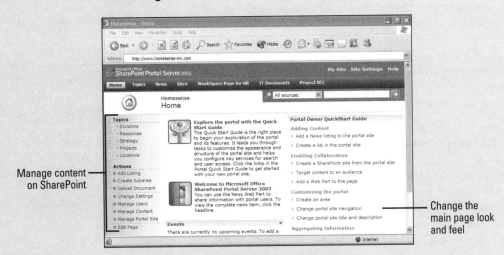

Manage content on SharePoint

Change the main page look and feel

Documents and Lists Page

Adds a new portal site

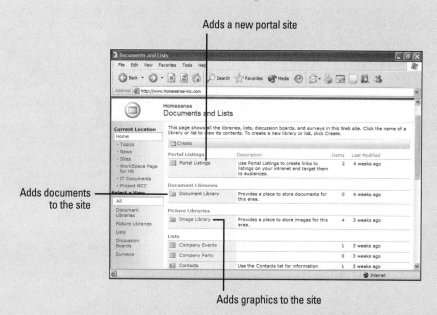

Adds documents to the site

Adds graphics to the site

Manage Users Page

Adds new users

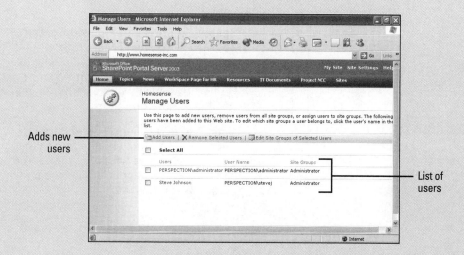

List of users

13

Administering SharePoint Team Services

Administering Microsoft SharePoint is easy within the site settings. The available pages are: The Home Page, Manage Content Page, Manage Users Page, Change Portal Site Navigation Page, Change Settings Page, and Site Settings Page. You can navigate within the site by clicking on each of the links within the home page. Certain Administrative Access rights are needed in order to view these pages.

Change Portal Site Navigation Page gives you a hierarchy structure to make changes to other portal sites within SharePoint. If you want to move your site to the top-level within SharePoint or modify your sub-level pages, you can do so with the SharePoint Portal Site Navigation Page.

Change Settings Page allows you to swiftly customize the look and feel of your portal site. You can change the title, description, and logo for the site. You can change the URL for creating sites based on the published templates for your site. You can also add a change management process by having the site approved by a manager before being published, and allowing you to change your contact information for your site.

Site Settings Page has four different categories: General Settings, Portal Site Content, Search Settings and Indexed Content, and User Profile, Audiences, and Personal Sites.

- ◆ **General Settings** offers additional security features, which allows you to manage the alerts settings, change your default SMTP e-mail server, change the location of your SharePoint Site, and modify the Regional Language Settings to your site.

- ◆ **Portal Site Content** allows you to manage the site structure, view your site lists and document libraries, import data into your SharePoint Server, and add link listings to your site.

- ◆ **Search Settings and Indexed Content** allows you to create Meta tags within your SharePoint Server, and create search crawlers to investigate your site for new key words which will create better search results within your site.

- ◆ **User Profile, Audiences, and Personal Sites** allows you to change and manage your user profiles within your site. You can also manage your audiences and personal settings.

Quick Launch bar

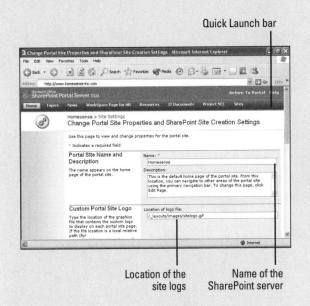

Location of the site logs

Name of the SharePoint server

Change Settings Page

Change publishing settings

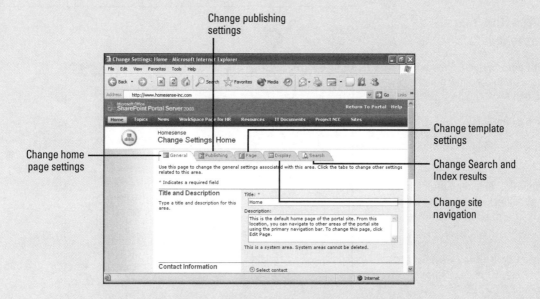

Change home page settings

Change template settings

Change Search and Index results

Change site navigation

Site Settings Page

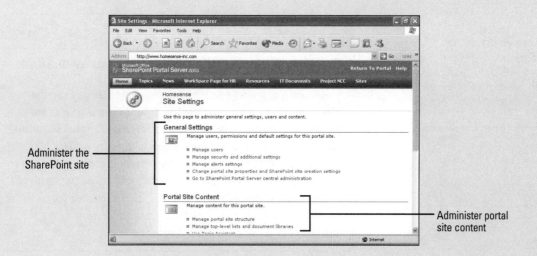

Administer the SharePoint site

Administer portal site content

Creating Sites Using SharePoint Templates

With FrontPage 2003, you can create a new SharePoint site using a SharePoint template. The SharePoint Web Site template creates a standard SharePoint Team Site with a team events calendar, library for shared documents, task list, and contact list. After you create the SharePoint site, you can use Site Settings to modify the initial setup.

Create a Web Site from a SharePoint Template

1. In FrontPage, click the New button list arrow on the Standard toolbar, and then click Web Site.

2. Click the General tab.

3. Click the SharePoint Web Site icon.

4. Enter the URL (including the path to a new folder) where you want the new SharePoint Team Site to reside.

   IMPORTANT *The URL must be a Web server running Windows SharePoint Services.*

5. Click OK.

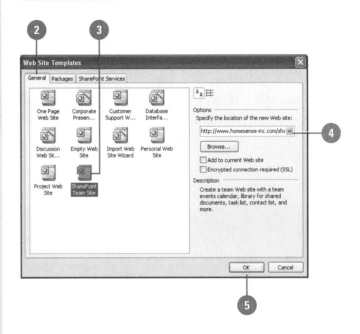

Did You Know?

You need to turn on support for SharePoint Services. Click the Tools menu, click Page Options, click Authoring tab, select the SharePoint Services check box, and then click OK.

For Your Information

Creating Windows SharePoint Services Web Sites

SharePoint also comes with templates that reside on the SharePoint Web server. You can use FrontPage to access these templates and create Web sites on the server. These templates include Team Site, Blank Site, Document Workspace, Basic Meeting Workspace, Blank Meeting Workspace, and Decision Meeting Workspace. To create a Web site on SharePoint Services, click the New button list arrow on the Standard toolbar, click the SharePoint Services tab, click a template icon, specify the URL, and then click OK. FrontPage passes the command to the SharePoint server to perform the command.

Creating Sites Using SharePoint Packages ▶

In addition to creating a SharePoint Web site using a template, you can also add SharePoint Web applications to create a related Web site using SharePoint package templates. The package templates allows you to create an issue tracking site with management tools, a news and reviews site with discussions and voting, and a Web log site with discussions, favorite links and a log search. A package template is different than a normal template; it consists of a single file and creates libraries, lists, and other database objects in addition to the ordinary Web content.

Create a Site from a SharePoint Package

1. In FrontPage, click the New button list arrow on the Standard toolbar, and then click Web Site.

2. Click the Packages tab.

3. Click the SharePoint package icon you want.

4. Enter the URL (including the path to a new folder) where you want the new SharePoint Team Site to reside.

   IMPORTANT *The URL must be a Web server running Windows SharePoint Services.*

5. Click OK.

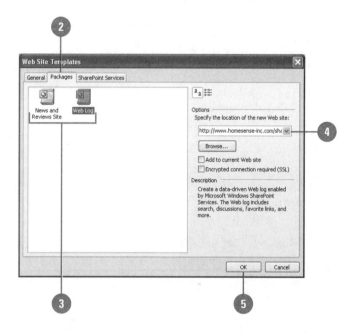

For Your Information

Exporting and Importing Web Packages

FrontPage enables you to export and import Web packages from Microsoft Windows SharePoint Services Web sites. Packages can export and import not only Web pages and related files, such as pictures and style sheets, but also SharePoint lists, and other related objects. Click the Tools menu, point to Packages, and then click Import or Export. In the Import Web Packages dialog box, specify the folder location in the destination box, clear the check boxes with the items you don't want and then click Import. In the Export Web Packages dialog boxes, use the Add or Remove buttons to add or remove files. Click Hide Dependencies or Show Dependencies, set properties if necessary, and then click OK.

Storing Documents in the Library

A SharePoint **Document Library** is a central depository of files you can share with company employees, team members and permissible members with access. Within the Document Library you can create a list of common documents for a project, documented procedures, and company wide documents for departments such as human resources or finance. When you first install SharePoint 2003, the Web site comes with a built-in document library called **shared documents**. This is located on the Quick Launch bar as well as on the Documents And Lists page.

Upload a Document

1. Log into your SharePoint server with your domain account and password.

2. On the main Home page, click Create Manage Content under the Actions Sidebar.

3. On the Documents And Lists page, click Create.

4. Click Document Library, and then type the name of the document library for creating a new page.

5. Click Upload Document.

6. Type the location of the document, or click Browse to search for the document on your system.

7. Type the name of the owner and a brief description.

8. Select the status of the document, and then click Save.

9. Click the Save And Close button.

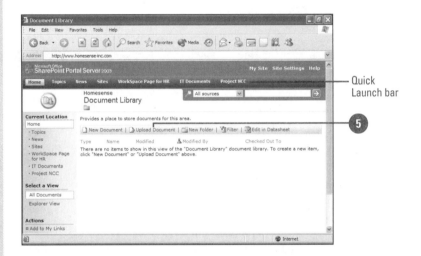

Quick Launch bar

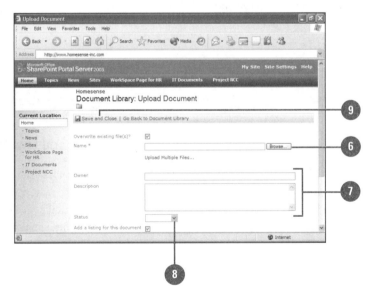

Did You Know?

You can check documents in and out. SharePoint's document management system ensures that only one person at a time can access a file. You can check out a document by clicking the Content menu in the Document Library, and then clicking Check Out.

Viewing Team Members

After you have setup a portal page, you need to specify a user access list to the site. Specifying a user access list controls who can access the site, as well as who has administrative privileges. With integration to Microsoft Active Directory, users can be managed with the same groups as your domain. The access will allow your users to perform a specific action in your site by assigning them to the appropriate groups.

Add New Members to the Site

1. Log into your SharePoint server with your domain account and password.

2. On the main Home page, click Give User Access To The Portal.

3. On the Manage Users page, click Add Users.

4. Type the name of their domain account.

5. Click the type of permissions you want to give this user:

   ◆ **Reader.** Gives the user read-only access to the portal site.

   ◆ **Contributor.** Gives the user write access to the document libraries and lists.

   ◆ **Web Designer.** Gives the user the ability to create lists and document libraries and customize the overall look and feel of the site.

   ◆ **Administrator.** Gives the user full access of the portal site.

   ◆ **Content Manager.** Gives the user the ability to manage lists, libraries, sites and moderate the discussions.

   ◆ **Member.** Gives the user the ability to personalize the portal site content and create lists.

6. Click Next, fill out any additional information, and then click Finish.

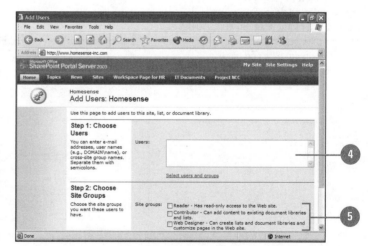

Setting Up Alerts

An Alert notifies you when there is new information which has been changed on the portal site. You can customize your areas of interests and define when you want to be notified after the site has been updated. You can define an alert to track new matches to a search query, changes to the site page, or a new site addition.

Create Your E-Mail Alert

1. Log into your SharePoint server with your domain account and password.

2. In a Portal Site, click Alert Me.

3. Define your delivery options, and then click Next.

4. Click Advanced Options if you want to set up filters.

5. Click OK.

Did You Know?

You can use the following filter categories to be alerted with: Search queries, document and listings, areas, new listings, sites added to the site directory, sharepoint lists and libraries, list items, portal site users, and backward compatible document library folders.

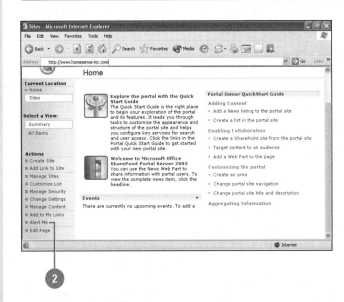

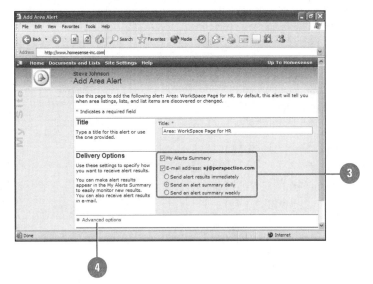

Assigning Project Tasks

Assigning a project task is another way you can use SharePoint to collaborate on the site. By creating a task, you can manage your team with status updates. You can also provide a central way to manage the effectiveness of a project. Since this is a Web based system, everyone can access this with a simple Web browser.

Add a Task Item to Your Site

1. Log into your SharePoint server with your domain account and password.

2. On the main home page, click Create Manage Content under the Actions Sidebar.

3. Click Create, and then click Tasks.

4. Type the name of the task, add in an optional description, click Yes, if you want to add the task to the menu bar, and then click Create.

5. Click New Item.

6. Type the title, set the priority, status, and completion percentage, assign your resource, add a description, and then set your due date.

7. Click the Save And Close button.

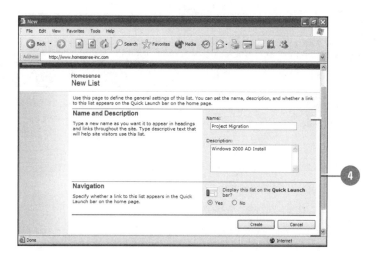

Did You Know?

You can use the Upload button to add an attachment. A general rule of thumb would be to keep your attachments under 1 MB, however, unless your administrator has set rights on your site, you are free to upload as much as you want.

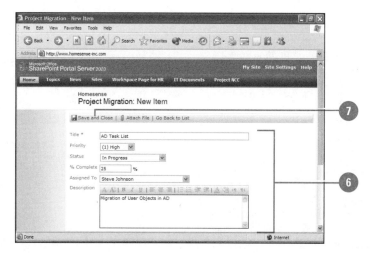

Creating an Event

Creating an event allows you to send out notices on upcoming meetings, deadlines, and other important events. This is helpful if you need to send out information to a wide range of people or in a project you are working on. If you are looking to set up a meeting to a large group of people, you may want to set up an event which is seen by everyone who logs in.

Setup New Events

1. Log into your SharePoint server with your domain account and password.

2. On the main Home page, click Create Manage Content under the Actions Sidebar.

3. Click Create, and then click Events.

4. Type the name of the event, add in an optional description, click Yes, if you want to add the event to the menu bar, and then click Create.

5. Click New Item.

6. Type the event title, select a begin and end event time, a description, the location, and then select an recurrence option.

7. Click the Save And Close button.

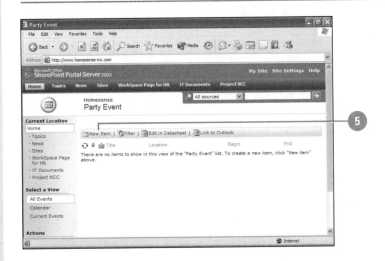

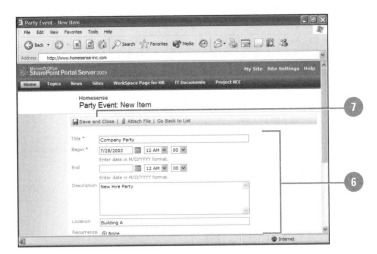

Link to Events in Outlook

① On the Events page, click Link To Outlook.

② If a security dialog box appears asking for your approval prior to adding a folder, click Yes.

You will be prompted to type in the credentials of your user account.

③ Type in your Domain User credentials and password, and then click OK.

④ Click Other Calendars to view your SharePoint calendar.

Did You Know?

You will not be able to change the events in your SharePoint calendar folder within Outlook 2003. You will only have read access rights within Outlook 2003. To change the SharePoint calendar information, return to your SharePoint Site, and then modify the information under your Events Site.

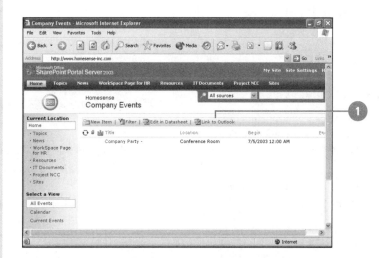

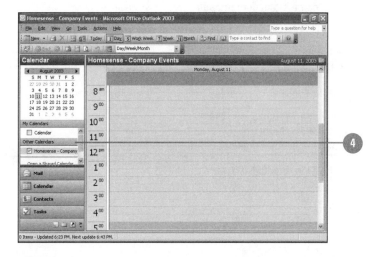

Creating Contacts

You can create a contact list when you want to have a central database of your team information. You will have the ability to manage information about sales contacts, vendors, and employees that your team has involvement with.

Create a Contact List

1. Log into your SharePoint server with your domain account and password.

2. On the main Home page, click Create Manage Content under the Actions Sidebar.

3. Click Create, and then click Contacts.

4. Type the name of the contact, add an optional description, click Yes, if you want to add the contacts list to the menu bar, and then click Create.

5. Click New Item.

6. Type the contact name, and then add in all the appropriate information on your contact.

7. Click the Save And Close button.

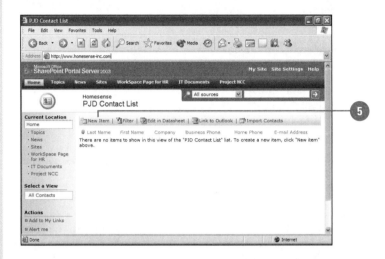

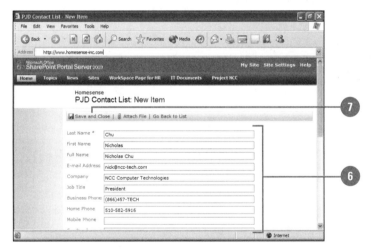

Link to Contacts in Outlook

1. On the Contacts page, click Link To Outlook.

2. If a security dialog box appears asking for your approval prior to adding a folder, click Yes.

   You will be prompted to type in the credentials of your user account.

3. Type your Domain User credentials and password, and then click OK.

4. Click Other Contacts to view your SharePoint contacts.

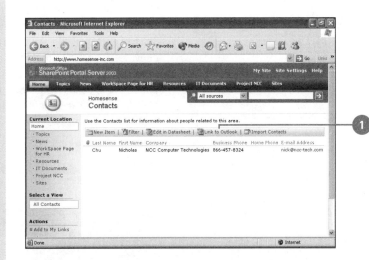

Did You Know?

You will not be able to change the contact information in your SharePoint contacts folder within Outlook 2003. You will only have read access rights within Outlook 2003. To change the SharePoint contacts information, return to your SharePoint Site, and then modify the information under your Contacts Site.

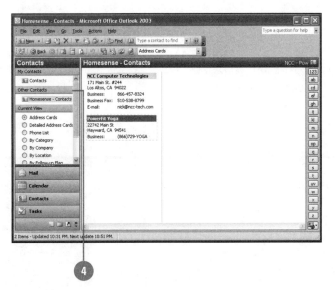

Holding Web Discussions

Web discussions are threaded discussions which allow users to collaborate together in a Web environment. Users can add and view discussion items, add in documents during the discussion and carry on conversations. Since the discussions are entered into a different area than the shared document, users can modify the document without effecting the collaborative discussion. Users can add changes to read-only documents and allow multiple users to create and edit discussion items simultaneously.

Hold a Web Discussion

1. Log into your SharePoint server with your domain account and password.

2. On the main Home page, click Create Manage Content under the Actions Sidebar.

3. Click Create, and then click Discussion Boards.

4. Type the name of the Discussion Board, add an optional description, click Yes, if you want to add this to the menu bar, and then click Create.

5. Click New Discussion.

6. Type the subject name, and then add in all the appropriate information on your discussion.

7. Click the Save And Close button.

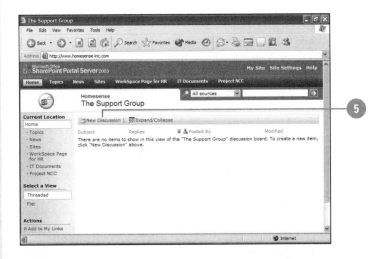

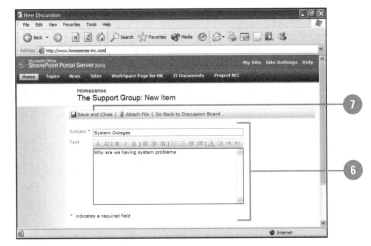

Working with Shared Workspace

Using Shared Workspace icons allow you to connect to your SharePoint Server in an Office 2003 program: Word, Excel and PowerPoint. Each icon displays different information on your document. Users can view the status of a document, see the availability of a document, display properties of a document, and list additional resources, folders, and access rights of a document. You can also show the current tasks which are assigned for your document, display the online team members of your group, and display the workspace information.

13

Use Shared Workspace in an Office 2003 Program

1. Log into your SharePoint server with your domain account and password.

2. In an Office 2003 program (Word, Excel and PowerPoint), click on the Tools menu, and then click Shared Workspace.

   If you open Shared Workspace for the first time you may be prompted to create a new workspace area.

3. Use the Shared Workspace Navigation bar tools.

   ◆ **Status.** Displays the checked-in/checked-out status of your current document.

   ◆ **Members**. Shows you who is online from your Team Members Group.

   ◆ **Tasks**. Shows you the current tasks assigned for this current document and the completion status.

   ◆ **Documents**. Displays the name and workspace of the selected document.

   ◆ **Links**. Displays additional resources, folders, and lists the access of files.

   ◆ **Document Info**. Displays the author of the document and the properties of the document.

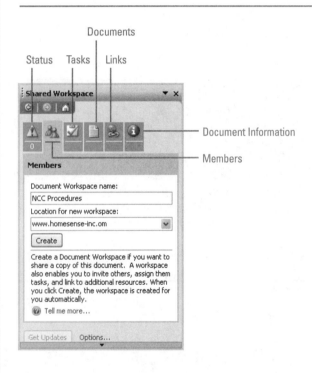

Documents

Status   Tasks   Links

Document Information

Members

Installing Windows 2003 and SharePoint Server 2003

In order for you to install the new version of SharePoint, you must Install Windows 2003 Server. Windows 2003 Server uses the new .NET Architecture Internet Information Server (IIS) 6.0, Microsoft SMTP (Simple Mail Transport Protocol) Service and Microsoft SQL Server 2000 Desktop Engine (MSDE 2000) or Microsoft SQL Server 2000 Enterprise or Standard Edition (64-bit), with Microsoft SQL Server 2000 SP3 or later.

Install SharePoint server

Ask for help before installing

Read the pre-install documents

Install database and additional components

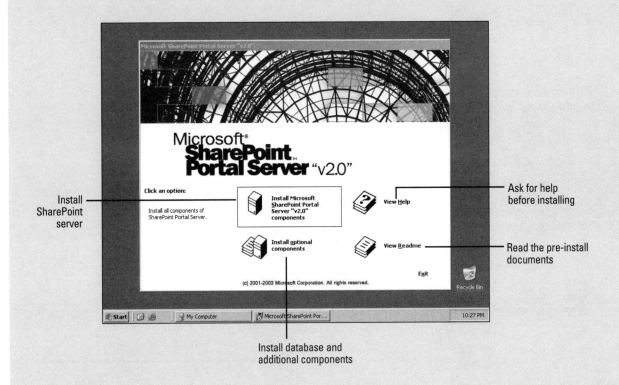

Customizing FrontPage

Introduction

Once you've become familiar with Microsoft Office FrontPage 2003 and all the features it contains, you might want to customize the way you work with FrontPage. You can change the way FrontPage starts up and whether it warns you about certain actions that you cannot undo. You can also configure FrontPage to associate editors on your computer with a specific file type you want to use, which makes it easy to open and work and with the files, or specify options to determine what information appears in reports.

You can set general options to specify when files are considered "Recent" or "Older", or the download time that qualifies a Web page for inclusion in the Slow Pages report. You can also set the connection speed, display row and column gridlines when viewing reports, and the maximum number of months shown in usage reports.

You can change the configuration of the menus and toolbars that you use. You can also create your own toolbar or menu for just the commands that you use when creating and formatting your pages. The Language bar performs a variety of functions. The Language bar allows you to control FrontPage with your voice, or execute various commands without having to use the keyboard. FrontPage will need to be trained to your voice in order to perform the voice recognition. You can also dictate text directly into your documents with the speech recognition feature. Or maybe, you want to add handwritten notes to a document.

Macros can simplify common repetitive tasks that you use regularly in FrontPage. Macros can even reside on a FrontPage toolbar for easy access. If a macro has a problem executing a task, FrontPage can help you debug, or fix the error in your macro.

Customizing General Options

You can customize several settings in the FrontPage work environment to suit the way you like to work. You can customize the way FrontPage starts up and whether it warns you about certain actions that you cannot undo. For example, one option automatically opens the last Web site you worked on when you start FrontPage. Other options check if FrontPage is the default editor for all Web pages or if Office is the default editor for Web pages created in Office programs.

Change General Options

1. Click the Tools menu, and then click Options.

2. Click the General tab.

3. Select the startup and general options you want. Some of the common options include:

   ◆ **Startup Task Pane.** Displays the Getting Started task pane every time you open FrontPage.

   ◆ **Open Last Web Site Automatically When FrontPage Starts.** Opens the Web site you most recently worked on.

   ◆ **Check If Office Is The Default Editor For Pages Created In Office.** Verifies file type associations for Office.

   ◆ **Check If FrontPage Is The Default Editor For Pages.** Verifies FrontPage is the standard editor for Web pages.

   ◆ **Warn Before Applying Themes To All Pages In A Web.** Displays a confirmation dialog box before you can apply a theme, which you cannot undo.

4. To change proxy firewall settings for the Internet, click Proxy Settings.

5. Click OK.

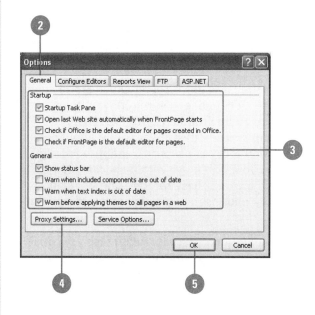

Configuring External Editors

You can configure FrontPage to associate any editor on your computer with any file type you want to use, which makes it easy to open and work with files. You can associate several editors with a file type. However, one of the editors is the default. FrontPage starts the default editor when you double-click the file in the Folder List, Folders view, and other file locations, or when you right-click the file and choose Open from the shortcut menu.

Configure External Editors

1. Click the Tools menu, and then click Options.

2. Click the Configure Editors tab.

3. To add a new extension, click the New Extension button, type the extension, select the editor you want to use, and then click OK.

4. To add a new editor, click the New Editor button, select the editor you want to use (if necessary, click Browse for more), and then click OK.

5. To add, rename, or remove an existing extension, select the extension, click the Modify Extension button, type the changes you want, and then click OK.

6. To set a default editor, select the extension, select the editor you want as the default, and then click Make Default.

7. Click OK.

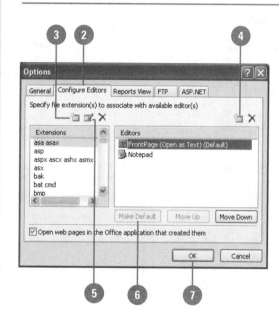

Customizing Reports View

You can customize the way information appears in Reports view by changing settings on the Reports View tab in the Options dialog box. You can set general options to specify when files are considered "Recent" or "Older", or the download time that qualifies a Web page for inclusion in the Slow Pages report. You can also set the connection speed, display row and column gridlines when viewing reports, and the maximum number of months shown in usage reports.

Customize Reports View

① Click the Tools menu, and then click Options.

② Click the Reports View tab.

③ Select the general and usage options you want. Some of the common options include:

◆ **"Recent" File Are Less Than *X* Days Old.** Determines which files appear in the Recently Added Files report.

◆ **"Older" Files Are More Than *X* Days Old.** Determines which files appear in the Older Files report.

◆ **Slow Pages Take As Least X Seconds To Download.** Determines whether a Web page appears in the Slow Pages report.

◆ **Number Of Months Shown.** Determines the maximum number of months shown in usage reports.

④ To display a grid, select the Display Gridlines When Viewing Reports check box.

⑤ Click OK.

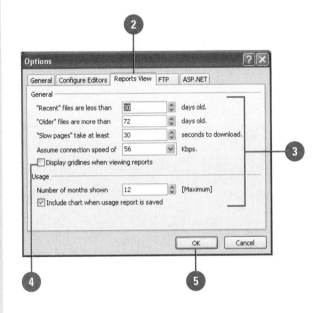

Customizing ASP Options

FrontPage allows you configure two settings applicable to Microsoft ASP.NET pages in your Web site. You can specify the folder that contains compiled versions of ASP.NET user controls available to the entire Web server and to the current Web site only. You can specify a folder or leave it blank to use the system default location.

Customize ASP Options

① Click the Tools menu, and then click Options.

② Click the ASP.NET tab.

③ Specify the default location for ASP.NET Control Assemblies (use Browse if necessary).

④ Specify the location for ASP.NET Control Assemblies For Pages In The Current Web Site (use Browse if necessary).

⑤ Click OK.

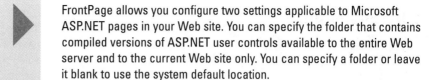

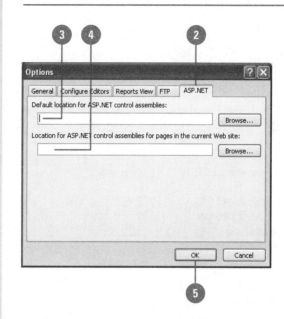

Did You Know?

You can customize FTP transfer options for text files. If you transfer text files between a PC and Unix, click the FTP tab in the Options dialog box, specify the extensions you want to be treated as text files, and then click OK.

14

Customizing the Menu Bar

You can customize the existing FrontPage menu bar by adding buttons, commands, and macros that you use frequently. Adding items to the menu bar is a great way to have easy access to features without adding more buttons or toolbars. The ability to drag features from different parts of the program window makes it easy to add items to the menu bar. Imagine, having a menu with all of your most commonly used formatting, sorting, or printing commands.

Customize the Menu Bar

1 Click the Tools menu, and then click Customize.

2 Click the Commands tab.

3 Select a category.

4 To add a command, drag the command to the appropriate place on the menu you want to modify. A solid horizontal line appears below the place where the new menu command will be placed.

5 To remove a command, drag the menu command you want to remove to an empty area in the workspace.

6 Click Close.

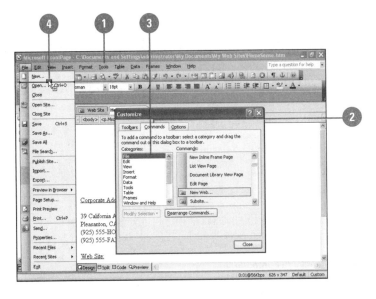

Did You Know?

You can assign an accelerator key to a menu. An accelerator key is the key you press to display a menu or run a menu command. For example, the accelerator key for the File menu is "F." To add an accelerator key to a menu item, type an ampersand (&) before the letter that will be the accelerator key. For example, enter the menu name "&New Menu" to create the menu entry New Menu with the accelerator key "N."

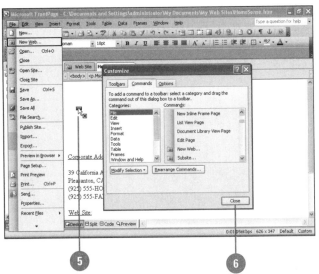

Create a New Menu

1 Click the Tools menu, click Customize, and then click the Commands tab.

2 Click New Menu in the Categories box.

3 Drag New Menu from the Commands list to an empty spot on the menu bar.

4 Click Close.

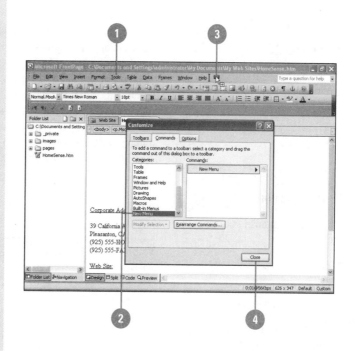

Name a New Menu

1 Click the Tools menu, and then click Customize.

2 Click New Menu on the menu bar.

3 Click Modify Selection.

4 Click the Name box, and then type a new name.

5 Press Enter.

6 Click Close.

Did You Know?

You can copy a command to toolbars and menus. Copy commands from other menus or toolbars to new menus and toolbars by pressing and holding Ctrl as you drag the new command.

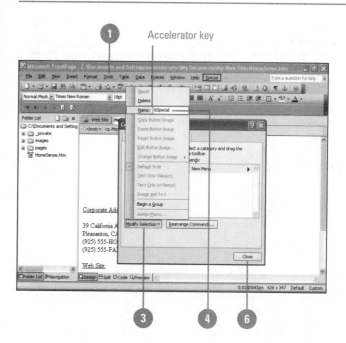

Accelerator key

Adding and Removing Toolbar Buttons

Each toolbar initially appears in a default configuration, but many toolbars actually contain many more commands than are displayed. When monitors are set to low resolution, sometimes not all toolbar buttons are visible. You can modify FrontPage's toolbars so that they display only the buttons you want. For example, you can add buttons to a toolbar for commands you frequently use, or you can remove buttons from toolbars that have too many. You can also use the Add Or Remove command on the Toolbar Options menu to quickly show or hide buttons on a toolbar. If a button doesn't appear on the button list for a toolbar, you can add it. If you no longer need a button on the button list, you can remove it.

Show or Hide a Toolbar Button

1. Click the Toolbar Options list arrow on the toolbar.

2. Point to Add Or Remove Buttons.

3. Click to select or clear the check box next to the button you want to show or hide.

4. Click outside the toolbar to deselect it.

Did You Know?

You can use the Customize dialog box to show and hide toolbars. Click the Tools menu, click Customize, click the Toolbars tab, select or clear the check box next to the toolbar name you want to show or hide, and then click Close.

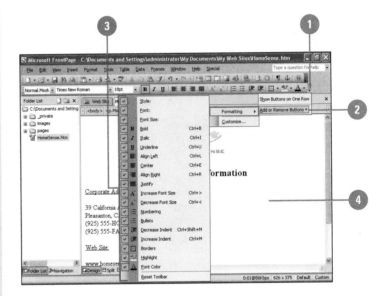

Add or Remove a Toolbar Button

1. Click the Tools menu, and then click Customize.

2. Click the Commands tab.

3. Click the category containing the toolbar button you want to add.

4. Drag a command from the Commands tab to the toolbar to add a button, or drag a button off a toolbar to a blank area to remove it.

5. Click Close.

See Also

See "Changing Menu and Toolbar Options" on page 353 for information on changing general options for menus and toolbars.

Did You Know?

The Customize dialog box uses a special operating mode. When you use the Customize dialog box, menus and toolbars don't act in the normal way. The special mode allows you to drag-and-drop items on menus and toolbars.

A solid vertical line appears to the right of where the new button will be inserted.

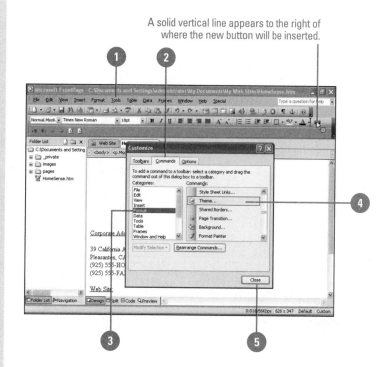

14

Customizing a Toolbar

You can create your own toolbars to increase your efficiency. You might, for example, create a toolbar that contains formatting and other features that you use most often when you are performing a particular task, such as editing Web pages. This will give you a greater workspace, since you will not have to have all the various toolbars up at once. Using one toolbar will help you achieve this.

Create a Custom Toolbar

1. Click the Tools menu, and then click Customize.

2. Click the Toolbars tab.

3. Click New.

4. Type a name for the new toolbar.

5. Click OK.

6. Add buttons to the new toolbar by dragging commands found on the Commands tab.

7. Click Close.

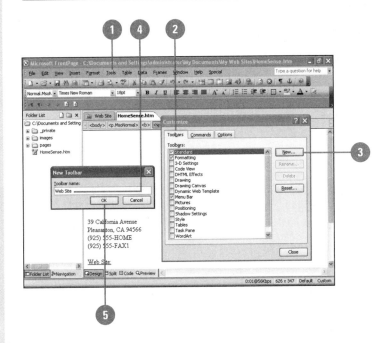

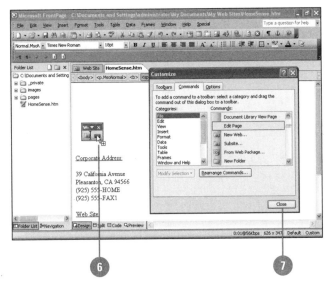

Delete a Custom Toolbar

1. Click the Tools menu, and then click Customize.

2. Click the Toolbars tab.

3. Click the toolbar name you want to delete.

4. Click Delete.

5. Click Close.

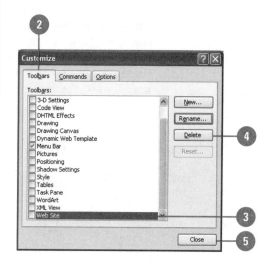

Rename a Custom Toolbar

1. Click the Tools menu, and then click Customize.

2. Click the Toolbars tab.

3. Click the toolbar name you want to rename.

4. Click Rename.

5. Type a name for the toolbar.

6. Click OK.

7. Click Close.

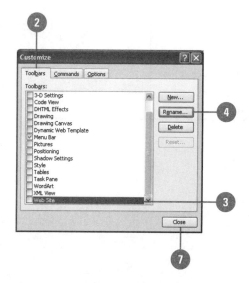

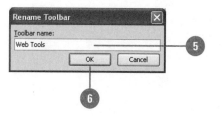

Editing Toolbar Buttons and Menu Entries

FrontPage includes tools that allow you to edit toolbar buttons and menu entries. You can specify whether the button or menu item will display text, an image, or both text and an image. If you choose to display an image, you can edit the image, copy it from another button or use one of FrontPage's predefined images. You can also use the Customize dialog box to makes these and other changes to your buttons and menus.

Edit a Button or Menu Entry

1 Click the Tools menu, and then click Customize.

2 Select the button on the toolbar or command on the menu you want to edit.

3 Click Modify Selection.

4 Choose the commands that will modify the selection in the way you prefer.

◆ Click Copy Button Image to copy the button image.

◆ Click Paste Button Image to paste the button image.

◆ Click Reset Button Image to reset the selected item to its default image.

◆ Click Edit Button Image to edit the button image.

◆ Click Change Button Image to select from a group of predefined images, as shown.

◆ Click Image And Text to paste a button image into the selected item.

◆ Click Begin A Group to begin a group of menu items, separated by horizontal lines.

5 Click Close.

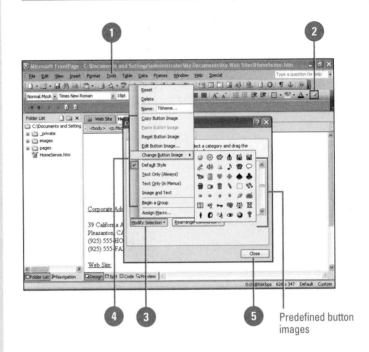

Predefined button images

Changing Menu and Toolbar Options

In addition to creating, adding, or removing menu command and toolbar buttons, you can also use the Customize dialog box to make global changes to menus and toolbars to personalize the FrontPage interface. The Options tab allows you to reset menu and toolbar changes, show the Standard and Formatting toolbars on one row to save space, and always show full menus so you don't have to wait or click the expand arrow. If you do not want to view ScreenTips, you can turn them off.

Change Menu and Toolbar Options

1 Click the Tools menu, and then click Customize.

2 Click Options tab.

3 Select the general options you want. Some of the common options include:

♦ **Show Standard And Formatting Toolbars On Two Rows**. Displays the Standard and Formatting toolbars on two rows.

♦ **Always Show Full Menus**. Displays the full contents of a menu as soon as you open the menu.

♦ **List Font Names In Their Font**. Displays fonts in the Font menu using the actual font.

♦ **Show ScreenTips On Toolbars**. Displays descriptive text when you move the pointer over a toolbar button.

♦ **Show Shortcut Keys In ScreenTips**. Displays the shortcut key for a button along with the ScreenTip.

4 To reset personalized menus and toolbars to the default, click Reset Menu And Toolbar Usage Data.

5 Click Close.

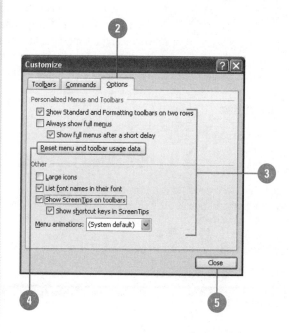

14

Controlling FrontPage with Your Voice

The Office Language bar allows you to dictate text directly into your document and also to control buttons, menus, and toolbar functions by using the Voice Command option. When you first install an Office program, the Language bar appears at the top of your screen. If you are using English as the default language, the toolbar is denoted by the letters EN. (Other languages have appropriate abbreviations as well.) Before you can use speech recognition, you need to install it first. You can choose the Speech command on the Tools menu in FrontPage, or you can use Add Or Remove Programs in the Control Panel to change the Office FrontPage 2003 installation. In Setup, look under Office Shared Features. Before you can use the Language bar for either dictation or voice commands, you need to connect a microphone to your computer, and you must train your computer to your voice using the Speech Recognition Wizard.

Work with the Language Bar

- **Open.** Right-click a blank area on the taskbar, point to Toolbars, and then click Language Bar.

- **Minimize.** Right-click the Language bar, and then click Minimize. The Language bar docks in the taskbar at the bottom right of the screen, near the system clock.

- **Restore.** Right-click the Language bar, and then click Restore The Language Bar.

- **Display or hide option buttons.** Click the Options button (the list arrow at the right end of the toolbar), and then click an option to display or hide.

- **Change speech properties.** Click the Speech Tools button, and then click Options.

- **Change Language Bar properties.** Click the Options button (the list arrow at the right end of the toolbar), and then click Settings.

Train Your Computer to Your Voice

① Click the Speech Tools button on the Language bar, and then click Training.

② Click Next, read the instructions, ensure you are in a quiet place, and then click Next again.

③ Read the sentence provided to automatically set the proper volume of the microphone, and then click Next.

④ Read the text with hard consonants to help determine whether or not the microphone is positioned too closely to your mouth. Repeat the process until you have a clear, distinct audio playback, and then click Next.

⑤ After you are reminded to ensure that your environment is suitable for recording again, read the instructions, and then click Next.

⑥ Read the following series of dialog boxes. The words on the screen are highlighted as the computer recognizes them. As each dialog box is completed, the program will automatically move to the next one, and the process meter will update accordingly.

⑦ At the end of the training session, click Finish and your voice profile is updated and will be saved automatically.

Did You Know?

You can create additional speech profiles. Click the Speech Tools button on the Language bar, click Options, click New, and then follow the Speech Profile Wizard instructions.

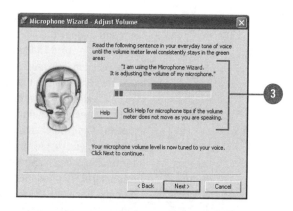

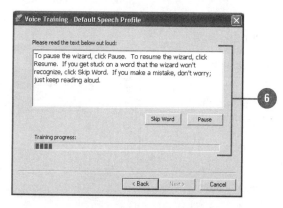

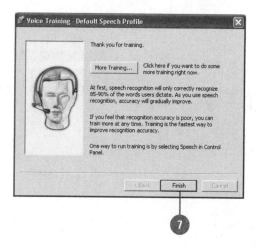

14

Executing Voice Commands

The two modes, Dictation and Voice Command, are mutually exclusive of one another. You do not want the word File typed, for example, when you are trying to open the File menu. Neither do you want the menu to open instead of the word File being typed when you are in the middle of a sentence. As such, you must manually click either mode on the Language bar to switch between them. The Voice Command mode allows you to talk your way through any sequence of menus or toolbar commands, simply by reading aloud the appropriate text instead of clicking it. For example, if you wanted to preview the current page in a browser you are working on, you would simply say File, Preview In Browser, Microsoft Internet Explorer 6.0 (without saying the commas between the words as written here). You need not worry about remembering every command sequence because as you say each word in the sequence, the corresponding menu or submenu appears onscreen for your reference.

Execute Voice Commands

① If necessary, display the Language bar.

② Click the Microphone button on the Language bar. The toolbar expands so that the Voice Command button becomes available on the toolbar.

③ Click the Voice Command button to shift into that mode.

④ Work with your Office document normally. When you are ready to issue a command, simply speak the sequence just as you would click through it if you were using the menus or toolbar normally (i.e. with the mouse or via keyboard shortcuts).

Say "File" to display the menu.

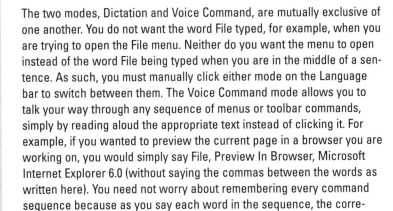
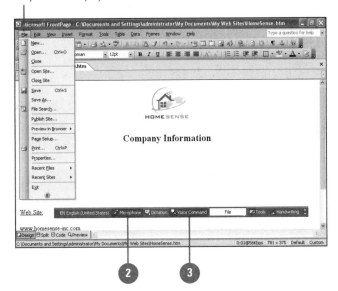

Did You Know?

You can have text read back to you. Display the Speak Text button on the Language bar. Select the text you want read back to you, and then click Speak Text.

Dictating Text

Dictating the text of a Web page using Office speech recognition functions may be easier for some users than typing, but don't think that it is an entirely hands free operation. For example, you must manually click the Voice Command button when you want to format anything that has been input, and then click again on Dictation to resume inputting text. Additionally, the Dictation function is not going to be 100% accurate, so you will need to clean up mistakes (such as inputting the word *Noir* when you say *or*) when they occur. Finally, although you can say punctuation marks, such as comma and period, to have them accurately reflected in the page, all periods are followed by double spaces (which may not be consistent with the page formatting you want between sentences) and issues of capitalization remain as well. Nevertheless, it is fun and freeing to be able to get the first draft of any document on paper simply by speaking it.

14

Dictate Text

1. If necessary, display the Language bar.

2. Click the Microphone button on the Language bar. The toolbar expands so that the Dictation button becomes available on the toolbar.

3. Click to position the insertion point inside the page where you want the dictated text to appear, and then begin speaking normally into your microphone. As you speak, the words will appear on the page.

4. When you have finished dictating your text, click the Microphone button again to make the speech recognition functions inactive.

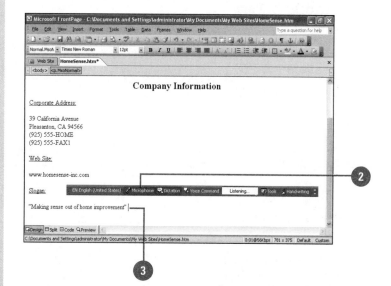

Recognizing Handwriting

Although entering information into a Web page through the keyboard is fast and efficient, you may find that you need to enter information in handwritten form. Office 2003 provides handwriting recognition to help you convert handwriting into text. Before you can insert handwritten text into a page, you need to have a mouse, a third party electronic stylus, an ink device, or a handwriting tablet, such as Tablet PC, attached to your computer. Although you can use the mouse, for best results you should use a handwriting input device. When you insert handwritten text into a page that already contains typed text, the handwritten text is converted to typed text and then inserted in line with the existing text at the point of the cursor. The program recognizes the handwriting when there is enough text for it to do so, when you reach the end of the line, or if you pause for approximately two seconds. In addition, the converted text will take on the same typeface attributes as the existing text.

Insert Handwritten Text into a Web Page

1 If necessary, display the Language bar.

2 Click the Handwriting button on the Language bar, and then click Write Anywhere.

3 Move the mouse over a blank area of your page, and then write your text.

After recognition, the characters that you write appear as text in the document.

4 Use the additional handwriting tools to move the cursor, change handwriting modes, and correct text.

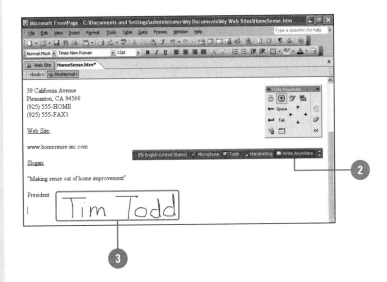

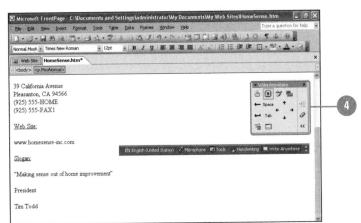

Insert Handwritten Text on a Writing Pad

1️⃣ If necessary, display the Language bar.

2️⃣ Click the Handwriting button on the Language bar, and then click Writing Pad.

3️⃣ Move the cursor over the writing area of the Writing Pad dialog box. (The cursor turns into a pen.)

4️⃣ Write your text with the pen.

After recognition, the characters that you write appear in the document.

5️⃣ Use the additional handwriting tools to move the cursor, change handwriting modes, and correct text.

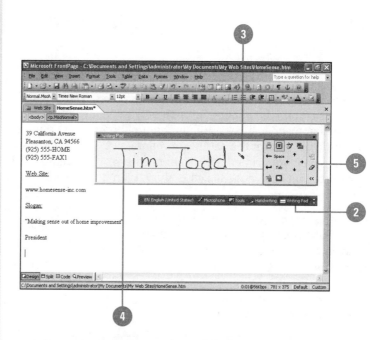

14

For Your Information

Using Additional Handwriting Tools

When you click the Handwriting button on the Language bar and then click the Writing Pad or Write Anywhere option, a dialog box opens on your screen with another toolbar. It has the same options that are available through the Handwriting button on the Language bar. In addition, the toolbar has the following buttons: Ink, Text, Backspace, Space, directional cursors, Enter, Tab, Recognize Now, and Write Anywhere. You use these buttons to control the input.

Understanding How Macros Automate Your Work

To complete many tasks in FrontPage, you need to execute a series of commands and actions. If you often need to complete the same task, you'll find yourself repeatedly taking the same series of steps. It can be tiresome to continually repeat the same commands and actions when you can create a mini-program, or macro, that accomplishes all of them with a single command.

When you create a macro, FrontPage stores the list of commands with any name you choose. You can store your macros in Microsoft FrontPage or All Open Projects. Storing your macros in FrontPage makes the macros available to you from any location in FrontPage, even when no project is open.

Once a macro is created, you can make modifications to it, add comments so other users will understand its purpose, and test it to make sure it runs correctly. You can run a macro by choosing the Macro command on the Tools menu, or by using a shortcut key or clicking a toolbar button you've assigned to it. When you click the Tools menu, point to Macro, and then click Macros, the Macro dialog box opens. From this dialog box, you can run, edit, test, or delete any FrontPage macro on your system, or create a new one.

If you have problems with a macro, you can step through the macro one command at a time, known as **debugging**. Once you identify any errors in the macro, you can edit it.

Indicates the project(s) from which you can access the selected macro.

You can create and edit a macro with the Microsoft Visual Basic Editor, which comes with FrontPage. Macro code is written in Microsoft Visual Basic, a programming language.

Each action listed in a macro either performs a step or states what attributes are turned on (true) or off (false). Quotation marks are used to indicate typed text, and the terms **Sub** and **End Sub** are used to indicate the beginning and ending of subroutines, respectively.

Because not everyone wants to read through codes to figure out what a macro does, comments are often included within the code. The comments don't affect the macro; they simply clarify its purpose or actions for a person viewing the code. Comments can be used to help you remember why you took the steps you did, or to help co-workers understand what is going on in the macro and how the macro should be used. A comment always begins with an apostrophe to distinguish it from a command code.

To learn more about macro code, check out Visual Basic titles on the Que Publishing Web site at *www.quepublishing.com.*

These comments tell the name the macro was assigned, when it was created, and its function.

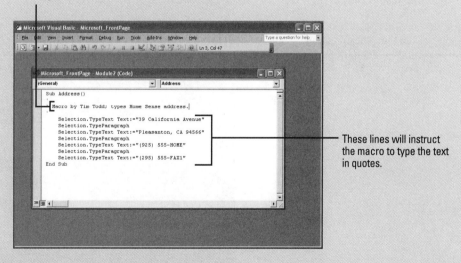

These lines will instruct the macro to type the text in quotes.

Automating Your Work with Macros

Do you often redo many tasks that require the same, sometimes lengthy, series of steps? Rather than repeat the same actions, you can work faster by recording the entire series of keystrokes and commands in a custom command, or **macro**. A macro is a sequence of commands and entries that can be activated collectively by clicking a toolbar button, clicking a menu command, typing a key combination, or clicking the Run command in the Macros dialog box. Macros are a perfect way to speed up routine formatting, combine multiple commands, and automate complex tasks. Any time you want to repeat that series of actions, you can "play," or run, the macro.

Record a Macro

1. Click the Tools menu, point to Macro, and then click Macros.

2. Type a name for the new macro.

3. Click Create.

   The Microsoft Visual Basic window opens, where you can create a macro.

4. Type your macro code.

5. When you're done, click the File menu, and then click Close And Return To Microsoft Office FrontPage.

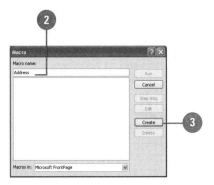

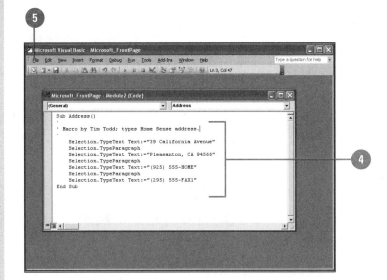

Run a Macro

1. Click the Tools menu, point to Macro, and then click Macros.

2. If necessary, click the Macros In list arrow, and then click the page that contains the macro you want to run.

3. Click the name of the macro you want to run.

4. Click Run.

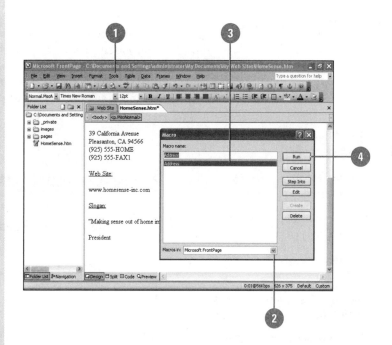

Delete a Macro

1. Click the Tools menu, point to Macro, and then click Macros.

2. Select the macro you want to remove.

3. Click Delete.

4. Click Yes to confirm the deletion.

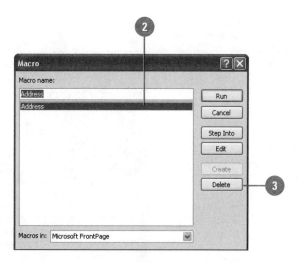

Modifying a Macro

If a macro doesn't work exactly the way you want it to, you can fix the problem. FrontPage allows you to **debug**, or repair, an existing macro so that you can change only the actions that aren't working correctly. When beginning the process, FrontPage will step through each of the actions that you supplied when you created the macro. Look carefully for any mistakes, and then correct as necessary.

Debug a Macro Using Step Mode

1. Click the Tools menu, point to Macro, and then click Macros.

2. Click the name of the macro you want to debug.

3. Click Step Into.

   The Microsoft Visual Basic window opens, where you can edit your macro.

4. Click the Debug menu, and then click Step Into to proceed through each action.

5. When you're done, click the File menu, and then click Close And Return to Microsoft Office FrontPage.

6. Click OK to stop the debugger.

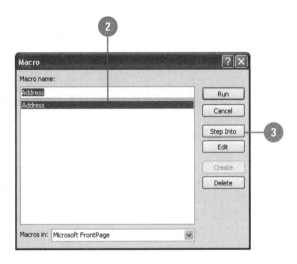

Module sheet

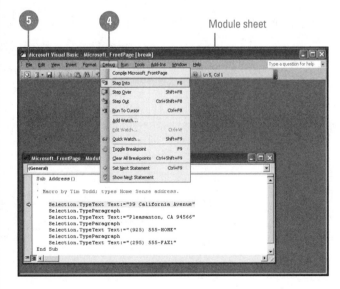

New! Features

Microsoft Office FrontPage 2003

Microsoft Office FrontPage 2003 is the Web site creation and management program that gives you the features that help you to build more powerful Web sites.

Designing your Web site

FrontPage 2003 provides an enhanced design environment, new layout and design tools, templates, and improved themes - all created to help you realize your Web site vision without any knowledge of HTML.

- **Larger design area (p. 7)**   Create Web sites in a larger work area that reduces the need to scroll and makes site design easier. FrontPage now uses task panes to centralize all of the Web design features and provides a Web Site tab for managing your site. The Views bar in previous versions is replaced with the Web Site tab and a much smaller set of tabs that appear below the main editing window. FrontPage also added new toolbars and task panes.

- **Themes (p. 44-45)**   Apply themes that use cascading style sheets rather than HTML, making to make your files smaller, more transparent, and easier to maintain and modify. Pages with HTML themes applied in previous versions retain their settings in FrontPage 2003.

- **Dynamic Web Templates (p. 72-74)**   Attach a Dynamic Web Template to a set of pages that you want to share the same layout. Protect that layout by specifying which page regions are available to coauthors for editing.

- **Graphics support (p. 114, 142, 343)**   Import images into your Web site using new intuitive user interfaces in FrontPage that enable you to edit images with ease. You have more control over how images are displayed and saved.

- **Tracing image (p. 121)**   Create a mock-up image of a Web page in a graphics program and then use it as a visual guide to create or trace the Web page design in FrontPage. Show or hide the image, set its opacity, and change its position.

- **Interactive Buttons (p. 166-167)**   Add professional-looking buttons to your Web page by selecting them from a list. Choose the font and button color, define a link, and then set the image and text settings for original, hover, and pressed states.

- ◆ **Layers (p. 128-131)** Use layers to position content anywhere on your Web page. You can overlap, nest, and show or hide layers on a page. Layers can contain HTML elements, such as text and graphics.

- ◆ **Support for Macromedia Flash (p. 150-151)** Enhance and update your FrontPage Web site by adding Macromedia Flash-based content - including movies, audio-enhanced animations, and previously recorded presentations or courses. Set options for automatic playback, such as playing a short animation one time when the site visitor first loads the page or looping the content to play continuously.

- ◆ **Page rulers and layout grid (p. 200)** Precision design and placement is a snap with helpful positioning guides, such as page rulers and the background layout grid. Customize the rulers or the grid by choosing a unit of measurement, line styles and colors, and spacing options.

- ◆ **Layout tables and cells (p. 202-209)** Create a framework for Web page content by using layout tables and cells. Automatically create professional graphic effects, such as rounded corners and shadows. Layout cells can contain text, images, Web Parts, Macromedia Flash-based content, and other elements.

- ◆ **Behaviors** Quickly add interactivity or increased functionality to text, images, or other Web page elements by using scripting-based Behaviors. For example, you can add a Behavior to an image so that when a site visitor moves the pointer over it, a different image appears. You can also view and edit the scripts associated with an element by viewing a list in the Behaviors task pane.

Developing your Web site

FrontPage 2003 provides an enhanced authoring environment, new graphic features, clean HTML, and more control over the code. In addition, its powerful coding tools help you to apply and increase your knowledge of various coding languages and to create interactive scripts.

- ◆ **Split view (p. 34, 53)** Review and edit Web page content in a split-screen format that offers you simultaneous access to the Code and Design views.

- ◆ **Quick Tag tools (p. 53)** Use the Quick Tag Selector to select any tag in your Web page. Use the Quick Tag Editor to insert, wrap, and edit HTML tags.

- ◆ **Typing aids** Speed up the code-writing process by using word-wrap, line numbers, automatic indentation, tag completion, bookmarks, and advanced code selection.

- ◆ **Code snippets** Reuse fragments of code that contain one or more lines of HTML or other code. Use the predefined code snippets or create and save your own.

- ◆ **ASP.NET controls**   Develop Web programs and Web services by using ASP.NET, a set of technologies in the Microsoft .NET Framework. Preview, reposition, and resize ASP.NET controls. IntelliSense support for scripting helps you to hook up, tailor, or even create new ASP.NET intrinsic controls.

- ◆ **Editing non-HTML files**   Edit file types other than HTML directly in FrontPage. Open and edit text files (files with a .txt file name extension), XML files, XSLTs, and files that contain ECMAScript as defined by the specification of the European Computer Manufacturers Association - such as Microsoft JScript or JavaScript (files with a .js file name extension). Text files are formatted as plain text; script files, XML files, and XSLT files are displayed with code formatting applied. When you edit XML and XSLT files, the XML View toolbar provides additional options for formatting code.

- ◆ **IntelliSense**   Reduce errors in your code by using Microsoft IntelliSense® technology in Code view. IntelliSense includes statement completion and shows the parameters available for the code you're writing, just as you would see in Microsoft Visual Studio. IntelliSense is available for HTML, Extensible Stylesheet Language (XSL), ASP.NET, Microsoft Visual Basic Scripting Edition (VBScript), and ECMAScript as defined by the specification of the European Computer Manufacturers Association - such as Microsoft JScript or JavaScript.

Developing a data-driven Web site

FrontPage 2003 enables your Web site to connect with people and information in new ways. Use Microsoft Windows Server 2003 with Microsoft Windows Share-Point Services to connect to, edit, and present live data from a variety of data sources - including Windows SharePoint Services data, XML, Web services, and OLE DB data sources - to build rich, interactive data-driven Web sites in a WYSI-WYG editor.

- ◆ **Web packages (p. 329)**   Package a portion of your Web site based on Windows SharePoint Services into a module that others can add to their sites. Web packages are cabinet files (with .fwp file name extensions) that can contain Web pages, templates, Web components, themes, graphics, style sheets, and other elements. FrontPage ensures that all dependent files are included in the Web package, so the deployed package works seamlessly on new Web sites.

- ◆ **Data Source catalog**   Use the catalog to access data sources that are already part of your Web site - such as Windows SharePoint Services lists or XML files - as well as external data sources, such as OLE DB data sources and Web services or URLs that return XML.

- ◆ **Data View Details**   View the data structure of a data source and walk through individual records by using the Data View Details task pane. Preview the structure and contents of a data source before adding a Data View to a page.

- **Web Part pages and zones** Create sophisticated master-detail data views by adding and connecting Web Parts. Changes to data or formatting in one Web Part can be reflected in others, providing site visitors with an interactive experience.

- **Data View Web Part** Author Data Views on live data by using the Data View Web Part. Data Views are transparent in both Design and Code views, and you can format them by using the standard formatting tools. When you format data in a Data View, FrontPage 2003 creates an Extensible Stylesheet Language Transformation (XSLT) file to apply that formatting to your page. The XSLT is presented inline in the HTML of your page, and you can edit it in Code view or Split view.

- **Customized Data Views** Change the overall look of data - either by manually formatting the data or by applying a prebuilt Data View style. You can apply additional manual formatting after you specify the style.

- **XML support** Use Extensible Markup Language (XML) to complement, rather than replace, your use of HTML. View or edit files, apply standard formatting to the structure of code in XML files, view the XML structure, and create custom displays of XML data on Web pages. For example, you can use FrontPage 2003 to create a Web page that displays data from an XML file, and then you can apply filtering, sorting, and conditional formatting to display the data the way you want.

Publishing your Web site

FrontPage 2003 contains a new publishing user interface, the Remote Web Site view. Using Remote Web Site view, you can publish files and folders to any location on a file system, between local and remote Web sites, an extended server, an FTP or WebDAV server, or you can synchronize a remote Web site with a local Web site.

- **Remote Web Site view (p. 300-301)** Display the files in both the local Web site and the remote Web site by using Remote Web Site view. Icons and descriptive text indicate the status of your files and folders, and the synchronization feature helps ensure that you don't overwrite any files or folders accidentally.

- **Publishing to any location (p. 3, 300-301, 304-305)** Publish entire Web sites and individual files and folders to any location - an extended Web server, a Web server that supports the File Transfer Protocol (FTP) or Web-based Distributed Authoring and Versioning (WebDAV), or a location in your file system.

- **Site-building tools for FTP and WebDAV servers (p. 300-301)** Work with others by using the new FrontPage site-building tools. WebDAV file locking is provided on WebDAV servers. On FTP servers, file locking is supported through the use of .lck files. These files are fully compatible with those used by Macromedia Dreamweaver, so you can work with Dreamweaver users on an FTP server without accidentally overwriting each other's changes.

- **Connecting to remote Web sites (p. 300-301)** Specify connection settings and manage connection types and protocols - including Secure Sockets Layer (SSL) or passive FTP - by using the Remote Web Site Properties dialog box.

Maintaining your Web site

FrontPage 2003 offers new compatibility and HTML tools to help you maintain your site.

- **Browser and resolution reconciliation (p. 66-67)** Target specific browsers or resolutions, or see how your site will look in various combinations of browsers and resolutions - including simultaneous preview your Web site in multiple browsers.

- **Smart find and replace (p. 90-91)** Quickly and accurately search and replace attributes or tags across an entire Web site or on specific pages. Save queries for later use, and share them with other authors. FrontPage includes basic find and replace functionality, as well as a rules engine for HTML searches.

- **Optimized HTML (p. 302-303)** Generate clean HTML code in files and folders either in your local Web site or when you publish pages to your remote Web site. Reduce the size of a page by removing empty tags, white space, redundant tags, unused and empty style definitions, and even certain tags that you specify.

- **Accessibility checking** Use the Accessibility Checker to select the guidelines (including U.S. government Section 508 guidelines) you want to follow in your Web site. Suggestions to improve accessibility are shown in a list, and you can jump back and forth between that list and your site to address the issues.

Troubleshooting

Views and page formats

Web structure

Index

toolbar, 38

working with, 38

.NET Architecture Internet Information Server 6.0, 340

.NET Programmability Support, installing, 4

New Page option button, 238

new pages, adding, 42-43

news, inserting, 262

New task pane

commands, 28

one page Web site, creating, 28

next links, link bars with, 265

No Frames view, 34

NSAPI script as form handler, 298

nudging drawing objects, 183

numbered lists, creating, 86-87

numbering for form fields, 288

O

objects. *See* drawing objects; graphics

ODBC-compliant database, saving form results to, 292

Office Assistant

character, changing, 21

help from, 20-21

Office Clipboard

deleting items from, 85

options, changing, 85

text, working with, 84-85

Office FrontPage Setup Wizard, 4-5

one-celled tables, creating, 214

one page Web site, creating, 29

One Page Web Site template, 30

Open dialog box, 16

search feature in, 17

opening

existing Web page, 16, 28, 32-33

Language bar, 354

recently opened Web page, 16

task panes, 11

optimizing published HTML code, 302-303

option buttons, 10

for forms, 272, 282

outline heading, selecting, 79

Outline view, selecting outline heading/subheading in, 79

ovals, drawing, 180

overlining text, 169

P

package solutions, 28

padding. *See also* cell padding

for tables, 210

page banners, 254-255

editing, 255

formatting, 255

Page Options dialog box, 176

Page Templates dialog box, 42-43, 236

page transitions, animating, 174

Page view, 34-35

paragraphs

for form fields, 288

indents, changing, 94-95

Parent page, 38

passwords. *See also* SharePoint Team Services

fields, 272

Paste Options button, 13, 84

pasting

exporting files by, 71

graphics from Web, 123

with Office Clipboard, 84

text between documents, 82

pattern fills, applying, 187

PDF files, hyperlinks to, 59

permissions for SharePoint Team Services members, 331

Personal Web Site template, 30

Photo Gallery

creating, 162-163

editing, 164-165

for thumbnails, 161

Picture Actions button, 126-127

Picture dialog box, 120

picture form field, 272

Pictures Properties dialog box, 132

Picture toolbar, 128